Customer Service For Dummies,® 3rd Edition

P9-DBJ-442

14.95

Six Keys to Becoming a Customer-Centric Company

The key to long-lasting customer loyalty and retention is to make the commitment to become a customer-centric organization in all areas. Becoming customer-centric is a process that requires focus, effort, and action in the following key areas:

- ✔ **Take a top-down approach** as a manager by practicing what you preach in the arena of quality service.
- ✔ **Ask for feedback and use it** by regularly surveying your customers and staff.
- ✔ **Train and educate** all your staff members and managers in service excellence and teach them the skills they need to be part of a customer-centric company.
- ✔ **Design customer-centric processes and technologies** that focus on the customer's convenience rather than on your own.
- ✔ **Set consistent service standards** that are measurable and specific, and spell out the actions that express the service qualities you value.
- ✔ **Reward and recognize service excellence** in both formal and informal ways. Remember, what gets rewarded is what gets done!

E-Mail Excellence

To ensure that your e-mails come across as professional and well-written:

- ✔ Use correct spelling, punctuation, and grammar.
- ✔ Avoid obscure acronyms, such as RTM (read the manual).
- ✔ Maintain a pleasant tone.
- ✔ Always include a salutation and sign-off.
- ✔ Provide a clear subject line.
- ✔ Don't "yell" at the reader by writing words and sentences in ALL CAPITAL LETTERS.
- ✔ Make your request clear.
- ✔ Provide sufficient background information.
- ✔ Use emoticons (also known as smileys) appropriately and sparingly.

Working Styles

Following are the four basic working styles you need to know in order to get in step with your customers and coworkers (see Chapter 12 for more details):

- ✔ **Driven:** These people focus on bottom-line results and want tasks done how they want them done, when they want them done, and with as few errors as possible.
- ✔ **Analytical:** These people want to know the facts, are less interested in a coworker's feelings, and look at the world through a veil of logic and details.
- ✔ **Expressive:** These people are enthusiastic and fun-loving, like to be around people, and put into motion the ideas they like now and worry about details later.
- ✔ **Amiable:** To these people, feelings are more important than tasks. They take time to decide and don't like to be pressured. They're usually on the quiet side.

For Dummies: Bestselling Book Series for Beginners

Customer Service

FOR

DUMMIES®

3RD EDITION

Customer Service

FOR

DUMMIES®

3RD EDITION

by Karen Leland and Keith Bailey

WILEY

Wiley Publishing, Inc.

Customer Service For Dummies®, 3rd Edition

Published by
Wiley Publishing, Inc.
111 River St.
Hoboken, NJ 07030-5774
www.wiley.com

Copyright © 2006 by Wiley Publishing, Inc., Indianapolis, Indiana

Published simultaneously in Canada

For general information on our other products and services, please contact our Customer Care Department within the U.S. at 800-762-2974, outside the U.S. at 317-572-3993, or fax 317-572-4002.

For technical support, please visit www.wiley.com/techsupport.

Wiley also publishes its books in a variety of electronic formats. Some content that appears in print may not be available in electronic books.

Library of Congress Control Number: 2006920629

ISBN-13: 978-0-471-76869-2

ISBN-10: 0-471-76869-3

Manufactured in the United States of America

10 9 8 7 6 5 4 3 2 1

3O/RS/QU/QW/IN

WILEY

About the Authors

Karen Leland and **Keith Bailey** are cofounders of Sterling Consulting Group, Inc., an international management consulting firm specializing in maximizing results through the people side of business. They have a combined 25 years of experience in this field and have worked with over 100,000 executives, managers, and front-line staff from a wide variety of industries including retail, transportation, hospitality, banking, and consumer goods.

Their consulting work in corporations and public speaking engagements has taken them throughout North America, Southeast Asia, and Europe. Their clients have included such companies as AT&T, American Express, Apple Computer, Avis Rent A Car, Bank of America, Bristol-Myers Squibb, The British Government, DuPont, SC Johnson Wax, Lufthansa German Airlines, Pacific Bell, Microsoft, and Oracle, to name a few.

In addition to their consulting work, Karen and Keith are sought after by the media as experts on quality service. They have been interviewed by dozens of newspapers, magazines, and television and radio stations including The Associated Press International, The British Broadcasting Company, CBS, CNN, *Entrepreneur* magazine, *Fortune* magazine, *Newsweek*, *The New York Times*, *Sales & Marketing Management* magazine, *TIME* magazine, and The Oprah Winfrey Show.

Karen Leland and Keith Bailey are the authors of the previous two editions of Customer Service For Dummies, which have sold over 200,000 copies to date and been translated into numerous languages including Spanish, German, Korean, and Polish, among others. In addition, they are the authors of *Watercooler Wisdom: How Smart People Prosper in the Face of Conflict, Pressure and Change* (New Harbinger, 2006).

For further information, please view their Web site at www.scgtraining.com.

Training, Consulting, and Keynote Speeches

Sterling Consulting Group offers a variety of training programs, consulting, and keynote speeches in the area of how to improve quality service.

Karen and Keith are among the highest-rated presenters on the training/ speaking circuit and offer programs that are

- ✔ Customized to reflect your specific needs, concerns, and industry
- ✔ Highly interactive, fun, and lively
- ✔ Based on practical, real-world information that attendees can use immediately

Among the customer service improvement programs that SCG offers are:

The Service Advantage — a one-day customer relations workshop for front-line staff. Also available as an online training program.

Service Management and Teambuilding — a two-day program for managers on how to create an environment for quality service

Building A Winning Quality Service Strategy — a one-day program for senior executives designed to facilitate developing a strategy for creating a more customer-focused company

The Quality Service Audit — a comprehensive survey and evaluation that helps a company or division identify how customer-focused they are currently and target specific areas for improvement

Essential E-mail — a half-day training session designed to help participants improve their overall email efficiency and compose messages with style and impact. Also available as an online training program.

To learn more about SCG, the above programs or any of our other training programs (including team building, conflict resolution, coaching) please visit our Web site at www.scgtraining.com. Some things you can do at this site are

- ✔ See a video clip of Keith and Karen in action
- ✔ Take a mini-audit to see how customer-focused your company is
- ✔ Check out our live and online training products
- ✔ Review the table of contents for our other books

If you are interested in speaking to us about any of the above, please contact Karen Leland/Keith Bailey at:

Sterling Consulting Group, Inc.
180 Harbor Drive #208
Sausalito, CA 94965
Phone: (415) 331-5200   Fax: (415) 331-5272
E-mail: service@quality-service.com
Please visit our Web site: www.scgtraining.com

Dedication

For my father, Cecil Frederick Bailey, 1919-2005

— Keith Bailey

To my parents, for encouraging education and imparting to me my love of learning

— Karen Frances Leland

Authors' Acknowledgments

First we would like to thank our clients who, over the years, have taught us more about customer service than we could ever write in one book. Thank you for helping us to turn good ideas into practical applications.

To our friends, family members, and colleagues, we thank you for putting up with those many months we spent in hibernation writing this book. We are especially thankful to Kaylyn Lehmann for being a gifted trainer and the technical advisor on this book.

Our deepest gratitude to Kathy Welton for contacting us about writing the original *Customer Service For Dummies*. Special thanks to the wonderful staff at Wiley who have helped us through this process: Chrissy Guthrie for keeping us on track, Stacy Kennedy for helping to make this third edition a reality, Melisa Duffy for the ongoing public relations support, and Joyce Pepple for being our champion for this third edition.

Publisher's Acknowledgments

We're proud of this book; please send us your comments through our Dummies online registration form located at www.dummies.com/register/.

Some of the people who helped bring this book to market include the following:

Acquisitions, Editorial, and Media Development

Project Editor: Christina Guthrie

Acquisitions Editor: Stacy Kennedy

Copy Editors: Neil Johnson, Jessica Smith

Editorial Program Coordinator: Hanna K. Scott

Technical Editor: Kaylyn Lehmann

Editorial Manager: Christine Meloy Beck

Editorial Assistants: Erin Calligan, Nadine Bell, David Lutton

Cover Photos: © Tom Grill/Getty Images

Cartoons: Rich Tennant (www.the5thwave.com)

Composition Services

Project Coordinator: Adrienne Martinez

Layout and Graphics: Carl Byers, Stephanie D. Jumper, Julie Trippetti

Proofreaders: Leeann Harney, Jessica Kramer

Indexer: Techbooks

Publishing and Editorial for Consumer Dummies

Diane Graves Steele, Vice President and Publisher, Consumer Dummies

Joyce Pepple, Acquisitions Director, Consumer Dummies

Kristin A. Cocks, Product Development Director, Consumer Dummies

Michael Spring, Vice President and Publisher, Travel

Kelly Regan, Editorial Director, Travel

Publishing for Technology Dummies

Andy Cummings, Vice President and Publisher, Dummies Technology/General User

Composition Services

Gerry Fahey, Vice President of Production Services

Debbie Stailey, Director of Composition Services

Contents at a Glance

Table of Contents

Part IV: Road Blocks: When the Going Gets Rough 215

Introduction

Customers love and cherish companies that treat them the way they want to be treated. They'll even pay more to get good service. Just look at these survey statistics that prove the point:

- Customers spend up to 10 percent more for the same product with better service.
- A customer will tell anywhere from 9 to 12 people when he or she gets good service.
- When that customer receives poor service, he or she will tell up to 20 people!

So, how well you communicate and establish a relationship with your customers is the essence of customer service. This relationship doesn't have to take a long time — it can often happen in an instant. For example, your customers will feel more recognized (and thus more connected) if they're greeted with smiles and are addressed by name. Simple actions such as these keep customers coming back for more.

It certainly pays to please!

About This Book

Customer Service For Dummies, 3rd Edition, is a down-to-earth, step-by-step guide that takes the mystery out of providing the best possible service to your customers. This book is filled with hot tips and techniques and lots of suggestions for giving your customers the kind of service that you would like to receive.

We've packed this book with lots of practical advice for getting through the everyday challenges at work. We show you how to keep your sanity when an angry customer is calling you (and your mother) unflattering names over the phone; how to manage and develop your staff so they can become service heroes to their customers; and how to implement tried-and-true techniques for achieving gold-level service at bronze-level cost.

For you business owners and entrepreneurs who want to build empires, we provide a blueprint that'll help you take over the world, or at least improve your market share. In fact, we've made it as easy as 1-2-3, with a specific and detailed service strategy that makes any company, large or small, more customer-oriented.

Finally, because the Internet has become such an integral part of business and of our everyday lives, we've included an entire part devoted to improving your online customer service. Here you find info on writing effective e-mails, creating a customer-friendly Web site, and using the latest in customer service software and Customer Relations Management (CRM).

Conventions Used in This Book

We've used a few conventions in this book that we want you to be aware of:

- ✔ Anytime we introduce a new term, we *italicize* it and then define it.
- ✔ Keywords appear in **boldface.**
- ✔ Web sites and e-mail addresses appear in monofont to help them stand out in the text.
- ✔ When we use the word "customer," we mean not only people who purchase items from your company, but also co-workers, clients, and anyone else you have dealings with.

What You're Not to Read

This book is chock-full of useful information, and we'd love for you to read every word we've written. However, if you're pressed for time (or perhaps you have the Driver working style discussed in Chapter 12) and just want the bare-bones necessary info, you can skip the following:

- ✔ **Sidebars:** These gray-shaded boxes contain interesting yet unessential material.
- ✔ **Anecdotes:** Any paragraphs that have the anecdote icon provide you with our own personal experiences. You can certainly benefit from our experience, but you can get by without it.

Foolish Assumptions

If you've picked up this book, we can assume a few things about you. You probably fit (more or less) into one of the following categories:

- ✔ You're an executive in charge of championing a service improvement process within your company and are looking for guidelines, ideas, and strategies for how to do this.

- ✔ You're a human resources or training expert and have been assigned the task of helping your organization, or a particular department within your organization, to become more customer-focused.

- ✔ You're a small business owner or entrepreneur and want to discover ways to give your business a competitive advantage by becoming as service-oriented as possible.

- ✔ You're a manager and want to improve your ability to coach and create a more customer-focused environment so that your staff will be better equipped to provide excellent customer service.

- ✔ You're an individual service provider who loves her job, loves her customers, and just wants to improve her skills at giving great service.

- ✔ You're an individual service provider who is burnt out by his job and his customers. You want to transform stress by finding out some new ideas and techniques for dealing with difficult customers, co-workers, and situations.

How This Book Is Organized

This book is organized into six parts, and chapters within each part cover specific topic areas in detail. Each chapter has lists of what to do, what to look for, and how to provide stellar service.

Part 1: Creating the Customer-Centric Organization

In this part, we explore the basic ingredients that make you and your company winners in the service game. Right from the get-go, you discover the core attitudes and strategies that all successful businesses and individuals have in common.

Part II: Take It from the Top: Service Management

This part is filled with real world suggestions and solutions that help you, as a manager, create a working blueprint for service improvement within your department. You gain real insights into how to build teamwork, morale, and accountability at all levels of your company.

Part III: Keeping Your Customers: Simple Actions, Significant Payoffs

Here we explore the seemingly little things — those simple actions that lead to significant payoffs in customer satisfaction. We provide you with time-tested techniques for dealing with people face-to-face and over the telephone, and we cover a variety of important communication skills that you can use every day at work and at home.

Part IV: Road Blocks: When the Going Gets Rough

In this part, you find out how to reduce the effects of stress when dealing with conflict situations and how to calm angry and upset customers (and co-workers!). This part of the book also contains a process that we have taught to more than 50,000 people in companies and jobs like yours for turning difficult situations into win-win ones.

Part V: Working in a Wired World: Customer Service on the Web

Both corporate giants and emerging companies alike know that in today's world, technology is fundamental to running a successful business. Tools such as e-mail, voice mail, and the Internet have become an integral part of the everyday workplace. In this part, we explore the many ways that you can use the online world to offer better service to your customers and enhance communication between co-workers.

Part VI: The Part of Tens

For this last part, we have added a few important topics that help round out your service education. The Part of Tens is a quick and easy way for you to brush up on the main points listed in this book — as well as a way to pick up some new tips and techniques.

Icons Used in This Book

These are stories that have happened to one or both of us that we feel are important enough to share with you.

If you're a manager, you want to be on the lookout for this icon. Wherever you see it, you find hot tips, techniques, and suggestions designed especially for managers.

When you see this icon, you know that the information is especially important and worth filing away in your brain.

The tip icon provides you with tricks, shortcuts, and suggestions for improving the customer service you offer even more.

This icon flags any potential pitfalls that people often make when dealing with customers and that we want you to be able to avoid. Don't skip these icons!

Where to Go from Here

As Julie Andrews sang in The Sound of Music, "Let's start at the very beginning!" Our recommendation is to begin your journey through this book by finding out where your customer service skills stand right now. The self-evaluation and company quiz in Part I will help you determine your personal, company, and departmental levels of service.

Once you know where home base is, you can go in any number of directions. Here are some suggestions:

- ✔ If you're hot to deal with those difficult customers, turn to Part IV, which shows you how to soothe the savage beasts hiding in your customers.

- ✔ If you're a manager, you may want to head for Part II to discover how you can create the strongest environment for service excellence.

- ✔ If you've mastered brick and mortar customer service but feel challenged by the Internet, you can surf on over to Part V to learn how to bring excellent customer service to your Web site and your other online interactions.

- ✔ If you need to brush up on core customer service skills and you want to learn some ways to create better rapport with both customers and co-workers, take a gander at the information-packed Part III. Here you find lots of specifics about making and keeping customers for life by using your tone of voice and body language to complement your words.

Even though this book gives great ideas for improving the service you offer your customers, you must have three basic elements in place in order for those ideas to take root and flourish. Smiling and saying please and thank you are important, but alone they don't lead to good service. You must have the following elements in place, even if they aren't easy (if they were so easy, everyone would be doing them):

- ✔ Expand your definition of service to go beyond saying "yes" or "no" to fulfilling a multitude of customer needs.

- ✔ Reconsider who your customers are and redefine excellent customer service to include co-workers.

- ✔ Develop, as a company, a customer-friendly attitude both personally and culturally.

If you hold the common idea that service is only giving customers what they want, you'll be in trouble every time a customer asks for something that is impossible for you to provide. However, if you expand your definition of service to include fulfilling the less obvious customer needs, you'll never be in a situation where you can't provide your customers with some level of service.

Now, go ahead and get started improving your customer service!

Part I
Creating the Customer-Centric Organization

The 5th Wave   By Rich Tennant

" Something I can help you with, sir?"

In this part . . .

An ancient Chinese proverb states that the journey of a thousand miles begins with the first step. In this part of *Customer Service For Dummies,* 3rd Edition, we explore the basic ingredients that make you and your company winners in the service game. Right from the get-go, you discover the key ingredient that all successful businesses and individuals have in common.

Included in this part is an eye-opening questionnaire that helps you evaluate how well your company is doing at creating an environment where service excellence thrives and delights your customers time and time again while leaving your competitors in the dust.

Lastly, this part of the book provides you with a whole bunch of specific surveys, memos, quizzes, and other tools that we've designed and used with clients for years in our consulting company. You can put them to use immediately in your own company.

Chapter 1

Championing Customer Service

*I*n the old days, nobody wrote books about service. It was simply a way of life. The pace of business was slower, and people had more time to talk and listen to one another. Mr. and Mrs. Smith could go to their corner grocery store to buy a pound of Muenster cheese and count on a warm welcome, friendly service, and familiar faces.

Then came the Great Depression. Price, always an important factor, became even more important, and life was about survival. Quality and service — never high on Abraham Maslow's hierarchy of needs — disappeared from everyday life and was reserved for the rich and famous. In the more prosperous 1940s, consumers began to consider value in addition to price as part of the service equation. By the 1960s, quality became important, with most customers willing to pay more for higher quality products and services. The era of convenience began in the 1970s with quick and easy foods, stores, banks, and so on. Today, all of these characteristics have converged; consumers want a competitive price, good value, convenience, and customer service — and they want it yesterday!

In this chapter, we introduce you to the tools and core values you can use to become a winner at providing good customer service. We even show you how to implement and maintain personal service in the often impersonal world of online business. Finally, to get you started on the right foot, we provide you with a short self-evaluating questionnaire, so you can determine what level of service you're currently achieving and what you can do to improve.

Benefiting from the Evolution of Customer Service

Since the 1970s, a variety of business movements have influenced what people know about making themselves and their companies customer friendly. In this section (and throughout this book), we highlight the best, time-tested ideas and show you how to make them work for your business.

Regardless of whether your business is large or small, domestic or international, online or off, the ideas and strategies contained in this book can help you use the wisdom of the past decades and current times to make your business a winner at the service game now and into the future.

Total quality management

During the 1980s, *customer service* and *quality improvement* were the buzzwords of the moment, and *TQM* (total quality management) became the most popular acronym since BLT. TQM, which was implemented to enhance customer service by delivering quality products, helped bring about modern manufacturing techniques. The idea is that you can gain the edge over your competitors by establishing optimal production processes, conforming to standards, and empowering members of your staff to blow their whistles when they spot any defects.

One of the most empowering tools to come out of the TQM movement is the idea of *quality groups* or *problem-solving teams.* These are groups of people who gather over a defined period of time (say once a week) to work on a specific problem. Using an agreed upon problem-solving method, they work to determine the core causes of and best possible solutions for the problem. In Chapter 9, we offer you a complete step-by-step process for using quality groups in your own organization.

Moments of truth

On the heels of TQM's moment of fame, Jan Carlzon, who was the CEO of SAS Airlines, quietly published his book *Moments of Truth* (Ballinger Publishing Company, 1987). It's an account of how the airline, under Carlzon's leadership, asked what influenced its passengers' perceptions of service. What the airline found was that perceptions of service depended on how customers remembered discrete encounters they had with the airline. These encounters — or moments of truth — can be either memorably positive experiences or memorably negative experiences. Each kind of encounter plays a critical part in an individual customer's future purchasing decisions. For example, a two-minute phone conversation can influence a customer's opinion about the entire enterprise — even more so than a two-hour flight!

The moment-of-truth approach still lives on because its premise can be applied to any business, large or small, and to any medium, such as voice mail, e-mail, and so on. The moment-of-truth method of thinking about customer service still holds up, because no matter what service or product you provide, your customers are, more than ever, making quick judgments based on fleeting contacts. Even though the quick judgment of your organization by customers may not seem fair, it, nevertheless, is customer logic.

For example: Imagine that a customer receives an e-mail from your company that has no greeting and sports several spelling mistakes. The sloppiness and carelessness of the e-mail, for many customers, can signify that your staff members aren't professional, your company doesn't care, and the quality of your product is questionable — and nobody wants that!

Customer perception is reality, and service excellence, to a large degree, is managing your customers' perceptions and expectations. In Chapter 7, we show you how you can determine and enhance your company's most significant moments of truth.

Sharing the market

Flash forward to the '90s, and *share of market* became the hot button in business/customer relations. Around this time, the speed of business began to increase exponentially. Fax machines, overnight delivery, and the Internet were beginning to present new customer-communication opportunities. E-mail soon joined the established channels of communication like the phone, regular mail, and the fax machine.

As technology advances by leaps and bounds, more and more magazine articles and business books are devoted to the *new* idea of developing deeper relationships with customers. Viewing each sale as a transaction is short-sighted. Customers are, after all, a finite commodity. Instead, you need to use every customer touch-point as an opportunity to establish a dialogue and create customer loyalty. Doing so makes sense, because acquiring a new customer after all costs five times more than keeping a current one — so why not increase efforts to retain established customers?

By listening to your customers and providing them with the services and products they really want, you can gain and keep your share of the market. Check out Part III of *Customer Service For Dummies* for simple, yet highly effective strategies you can put in place to keep your customers happy and coming back for more.

In-focused versus customer-focused

Nowadays, quantity is being replaced by quality. Every interaction with a customer or potential customer is an opportunity for gathering feedback, searching out needs, and implementing changes that can make your organization more customer centric. For service champions, the idea of converting *transaction buyers* (customers whose sole purchasing criterion is price and who have no vendor loyalty) into *relationship buyers* (those who value a long-term vendor partnership) is possibly the most important service development since Carlzon's moments of truth.

Simply put, a customer-focused company is one that listens to the needs of its customers and then does whatever it can to satisfy those needs. In-focused organizations care little about the needs of their customers and focus on what is convenient and expedient to them. Because customer-focused companies have more respect for and more understanding of their customers, they foster more customer loyalty, garner more positive word-of-mouth from their customer base, and enjoy a high level of service initiative from their staff. Part I of this book tells you everything you need to know about how to transform your organization from in-focused to customer focused.

CRM: The latest and greatest in customer service

CRM (customer relationship management) is the acronym that customer-service professionals are using today. CRM is simply the marriage of process and technology for tracking every contact point that customers have with your organization.

Many companies believe that the CRM strategy is the digital key to becoming customer centric in a fast-paced world. For small- or medium-sized enterprises, CRM can smack of hype or be too confusing to really understand. However, if you dig deep enough, valuable lessons can be learned from CRM — lessons that can improve your bottom line, such as discovering specific and often unspoken customer needs that enhance both loyalty and sales.

Head to Chapter 21 for a complete discussion of CRM. We tell you what to take from CRM and what to leave behind. We extract and simplify the key elements so you can move beyond the acronym-of-the month to the real, cutting-edge issues. New technology presents new opportunities and new challenges that will, no doubt, impact your business's ability to provide great customer service in the years ahead.

We're not suggesting that you ignore changing markets or new ways of serving them. We simply believe that embracing today's latest and greatest doesn't mean waving goodbye to everything useful from the past and forgetting everything you already know about making customers happy.

Standing for Real Values — Even in the Virtual World

If you look through the shelves of your local bookstore or search for the key-words "customer service" on your favorite bookseller's Web site, you'll find a long list of titles to choose from, including the one you're now reading! The books spell out customer-service strategies for making it in today's high-tech world. However, service strategies — like the seasons — come and go. Ultimately, the success of your enterprise has more to do with your core values (and a commitment to delivering them) than it does with the latest and greatest business trends.

Amid the hubbub caused by new and better technology, businesses that differentiate themselves as customer centric are the ones that will see online service as an exciting opportunity for delivering their *existing* values of service, quality, and excellence to a wider group of customers. The root of these values is a genuine customer-care attitude that compels companies to create a feeling of closeness with their customers and use technology to design systems with their customers' concerns and convenience in mind. Even in this fast-paced, technology-driven world, the timeless aspects of human relations still apply.

Valuing customer loyalty

Numerous studies highlight one key to business success: developing customer loyalty. When it comes to e-commerce, the cost of enticing customers to use your online service is expensive at the front end and light at the back end. In other words, the longer you keep your e-customers and the more loyal they are, the more lucrative they become!

Placing a greater emphasis on customer loyalty isn't a new phenomenon — even though many books and magazines seem to trumpet loyalty as though it were a recent innovation. Adapting your customer satisfaction efforts to a digital world is easier when your company already values customer loyalty and has experience creating it.

Building relationships

Many years ago, service gurus counseled senior executives to create customer-centric organizations. Becoming customer centric often meant moving away from an intense focus on product development to placing an equal amount of emphasis on relationship development. After all, even great products fail occasionally, and a strong bond between company and customer can overcome most problems.

If you're a business owner today, you still need to develop trusting relationships with your customers. The differences between today's business world and the business world of the past are the tools that you have at your disposal. A courteous voice on the telephone and a friendly face across the counter still are important; they're just so expensive nowadays that they have to be rationed. Replacing these luxuries are software and hardware that can be as rewarding to your customers as they are to your company's bottom line when they're designed, integrated, and used with a focus on customer service.

Staying close to your customers

Customers rarely describe doing business over the Internet as a warm and fuzzy experience. The absence of face time is, for many, the downside of today's Internet-heavy service environment. And yet, never before have businesses had the opportunity to be in such close and direct contact with their customers. The Internet enables your company to be in direct communication with all of your customers — regardless of where they reside on the planet — as long as they have an Internet connection.

You can assess individual customers' needs, apologize, say thank you, ask for input, and suggest new products or services suited to each one of them rather than to an entire demographic group — all online. Think of the Internet as a direct line to your customers and a new, exciting opportunity for any company that knows the value of listening and staying close to its customers.

Making it personal

In a wired world, your company must find ways to communicate a caring attitude through computer screens and digital technology. The field of e-business technology uses sophisticated software programs to track inventory, accept payments, trace deliveries, predict customer needs, and send thank-you notes. In short, it attempts to automate the personal touch — thus making the most efficient use of your human resources by minimizing human interaction. At the same time, e-business technology offers fast, convenient, and personalized service.

Ultimately, though, investing in e-business software solutions doesn't guarantee the personal touch — people like doing business with people. That doesn't mean that customers don't like quickness and convenience; they obviously do. But they also crave a human who can help them when they have a question or concern that doesn't fit into the templates of an online help desk. Best-in-class companies demonstrate their caring attitudes by using technology to support their relationships with people. They don't use technology to replace human relationships, but rather only to enhance them.

Mirror, Mirror on the Wall: Taking an Honest Look at Your Service

Remember when you were a kid and your parents took you to see *Snow White and the Seven Dwarfs* for the first time? Snow White's evil stepmother stood in front of her mirror and asked, "Mirror, Mirror on the wall, who's the fairest of them all?" Even though you were only a kid, you knew that if that mirror was smart, only one answer could be right: "You, my queen, are the fairest in the land."

Unlike the wicked queen — who had a hard time facing reality — your survival in today's business world depends on you telling the truth about your strengths and weaknesses as a service provider. After all, you have to know where you are before you can move forward. To that end, we provide you with a paper mirror — a questionnaire highlighting key service criteria that mark individuals who are service winners.

Taking this evaluation can help you discover the quality of service you provide as an individual and give you a good place from which to start improving. Congratulations, you and your company are on the way to being service stars!

Self-evaluation questionnaire

Use the following ten questions to find out whether you're delivering bronze-, silver-, or gold-level customer service. Stepping back and objectively assessing yourself helps you determine your personal service strengths and shows where you may need to devote some extra attention.

Use the following numbers to rate your response to each question.

0 = Rarely

1 = Sometimes

2 = Often

3 = Almost always

___ When having a conversation with a customer, do I give him or her my complete attention and avoid doing other activities (working on the computer, writing unnecessarily, doing a crossword puzzle, and so on)?

___ Do I make eye contact when speaking with a customer to show that I am paying attention?

___ When speaking to a customer over the phone, do I make an effort to use inflection in my voice to convey interest and concern?

___ Do I pick up the telephone by the third ring?

___ When I need to put a customer on hold, do I ask his or her permission and wait for a response before doing so?

___ Do I avoid technical jargon and use language that the customer can understand?

___ When I cannot provide my customer with exactly what he or she wants, do I suggest options and alternatives?

___ Do I sincerely apologize to the customer when a mistake has been made by me or my company?

___ When a customer is voicing a complaint, do I remain calm and understanding — even if I think he or she is wrong?

___ Do I view customer complaints as an opportunity to improve service rather than as a problem that is taking up valuable time?

___ **Total score**

So, how's your service?

Add together the scores you gave to all ten questions and then look below to see how you did. If you scored:

- ✔ **0-12 points:** You're at the **bronze level.**
- ✔ **13-22 points:** You're at the **silver level.**
- ✔ **23-30 points:** You're at the **gold level.**

For specifics about what your score means and where to go from here, find the description of the level you achieved in the sections that follow and read on.

Bronze level

Scoring at this level doesn't mean that you don't care about your customers. We find that a score in the bronze level is caused by one of the following three reasons:

- You're a newcomer to the service field and are still discovering the ins and outs of dealing with customers. If this statement applies to you, then using the information in this book can help bring you up to the silver level and higher.

- You're a seasoned service provider, but you may have become a little rusty on some of the basics that you once practiced. Refresh yourself on the basics by attending a customer-service training program.

- The last reason has to do with job suitability. Through the years, we've met certain people who just don't enjoy dealing with customers or helping others solve problems. Nothing is wrong with them; they just work better by themselves. If this situation applies to you, you may want to consider changing jobs or changing the focus of the job you're now in.

Silver level

You have a solid understanding of the basics, but you're not using them consistently. The probable reason for your inconsistency is that you're overwhelmed by the functions of your job. On good days, you give good service, and on bad days, you give bad service. The key is to become more consistent. Remember that regardless of the time you spend with a customer (be it a 30-second phone call or a one-hour meeting) and regardless of how busy you are, you always have a personal choice about the attitude you project. It takes about 30 days to form a new habit, so make a point of practicing the items covered by the questionnaire every time you deal with a customer — especially when you don't feel like it.

Gold level

Congratulations! You're a professional at providing service. You seem to have a firm understanding of the basics and are ready for bigger and better challenges. To continue to grow, consider the following suggestions:

- After you've finished evaluating yourself, get another perspective by having a co-worker you know and trust evaluate you. He or she may see areas for improvement that are blind spots to you.

- Go beyond the basics of service. Educate yourself in the more sophisticated service skills by learning to take initiative (see Chapter 7).

We suggest that you go through this questionnaire a second time and replace the word *customer* with the words *staff member*. Doing so can help you evaluate how well you're treating members of your staff as customers.

Chapter 2

In-Focused or Customer-Focused: Where Do You Stand?

In This Chapter

▶ Identifying the two common threads of a service attitude

▶ Revisiting the definition of a customer

▶ Measuring how customer-focused your company is

*R*egardless of whether your company is large or small, local or international, in the manufacturing, technology, service, or public sector, the key to successful customer relations is infusing your company to the core with the principles of quality customer service. As a manager, executive, or business owner, you have to deliver first-rate service to your customers, instill a commitment to service in every person who works for you, and strive to create a customer-centered company culture. The path to excellence in customer service isn't simply a matter of hiring the right people and training the front-line staff, it's a genuine commitment to create a customer-focused rather than an in-focused company.

In this chapter, we compare the in-focused company with the customer-focused one, and then we show you how to evaluate just how customer-focused your company currently is. After you get a clearer picture of where your company currently stands, you can read the rest of Part I where we provide you with a strategic outline and specific activities that help your company become more customer focused.

The In-Focused Company

If the companies we refer to as in-focused were people, you'd probably be inclined to call them selfish, because their main concern is pleasing themselves rather than their customers. *In-focused companies* are fixated on achieving internal goals that benefit the company, such as cutting costs, earning profits, and budgeting, but customer-satisfaction goals are either low on the list or may even be nonexistent (see Figure 2-1). Some typical qualities that identify an in-focused company are

✔ Recognition usually isn't given to the staff members who provide good service but rather to those who excel at accomplishing internal company goals.

✔ Staff members must focus most of their efforts on making their managers, rather than their customers, happy.

✔ Promotion is based on seniority and favoritism rather than on merit.

✔ Staff members, if trained at all, are trained in the functions of the job but rarely in communication and interpersonal skills.

✔ Departments that don't deal directly with the external customer don't see themselves as responsible for customer satisfaction.

✔ Decisions that affect the customer are made at the top (behind closed doors) and then pushed down without consulting the front line.

✔ Short-term, bottom-line fixes always win out over long-term solutions.

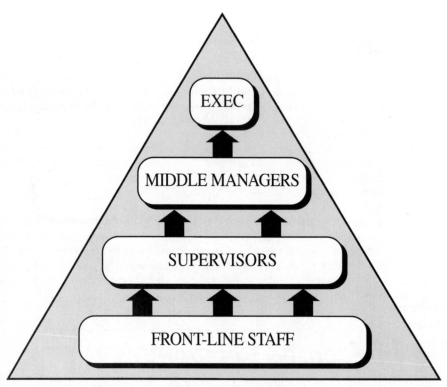

Figure 2-1:
The in-
focused
organization
pleases
itself.

ANECDOTE

In-focused from the top down

A company we know had received dozens of complaints about how discourteously its corporate headquarters handled telephone calls. In response, senior management asked the company's human resources department to design and present a two-hour training seminar on customer service to resolve the problem. The HR department did so and invited all the upper management to attend, since they were some of the worst offenders. The indignant response of the higher ups was that they didn't have time to attend such a program and that the lower ranks were the ones who needed the training anyway — not them. The training program was held, with junior staff in attendance. However, the lack of clear management support and participation left a bad taste in everyone's mouth, and created an attitude of 'this is not really that important'. The moral of the story is that service excellence starts at the top. If you don't have the right attitude at the top, don't expect it from your front line.

The Customer-Focused Company

A *customer-focused company,* on the other hand, has one eye on profits and the other eye on how best to serve its customers. This company has discovered that profits and market share are the products of listening to customers and acting upon their needs (see Figure 2-2).

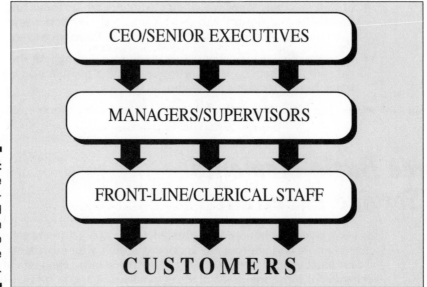

Figure 2-2:
The customer-focused organization seeks to please customers.

CEO/SENIOR EXECUTIVES

MANAGERS/SUPERVISORS

FRONT-LINE/CLERICAL STAFF

C U S T O M E R S

A real-life customer-focused company

One of our clients, an international hotel chain has made being customer-focused a way of life. This company has put a system in place that makes it clear to all managers and staff that customer excellence is a top priority. They do quarterly guest tracking to monitor customer satisfaction. The results are then forwarded to the general managers at each location. Information, such as how one hotel site compares with the others in the same region and specific information on each department (front desk, check out, restaurant, and so on), is made available. Management bonuses are based on these guest-tracking results, and a yearly achievement forum acknowledges staff members and locations whose guest-tracking scores are the highest.

Qualities that characterize a customer-focused organization are

- ✔ Recognition is earned by staff members who balance job efficiency with customer satisfaction.

- ✔ Managers focus on supporting their staff members in doing their jobs well so that they can focus more attention on taking care of customer needs.

- ✔ Promotion is based on good service skills and on seniority.

- ✔ Training the staff is a high priority, focusing on technical and interpersonal skills.

- ✔ All staff members know who their customers are (external and internal — see the "Reconsidering Who Your Customers Are" section later in this chapter) and understand how they're part of the customer-service chain.

- ✔ A participative management style is common throughout the company, and staff members have opportunities to offer feedback on key customer issues *before* decisions are made.

- ✔ Long-term thinking is the rule rather than the exception.

Three Basic Elements of Service Excellence

This book gives you hundreds of great ideas for how to create a customer-focused culture and improve the service you offer your customers. However, you first must gain an understanding of the three basic elements of service excellence for those hundreds of ideas to take root and flourish. Otherwise, no amount of smiling, saying please and thank you, or customer-loyalty programs will help your company develop good service. The three basics are

- ✔ Developing a customer-friendly attitude.
- ✔ Expanding your definition of service.
- ✔ Reconsidering who your customers are.

You may find yourself looking at these basics and thinking, "That's no big deal. These ideas are obviously from Business 101." But beware, looks can be deceiving. Although these elements may seem obvious, they're not necessarily easy to accomplish. If they were, everyone would be using them. The difference between knowing them and living them takes commitment and practice. Check out the three sections that follow as we discuss these elements in detail and show you how to apply them to your business.

Developing a Customer-Friendly Attitude

All companies and individuals who provide great service have a genuine customer-friendly attitude in common. By customer-friendly attitude, we mean they view their customers as the most important part of their jobs and have a sincere appreciation for the way their customers do business with them. We don't mean viewing your customers as interruptions to your work routine for which you have to paste on a false smile, all the while wishing they'd just leave so you can get on with your work. For you and your staff to be able to understand how to create a customer-friendly attitude, you all need to step back and take a look at what you do during the workday.

Imagine a busy Monday morning at the office when suddenly Oprah Winfrey shows up and announces she's doing a special on "A Day In The Life Of The American Worker," and she wants to follow you around with a camera for an entire day, videotaping everything you do (with the exception of a few personal moments). At the end of the day, Oprah invites you to view the tape. As you watch, you notice that you're resourceful under pressure, productive, efficient, and good looking. That's probably the reason they picked you.

However, seeing yourself on the video confirmed your suspicions: A day at work is rather like a trip down a raging river. After you walk in, everything switches into high gear and is a crazy and fast-moving whirl of doing this, that, and the other thing until you leave for the day. The tape demonstrates how surrounded and submerged you are by ringing telephones to answer, e-mails to read and write, paperwork to process, meetings to attend, problems to solve, fires to put out, and so on. (We, of course, recommend that you show the video to your boss, point out all that you do, and ask for a raise. If you're self-employed, take yourself out to dinner — you deserve it!)

It pays to please

Customers love and cherish companies that treat them the way they'd like to be treated. In fact, some consumers will even pay more to obtain those kinds of services. Here are some survey statistics proving the point:

✔ Consumers spend up to 10 percent more for the same product with better service.

✔ When consumers receive good service, they tell an average of 9 to 12 other people about it.

✔ When consumers receive poor service, they tell up to 20 people about it.

✔ The likelihood that customers will repurchase from or patronize a company whenever their complaints are handled quickly and pleasantly is 82 percent.

✔ When service is poor, 91 percent of retail customers refuse to go back to a store.

Communicating and establishing relationships: Two common threads

The incessant tasks that make up your day are the *functions* of your job. Thinking that all the paperwork, e-mails, memos, and meetings are the whole story is tempting, but if you look a little deeper, you find two common threads that link together the fabric of everything you do at work, regardless of whether you're a plumber, a teacher, or an IRS auditor.

The first common thread is communicating with other people. Although plumbers may spend most of their day alone under a sink with only a wrench for company, their communication skills are what count when they explain to you what the problem is and what it will cost to fix it. A teacher's ability to make a subject utterly fascinating or boring has a great deal to do with the way he or she talks about it. Even the IRS has instituted customer communication improvement programs during the past few years! The bottom line is that everyone, regardless of whether they work alone or in a group, uses some form of communication to get their jobs done.

 Communication isn't just about talking. It's also body language, writing, and, in today's world, online interaction. Part III of *Customer Service Excellence For Dummies* offers you some valuable techniques for enhancing your communication skills.

The second common thread of the workplace routine is establishing relationships with other people. *Relationship* usually refers to a personal connection, such as a friend, spouse, or family member. However, in the service game, we use the word relationship to mean connecting with another person to accomplish something. Go back under the sink and visit with your seemingly solitary plumber and you'll discover that he or she has relationships with customers, vendors, and fellow plumbers. The same applies to the school-teacher, who not only has relationships with the students but also with their parents, fellow teachers, and school administrators. IRS auditors likewise have relationships with tax accountants, citizens, and the United States Government. (Now that's a lot of relationships.)

Although your job has many functions, communicating and establishing relationships are at its *essence*. At a department store, for example, a sales assistant may have many tasks to complete, such as stocking, merchandising, and running the register, but the essence of his or her job is keeping customers happy and coming back. As a customer, you feel more recognized — and consequently more connected — whenever the sales assistant takes the time to smile at you and call you by your name when handing your credit card back to you.

On the other hand, a bad impression can develop just as fast. When you call a company on the phone, and the telephone rings ten times before someone answers it, what kind of bond has that company established with you? More than likely, the poor response created a negative relationship before any business ever was transacted.

Create positive moments of truth

These brief actions or instant connections are what Jan Carlzon (the former President of SAS Airlines) calls moments of truth. A *moment of truth* occurs whenever a customer comes in contact with your company and forms either a negative or positive memorable impression. These moments of truth usually take no longer than 20 seconds, but have a lasting impact on a customer's perception of the service your company offers.

Imagine a prospective customer coming to see you and walking up to the receptionist in your office and telling him that she's here for her 2 o'clock appointment with you. The receptionist (a temp you just hired) is busy doing e-mail and doesn't respond or look up for several seconds. When he finally looks up and speaks, his go-ahead-make-my-day expression and get-out-of-my-face tone form a brief but off-putting negative moment of truth for your potential customer. The problem doesn't end there, however. The negative impression your customer has of the receptionist is unwittingly applied to the rest of your company (including you). Okay, so we know it isn't fair, but it is after all the way customers think. We call this type of thinking *customer logic* — the logic being that the one equals the many.

Next imagine the opposite situation. Your customer walks in, and the receptionist immediately looks up, greets her with a smile, and says, "Good morning. How may I help you?" When the customer asks for you, the receptionist tells her you'll just be a moment and offers her a comfortable chair and a cup of coffee or tea. A positive moment of truth like this puts the customer on your side and paves the way for a successful meeting.

Friendly is more efficient

We recently took a flight from San Francisco to New York. While about 100 weary travelers patiently waited for their luggage to appear on the carousel, a voice came over the loudspeaker and announced that a loading mix-up in San Francisco meant the luggage (our luggage) would arrive on the first flight the next morning. Amid quiet moans and louder curses, we were herded over to the lost-luggage area and asked to form two lines. As we moved closer to the front of our line, we became painfully aware that the other line was moving faster (don't they always). We also observed that the agent in the fast-moving line seemed much more friendly, empathetic, and energetic than the grumbling and resentful counterpart who was taking care of our group.

The friendly agent was going out of her way to be nice to disgruntled passengers. She smiled and apologized, saying that she understood her customers' frustration and so on. The passengers moved quickly through her line, apparently satisfied that everything that could be done was being done. At the head of our line, the story wasn't so pretty. We could tell that our agent was upset, because she had a tortured expression on her face, a loud, cranky voice, and an overall bad attitude. Her conversation was peppered with phrases like: "What do you expect me to be able to do about it?" "You'll just have to make do until the morning," and the ever popular "The sooner you give me the information I need, the sooner I'll be able to help you." We started talking about how each of the agents might talk to her family about her day at work. We imagined the one with the customer-friendly attitude saying, "We had a problem with luggage on the San Francisco flight tonight, but most of the passengers were understanding." But the other agent's report would be more like, "You won't believe what a terrible evening I've had. The passengers on the San Francisco flight were a total pain in the neck about a problem with their luggage, and I'm stressed out!" What this agent failed to realize was that being friendly to the customers would not have taken any longer, but it would have been much less stressful and more effective had she done so.

For a great story about how one company became a service winner, read *Moments Of Truth,* by Jan Carlzon (Perennial Library, Harper & Row). Even though the book is written about the airline industry, we've never found a business that couldn't benefit from Carlzon's advice.

Don't put functions before essence

Creating positive moments of truth is easy when you're not under pressure. However, when you're faced with having too much to do and too little time to do it, you can get so caught up in your daily *To Do* list that it's all too easy to forget that the essence of your job is serving the customer.

If you forget this principle, the customer suddenly becomes an inconvenience, and you project an attitude that the customer somehow is interrupting your job. That attitude is what leaves customers with the feeling they're unimportant to you and that the company has little or no regard for their needs. Alternatively, when you create a customer-friendly attitude by viewing the customer as the job, the customer feels valued by your company.

"I don't have the time to create a relationship with every customer." If we had a dollar for every time we've heard this statement, we'd be writing this book from the warm sands of our tropical beach vacation home. When you have a customer-friendly attitude, you naturally develop a partnership with the other person, and solving a problem with a partner takes much less time than it does with someone who's an adversary. In a survey that we conducted for a client, we found that 98 percent of customer interactions were faster and more efficient when the service provider took enough time to establish a relationship and create rapport with the customer.

Here are some clues that you may have slipped into the habit of viewing your customers as interruptions of your job:

- ✔ Your shoulders hug your neck every time the phone rings.
- ✔ Switching on voice mail has become a reflex — even when you're in the office.
- ✔ Every customer or co-worker looks like he or she is out to get you.
- ✔ You enjoy saying, "No," more and more.
- ✔ Every sentence you utter to a customer begins with a sigh.

Although your job functions are important, they never are more important than the customers they were designed to serve.

Expanding Your Definition of Service

Your definition of service shapes every interaction you have with your customers. If you hold the common belief that service is giving customers only what they want, you may as well paint yourself into a corner every time a customer asks for something that's impossible for you to provide. If, on the other hand, you expand your definition of service to include fulfilling the multitude of less-obvious customer needs, you'll never encounter a time when you can't provide your customers with at least some level of service.

By addressing less-obvious customer needs, such as listening with empathy when customers have a problem or providing options and alternatives when you can't give customers exactly what they want, you widen the gap between you and your competitors. You can find out more about these less-obvious customer needs and how to fulfill them in Chapters 14 and 15.

Service has a feeling

Think of a company (restaurant, store, bank, and so on) with which you enjoy doing business. Why do you like being a customer there? Are customer-service representatives friendly, courteous, and knowledgeable? Imagine for a moment that you're there right now. How do you feel? Okay, now we're going to transport you instantly to a new location. You're now standing in line at the Department of Motor Vehicles waiting to renew your driver's license. How do you feel now? If you don't feel any different, you may need psychiatric help!

 Customer service is not a department somewhere within your company. Rather, it's a company culture in which every individual at every level is customer-oriented.

Reconsidering Who Your Customers Are

Who are your customers? Do you really know? All too often businesses and employees limit their definitions of a customer to someone who is outside of the company. Look up the word "customer" in your dictionary. The first definition of customer is "a person who buys," but the second definition is "a person with whom one has dealings."

In fact, everyone who works for a company has customers regardless of whether they work with external, paying customers or internal co-workers.

The external customer

External customers are the people you deal with either face to face or over the phone. They're the ones who buy products or services from you — customers in the traditional sense of the word. Without them, you'd have no sales, no business, and worse yet, no paycheck. If your definition of a customer stops here, however, you're seeing only half the picture.

The internal customer

Internal customers are the other half of the picture. They're the people who work inside your company and rely on you for services, products, and information they need to do their jobs. They're not traditional customers, yet they need the same tender, loving care that you give to external customers.

Having an indirect effect

Many years ago, coauthor Keith Bailey worked as a waiter in a restaurant. One of the cooks was moody and had a bad habit of throwing kitchen utensils at the wall on the far side of the kitchen. The noise of clattering metal let all the waiters know when the cook wasn't a happy camper and to beware! One day, Keith was taking an order from two dinner patrons, and one of them asked to substitute steamed vegetables for the French fries that usually accompanied such an order. As his smile congealed, he immediately thought of the unhappy cook and his desire to live. Eventually, Keith nervously said, "I'm sure that'll be no problem." On the trip back to the kitchen, he felt like he was walking up the steps of the gallows. He poked his head into the kitchen, quickly threw down the order and left before the spoons started flying. As Keith waited on his next table, he noticed that the cook's attitude had put a wet blanket on his own enthusiasm. The cook's job, as written on his job description, was to prepare food. No mention was made about how his dealings with or attitude toward other employees might indirectly affect the customers' dining experience.

By expanding your definition of a customer to include co-workers, you take a vital step toward providing excellent service.

REMEMBER

At work you play the dual-role of customer and service provider at different times. For example, a co-worker may come up to you and ask for a printout of a report. In that case, since you're the one providing the service, information, product, you're the service provider. However, ten minutes later, you may turn around and go to that same co-worker and ask for help with a project. Now he's the one providing the service, information, product, and you're his customer. In less than one hour, you've changed hats!

The customer chain

The relationship between internal customers and external customers forms the *customer chain*. So, if you have a backroom kind of job where you rarely see the light of day, let alone a living, breathing customer, you can easily begin to feel that your work has little or no impact on external customers. But if you look at the bigger picture, you can see that everyone in a company plays some part in fulfilling the customers' needs. Barely an hour goes by during the day when you're not providing something for somebody in some form or another. Each interaction between internal customers is an important link in a chain of events that always ends up at the external customers' feet.

Breaking news: Staff members are customers

We once were invited to present our ideas about providing service to senior executives at a large and well-known manufacturing organization. They were puzzled about why surveys of customers continually revealed one central weakness: They were *not* service-oriented. We began the meeting, and the executives became less and less comfortable with the idea of treating co-workers and employees as customers. During an afternoon break at this rapidly deteriorating meeting, a vice president of human resources shuffled us into a darkened corner of the boardroom and said with fear in his eyes, "Are you trying to tell me that the way I treat my staff has an effect on how they treat their customers?" "Yes," we said in unison. He shook his head in dismay, lit his pipe, and wandered off through his own smoke. We never were invited back. Here was a group of educated, experienced professionals apparently unaware of one of the basics of excellent service: Treat your staff like customers.

About two years ago, *The Wall Street Journal* ran an article titled, "Poorly Treated Employees Treat the Customer Just as Poorly." Boy, does that hit the nail on the head. We've dealt with a frightening percentage of managers who don't realize that their staff members are internal customers. We're convinced that the quality of service that a company provides to its customers is a direct reflection of how a company's staff members are treated by their managers. Viewing your staff members as customers is a priority. When you see them as customers, you can then treat them accordingly. Doing so means focusing not on what your staff can do to make your job easier, but rather on what you can do to make their jobs easier.

Many companies seem to overlook an important link in the service chain — their vendors. By using the techniques in this book with your vendors, you'll not only enhance your relationship with them, but you'll also receive better service. In our business, we know that we're dealing with truly customer-focused companies when they treat us as customers even though *they* are *our* clients.

Measuring Your Customer Focus: A Questionnaire

The answers to the many questions we present in this section are meant to give you an idea of how customer-focused your company or department is today. You can complete the questionnaire that follows on your own, or you may want to gather together four or five of your co-workers and, as a group, discuss the questions and reach a consensus on the score you give yourself for each one. More often than not, the ensuing conversation — including each person's reasons for their ratings — proves to be as valuable as the scores. In fact, many people view the survey as an opportunity to talk about the state of the company's customer service.

Before you begin

The 38 questions that follow are designed to be equally applicable to the evaluation of an individual department or an entire company. Before you begin, decide whether you're focusing on a specific department or the company as a whole. Some general do's and don'ts to keep in mind as you go through the questionnaire include

- ✔ Do be honest and discerning in the ratings you give.
- ✔ Do go with your gut feeling when responding to each question.
- ✔ Do base your ratings on where things stand today.
- ✔ Don't base your ratings on what you're planning to do in the near future.
- ✔ Don't base your ratings solely on other people's opinions — although building a consensus when working as a group is fine.
- ✔ Don't overestimate where your company is.

Using the following rankings, consider each question separately and assign a score that you think reflects where your company is today. Each question needs to receive a score from 0 to 3, according to the following criteria:

> 0 = Not at all
>
> 1 = To a small degree
>
> 2 = To a moderate degree
>
> 3 = To a large degree

As you read the questions, you may find yourself thinking, "Aren't these subjective?" Well, of course they are! This questionnaire is designed to give you a feel for where you stand today and to highlight some key areas for improvement. This questionnaire is not meant to replace formal customer and staff surveys that give you hard data about the way your customers and staff view your company.

And now the questions . . .

___ Is it customary to regularly survey our customers to find out how satisfied they are with our service and products?

___ Do we have a written, clearly articulated mission statement that stresses our commitment to providing customers with quality products and an excellent level of customer care?

___ Do we have specific, long-range goals for improving and enhancing customer satisfaction within our company?

___ Do we make day-to-day decisions that are consistent with our customer-satisfaction goals and stated mission?

___ Does taking care of our customers have a higher priority than do the internal politics of our company?

___ Do we collect data on the aspects of our service that are statistically measurable, such as telephone waiting times, e-mail response time, the percent of deliveries that are made on time, defect dates, and so on?

___ Do we focus an equal amount of attention on service excellence and cost-cutting to increase our profits and earnings?

___ In their everyday dealings with their staff and customers, do our managers consistently demonstrate the service attitude and skills we expect our staff to show toward our customers?

___ Do we have an effective process for handling complaints so that the feedback we receive is translated into preventive measures?

___ Do we regularly survey our employees to find out how satisfied they are with their jobs, their managers, and the company?

___ Is it customary for us to meet with our employees to get their ideas on how our service and products can be improved?

___ Do we provide our staff members with job descriptions that include specific, measurable criteria and standards for service excellence?

___ Do we collect and make available data on the effects of poor service (mistakes, waste, redoing work, lack of communication, lost customers) and what it costs our company in terms of time, effort, money, and morale?

___ Do we regularly meet with staff members to keep them updated on relevant objectives, changes, and plans within the organization that affect their jobs?

___ Do we have a means of internal communication, such as a company newsletter, that regularly focuses on service excellence as the key to our company's success?

___ Do we train our managers to fulfill their roles in creating a service-oriented organization?

___ Do we train front-line staff in effective telephone, face-to-face, and e-mail customer relations skills?

___ Do we educate internal service staff about the important role they play in customer care and satisfaction?

___ Do we put new hires through an orientation program that stresses the importance of service excellence and their roles, as individuals, in creating excellence?

___ Do we consistently look for ways to reduce bureaucracy, red tape, and other obstacles that get in the way of our staff being able to best serve the customer?

___ Do we promote staff members who demonstrate excellent service and people skills to management positions?

___ Do we have an organizational structure that minimizes the number of levels between the customer and senior management?

___ Do we have telephone systems that reduce the amount of customer waiting time and enable customers to get through to us easily and quickly?

___ Do we maintain an atmosphere that informally recognizes employees who provide service excellence to customers?

___ Do we have computer systems that enable our staff to provide fast, efficient, and responsive service to our customers?

___ Are our current policies and procedures customer-friendly and centered on the customer's convenience in addition to our own?

___ Do we have a process in place that enables us to make specific changes in our policies, procedures, and systems, based on customer feedback?

___ Do we have minimally acceptable customer-care standards in place for customer satisfaction?

___ Do our performance reviews evaluate the degree to which staff members are meeting the specific standards set for service excellence?

___ Do staff members understand the connection between our mission statement, their jobs, and the established service standards?

___ Have we established an executive task team to review the status of service within our organization and to create a plan for its continued improvement?

___ Do we use feedback we receive from customers as the basis for determining what our service standards will be?

___ Do we periodically review and update these standards of performance?

___ Do we have a formal recognition program that rewards excellence in customer care and service?

___ Do we discipline and council employees who do not demonstrate the desired service attitude and skills or who aren't performing up to the established standards?

___ Do we have examples of individuals in our organization who have gone beyond what was expected to perform an almost heroic act to serve a customer?

___ Do our senior managers make a point of regularly meeting with customers?

___ Do we go out of our way to acknowledge staff members for their efforts on behalf of customers, rather than reprimanding them for going beyond the scope of their authority?

___ **Total score**

Scoring your responses and making improvements

Add your numbers up for all of the questions and get a total score. Look at the list below to determine what stage your company or department currently is at with regard to being customer-focused.

- ✔ **Level 1:** Bean counting (0 to 26 points)
- ✔ **Level 2:** Posters, pins, and plaques (27 to 57 points)
- ✔ **Level 3:** Tiger by the tail (58 to 83 points)
- ✔ **Level 4:** Bull's-eye (84 to 114 points)

You can find out more about the *dangers* and *recommendations* at each level by reading on.

Level 1: Bean counting (0–26 points)

If your company or department scored in Level 1, the bean counters are running your company. Your organization probably views customer service as a low priority and focuses most of its attention on financial goals and activities that impact the bottom line, such as cost cutting, budgets, and so on.

Short-term results are considered more valuable than long-term gains, and results are measured by quantity not by quality. At this level, pursuing financial gains to the exclusion of customer satisfaction is like jumping over a dollar to get to a dime.

Danger: You won't see the importance of customer service until it's too late and an emergency, such as lost accounts or reduced market share, forces you to make customer service a higher priority. When your company gets to this point, you often face the additional pressure of uncertainty regarding the future, which makes improving service even more challenging. We have witnessed the panicked look on the faces of people at our workshops who realize that they needed to be paying attention to their service long before it became an emergency.

Recommendation: Do something about service before it's too late. Examine how important customer service is to the overall, long-term success of your business. You may want to begin by building your company's awareness of the importance of customer service by:

- Conducting a survey to measure current levels of customer satisfaction.
- Sending managers and staff to customer-service training.
- Gathering information that shows the effect providing poor service has on your company.

Level 2: Posters, pins, and plaques (27–57 points)

The walls of your business tell the entire story. Having seen the light, management has put up posters, handed out pins, and designed plaques declaring such popular platitudes as:

- The customer is *job one*.
- The customer is *king*.
- The customer is *always right*.

Actions speak louder than words

A transportation company we know spent a great deal of time telling its staff that customer service was the future of its business. The problem: The staff had seen little action from management that demonstrated this commitment to customer service. Executives eventually realized that they needed to do something to prove to their staff that they were serious about doing whatever was necessary to improve service. For years, staff and customers had complained about how far one of the service buildings had fallen into disrepair. It needed new carpet and a coat of paint. In a move that surprised everyone, executives refurbished the building. This simple, low-cost, yet highly visible action said more to the staff than anything else management had done. This step was the beginning of a service-improvement process that continues to this day.

Improvement takes time

A couple on TV has a show about how to remodel houses. In one show, I watched them put in a complete drainage system in three minutes. In the first 30 seconds, they showed how to mark off the trench. In the next 60 seconds, a backhoe arrived and began digging the ditch. Effortlessly and without any mishaps, they next installed the drainage pipes, all of which fit perfectly. Leaning on their shovels and wearing protective eyewear, they wiped their brows and moved on to replacing the roof! "This is fiction!" I thought. Nobody I know would expect to go out and redo his or her drains so effortlessly. Neither should you expect to remodel a business in record time — especially where customer service is concerned.

Management now is convinced of the importance of providing customer service but has yet to make customer service a part of everyday business. Management has begun promoting the ideas behind customer service and probably has taken one or two highly visible actions to this end. At this level, the attitude of the staff is: "This sounds good, but we'll see whether management follows through."

Danger: Your company may get stuck in talk and theory but not go into real changes, thus creating an attitude that customer service is just another program of the month. If this issue is not resolved, skepticism among the staff makes any future attempts at improving customer service more difficult.

Recommendation: Take a highly visible action that clearly demonstrates the company's commitment to customer service. Follow the advice from old adages: "Put your money where your mouth is" and "Walk what you talk." Your staff probably will view the actions you take as a benefit to them or to the customer. Something to think about: What customer-service problem can you fix that your staff has been complaining about forever?

Level 3: Tiger by the tail (58–83 points)

You've grabbed a tiger by the tail! Good job! Even though you're in the middle of creative chaos and may feel as if you're continually on the brink of being out of control, your company is well on its way to customer-service excellence. Your staff members are excited by all the positive changes and are cautiously optimistic about the future. A feeling that "We still have a ways to go" permeates throughout the company. Like a trip to the moon, you've achieved liftoff, and it's too late to go back but too soon to see exactly where you're going.

Danger: You've opened Pandora's Box, and all your company's service weaknesses and problems are laid out before you. Now that you see all that needs to be fixed, you may become overwhelmed and paralyzed, and you may, consequently, throw in the towel before you've accomplished all that you want to.

ANECDOTE

Requiring an ongoing commitment

We had the privilege a few years ago of working with an international hotel chain that has a great reputation for service. In meetings with senior managers, we were continually impressed by their appetite for continuously improving service. Even though their customer surveys showed they were doing an excellent job, they still said things like:

✔ "We're only as good as the guest's last visit."

✔ "We want to continue to be the best."

✔ "We can always improve."

The ongoing commitment of these managers to continued improvement is what sets them apart from their competitors and continues to make them winners in their field.

Recommendation: Keep the big picture in mind, and don't try to fix everything all at once. Remember, Rome wasn't built in a day. One way to keep your focus without losing your mind is to select one specific service problem (not necessarily a big one) and completely resolve it before going on to the next. If you follow this routine for six months, you'll be amazed by how many indirect problems also are solved. Just remember that the light is at the end of the tunnel, but it isn't the headlight of an oncoming train.

Level 4: Bull's-eye! (84–114 points)

Congratulations! Your company makes service a way of life. You've created a strong focus on customer satisfaction that influences the way managers and staff members do their jobs every day. The service culture is so strong that it has taken on a life of its own, and you see quick returns from the efforts you put into service improvement. Your staff members see customer service as an important part of the jobs they do, and they know that the company will back them up in doing what it takes to please the customer.

Danger: When all systems are ready to go, becoming complacent is easy, and you may get blindsided by the arrogance of success. In other words, don't read or believe your own press releases. At this level, the biggest danger is the tendency to rest on your laurels, thinking that you've arrived.

Recommendation: Look for new ways to be innovative. Take a risk and do something that hasn't been done before in your company or industry. Ask yourself: "How can we move our existing services to the next level?" The president of a major airline put it this way: "Our job is to make our existing services obsolete before our competitors do."

Chapter 3

Building a Winning Service Strategy

Standing face to face with the inevitable task of coming up with a plan for improving service can be paralyzing. Many companies know that customer service is important, and they genuinely want to improve the quality of service they offer. Unfortunately, few realize that doing so requires developing an overall strategy that translates this desire into day-to-day reality.

One of the hardest lessons for business leaders to deal with is that neither excellent product quality nor the latest, greatest technology is the cure for all their customer relationship ills. Ultimately, the key to long-lasting customer loyalty and retention is to go *beyond* the strategy of technological excellence and embrace all the key strategic elements that can make your company a winner at the service game.

In this chapter, you'll explore the six key areas that your company must take action on in order to achieve a true customer focus. These areas are time-tested and are at the core of what truly successfully companies do to make their business a place where customer loyalty and satisfaction are paramount.

Six Key Strategies for Customer Service

Becoming customer-centric is a process that requires focus, effort, and action in certain strategic areas. In this section, we discuss each of these six key strategic areas and show you how to implement them.

Fish stinks from the head down

An old Dutch adage says, "Fish stinks from the head down." We gained firsthand experience of this sage wisdom when we were invited to present our ideas on how to create a customer-centric organization to the senior executives of a large and well-known manufacturing company. The execs had just completed a $2 million, two-year overhaul of their manufacturing capabilities aimed at improving overall quality. Although they were pleased with the progress they'd made — especially in product quality — they were scratching their heads in wonderment about the results of their most recent customer and employee surveys. Despite their efforts, they still were getting relatively low scores when it came to the company's overall responsiveness to customer and staff problems and concerns. They asked us to meet with them to help figure out why and strategize a plan to address the problem.

As soon as the meeting started, it became apparent that the president and his senior management team were uncomfortable with our core beliefs on what it takes to create a customer-centric organization. At almost every turn, they took issue with the guiding principles of a customer-centric organization. They were ambivalent about modeling service from the top down, making meaningful use of feedback, educating every person about quality service, setting service standards, and recognizing employee service excellence. (Rest assured: All these principles are explored in detail in this book.)

Realizing that we needed to give them a bit of time to digest what we were saying, we took a break. During the break, one of the senior vice presidents shuffled us into a dark corner of the boardroom. He said, with fear in his eyes, "Are you trying to tell me that the way I treat my staff has an effect on how they treat their customers?" "Yes," we said, relieved that our message had, at last, gotten through to one person. Unfortunately, we were mistaken. In disgust, he shook his head, lit his pipe, and wandered off through a billowing cloud of smoke.

As the meeting went on, it became crystal clear to us why this company had the problems it did. The final straw came when we boldly (in their opinion) dared to put forth the idea that there might be a direct connection between their survey results and their lack of focus on the quality of service the customers received. The body language of the group said, unmistakably, "Heretics!" The day eventually ended. Much to our relief, the company didn't call us again.

Don't fall into the trap of thinking that developing a strategy and taking action in only one of these six essential areas can do the trick — because it won't. We've seen countless companies try to shortcut this process by just doing the training or putting the extra service blurbs into the company newsletter. Although these aren't bad actions to take, they can't stand alone. If you're committed to making your company more customer-focused, then by default you're also committed to changing your company's culture. Doing so requires a willingness to reevaluate and even redesign how you do business. No shortcuts are available. If there were, then everyone would be using the same shortcuts, and no shortage of good service would exist. Moreover, you wouldn't be able to create the service advantage that leaves your competitors eating your dust!

Taking a top-down approach

Most business owners, executives, and senior managers, when asked, nod their heads in complete agreement that excellent customer relations are the cornerstone of a successful business. In the final analysis, however, what matters isn't what they say, it's what they *do*. A manager's actions can greatly enhance the staff's commitment to providing improved service.

Many managers express their commitment to service by taking a roll-up-your-sleeves approach and modeling excellent service skills. Examples of this approach include

- ✓ **Executives at a well-known communications company who took complaint calls in the customer-service department once a month.** They personally followed up on all the calls they answered until the issues were resolved.

- ✓ **Executives at a rental car company who took a trip every week on a shuttle from the rental location to the airport terminal to speak with passengers and get their impressions of the service the company offered.** Each of the executives brought back stories and suggestions to their monthly management meetings.

- ✓ **A general manager in a transportation company who started holding informal lunch gatherings on a regular basis.** The meetings gave employees an opportunity to ask him questions and make comments or suggestions related to improving the conditions at work and the quality of the customer service they offered.

No quicker way exists for an executive to hinder a company's progress toward becoming customer centric than by promoting service excellence with her words and expressing mediocrity with her actions — for example, a senior manager who recommends service training for employees but refuses to participate in the training herself.

Asking for feedback (and actually using it)

Many companies mistakenly assume that they know what their customers want. One of the first and most important steps in becoming customer centric is taking steps to find out — rather than just assuming that you already know — what your customers want and expect of you. You need to discover whether you're meeting, and hopefully exceeding, their expectations. You can put your fingers on the pulse of your customers' experience by conducting surveys and forming focus groups. See Chapter 4 for specific details about how to develop customer and staff surveys.

ANECDOTE

Know thyself! (and know thy customers!)

As part of a survey we conducted for one division of a large multinational, we asked senior executives, middle managers, and front-line staff to choose from a list of 100 service qualities the ones they thought were most important to their customers. We then asked those same customers to choose from the same list. The three qualities the supplier thought were most important were ranked by the customers as the least important service qualities on the list. The three items listed by the customers as the most important were listed by the supplier as the least important!

After you gather and analyze the data, be sure to close the loop by reporting any appropriate findings back to the people you surveyed. At the conclusion of the surveys, after you digest the feedback, you can get in touch with your customers any number of ways, including:

- ✔ Sending a letter thanking your clients for their feedback, outlining your major findings, and proposing the next steps.
- ✔ Sending an e-mail, no longer than three or four paragraphs, that summarizes the findings from the report and highlights any actions you plan to take.
- ✔ Inviting customers who participated in the survey to a meeting where you present the overall survey results and conclusions.

As a byproduct of conducting the survey and sharing the results (good and bad), your company can enjoy an enhanced image and greater prestige among customers who played an active role in the evaluation process.

TIP

Gathering feedback from staff is another significant step in discovering where you stand as a company. We often begin consultations with a client by conducting an employee survey that focuses on how the company treats *its own staff*. This "cultural X-ray" provides an inside look at the organization's internal focus that gives us an insight into how the current company culture is affecting customer service. A company that treats its staff poorly can't expect the staff to treat customers like royalty.

Educating everyone, everywhere

Your front-line staff has the greatest amount of interaction with your customers. Many times, however, these are the workers within the organization who receive the least amount of education. In this context, *education* means formal classroom-style training in which the objective is to build skills and awareness in specific areas of service excellence and any *general improve-ment activities,* including coaching sessions, team problem-solving meetings, and so on that illuminate the importance of service in those staff members' specific jobs.

The overarching activities of service education can take the form of newslet-ters, briefings, meetings, videos, and so on. Maximum effectiveness is gained when formal training and general education are combined — as in the follow-ing case:

> One company we know waited a full year into its customer service improvement program before introducing service-skills training to its staff. The reasoning: The company's managers wanted to wait until they were sure that the staff was well informed (general education) about the company's long-term sales and service strategies and some planned changes in the organizational structure and systems. By preparing the soil in such a way, the formal service training, once initiated (with ses-sions focusing on such topics as dealing with difficult customers, going the extra step, and so on) took root quickly. This approach produced immediate positive feedback from customers who noticed a definite atti-tude change.

Educating the front-line staff alone isn't enough to create a customer-centric company. Equally as important as educating your front-line staff is training the managers of your company about how to create an environment that favors service excellence. "Train those people (the front-line staff), and the wheels of the corporate machine will keep running smoothly" is a manage-ment mentality we often run into in our consulting work. Merely focusing on the front lines rarely leads to improved service and almost always leads to resentment.

For example, enthusiasm generated by participants in a training workshop is fragile; it's easily extinguished by the environment to which they must return. The manager must take steps to reinforce what was learned in the workshop. Otherwise, the training may be quickly forgotten, and the money spent for naught.

Creating customer-centric systems

In our work, we see that *in-focused systems,* systems that work favorably for the company but unfavorably for the customer, serve as the fulcrum on which a successful move toward being customer centered rests. Companies must be willing to examine and change these systems to become more cus-tomer centric. Until the inherent service problems caused by such systems are resolved, any service improvements are limited.

The prospect of creating customer-centric systems can be overwhelming. Part of the problem lies in the tangled web of procedures, policies, and actual technology that make up the systems and act as a blueprint for the way a company does business. Although obviously indispensable, these systems can help or hurt your customers and staff, depending on how they're designed.

Some systems are set up with an objective of preventing employees and customers from taking advantage of the company — a protective measure. For example, the delivery procedure for a large consumer-products company involved delivery personnel having to call the distribution center for authorization to accept merchandise for return to the warehouse. The call to the distribution center was then routed to the warehouse manager, who then called the sales manager for approval, and so on, ad nauseam. This time-consuming procedure delayed the driver enough to make him late for his next delivery. This inefficiency was further compounded (and confounded) by the fact that permission for the return of merchandise was granted in nine cases out of ten.

Customers suffered as a result of a system that made returns unnecessarily difficult and prevented drivers from completing their routes on time — even though the company derived some benefit by slightly reducing the amount of returned merchandise.

Other systems still exist because they're the way the company always has done business. No one questions their validity or effectiveness. One woman at a workshop that we led stated the problem perfectly when she said, "In our company, adhering to the procedures and policies overrides common sense!"

Quality groups or service-improvement teams (see Chapter 9) work well when developing procedures and processes. They empower the entire staff to take ownership of the new procedures and processes and ensure that staff members who are the closest to the customers and know the most about the issues are an integral part of brainstorming service solutions. Remember that changes in processes and technology need to be based on customer and employee feedback. After you've gathered feedback, you can use quality groups to design the new procedures and processes.

Using a broken ceiling to boost morale

In an earthquake in San Francisco a few years ago, downtown businesses sustained a considerable amount of damage to their offices. In one case, most of the ceiling tiles in the customer-service department crashed down onto staff members' desks. No one was hurt, but the place was a mess. The manager wanted to lift his staff's morale, so he took one of the ceiling tiles, spray-painted it gold, and with an inscription dubbed it "The Mover And Shaker Award." Each month, he put the award on the desk of the best performing customer-service representative. This manager proved that it isn't so much the award as it is the spirit in which it's given.

The six keys to customer service in the real world

One major airline has developed a system that links all six customer-service strategies together. Once every quarter, the airline surveys several thousand passengers while they're waiting to retrieve their luggage in baggage claim. The results of the survey are turned over to task teams who look for trends and make service improvements based on the customer feedback. Training courses are then updated to reflect concerns highlighted in the surveys. The next quarter the whole process starts over again, thus creating a loop between all six essential strategic areas.

Developing consistency

Friendliness, courtesy, responsiveness, and accuracy are worthy goals, but how do you achieve them, given that they mean different things to different people? If you ask ten people what being friendly to a customer means, you'll more than likely receive ten different answers. You have to quantify *service quality* by developing specific, objective, and measurable service standards that translate service quality into specific behaviors and actions. *Service standards* provide a basis for the objective evaluation of staff performance and ensure consistency of treatment for customers across the board.

You must clearly communicate to your staff the behaviors that are required to meet these standards. For example:

A manager for a large hotel chain with whom we were working received multiple complaints from customers that his senior front-desk clerk was difficult to deal with. In an attempt to remedy the situation, the manager explained to the clerk the importance of being friendly. Much to the manager's dismay, none of his coaching produced the desired result. Finally, the front-desk clerk asked the manager to detail specifically what he should do to appear friendly. The manager realized that he had wrongly assumed the clerk knew how to translate the service quality of *friendliness* into specific behaviors. Obviously, the clerk didn't know the specific behaviors, so the manager explained that the clerk should smile, make eye contact, use the customer's name, and so on. Within a few weeks, the manager received numerous compliments from customers on the front-desk clerk's friendly manner.

Recognizing excellence every chance you get

In a company's culture, what gets recognized and rewarded is what gets done. Every recognition program needs to have three important elements:

✔ **A formal recognition program:** Formal recognition can be department-, division-, or company-wide. It needs to provide rewards for the individual or team that best fulfills specified service criteria. The rewards can include cash, movie tickets, vacations, and so on.

✔ **An atmosphere of informal recognition:** Casual, everyday acknowledgment of staff that's often expressed by the manager's spontaneous gestures is what we're talking about here. It can be in the form of thank-you notes, pizza parties, sharing customers' complimentary letters, and so on.

✔ **Salary and advancement:** In the final analysis, all staff must see some personal benefit in increasing their sensitivity toward customers. If providing quality customer service isn't central to the possibility of advancement in pay and position, then the gospel of service becomes just so much hot air.

Implementing Your Strategy

In the immortal words of Will Rogers:

> *Even if you are on the right track, you'll get run over if you just sit there.*

Being aware of the key areas in building a winning service strategy is only half of the picture. Your next step is creating an overall implementation plan that takes your strategy from paper to reality. This plan has four phases, each of which we discuss in detail in this section. We've used this strategy and have seen similar ones used with great success in the United States and abroad with:

✔ Manufacturing and service businesses

✔ Public and private sector companies

✔ Fortune 500 and small businesses

Think of this four-phase plan as akin to putting together one of those really big 3-D puzzles of New York's Manhattan skyline. At first, you excitedly open the box and dump the contents onto the dining room table. As you begin to work on the puzzle, you're amazed by how easily things fit into place. After a while, though, you hit the hard spots and become frustrated because you just can't find the top of that darn Empire State Building. Eventually, you arrange all the pieces perfectly, and the completed puzzle is proudly displayed on your dining room table.

Just like working a puzzle, creating an overall strategy for making your company more service-oriented takes patience, careful attention to detail, and diligence to get positive results. However, when the strategy is complete, the clarity you gain for where you're going and how you'll get there, not to mention your sense of satisfaction, is well worth your efforts.

We recommend that you use the following sections as a general guideline to creating an overall service strategy, modifying it where necessary to suit the unique needs and circumstances of your organization.

Phase 1: Awareness building

If you've already invested some time in improving the quality of service your company or department is providing, much of your effort still may be focused on other priorities and goals, such as generating revenue, cutting costs, and budgeting — with more attention going toward quantitative rather than qualitative aspects of the company.

This first phase of implementing your service strategy is designed to help you build awareness throughout your company (from the top to bottom) of the overall importance of the role that service plays in your company's future. The main activities that we recommend in this phase are

- **Conducting formal surveys of your customers to assess overall satisfaction levels and determine the main customer-service issues.** Benchmarking your starting point before you begin any service improvement program is essential. Various methods you can use to gather feedback include

  - Telephone interviews
  - Mail surveys
  - Face-to-face interviews
  - E-mail surveys
  - Complaint-analysis tools
  - Lost-account surveys
  - Focus groups

  If you haven't done your customer research, stop dead in your tracks; go no further. Don't waste your time by moving on to other phases before you actually know what your customers and staff think.

- **Creating an executive task team to champion the service improvement effort.** This task team should be composed of managers and executives with enough clout and authority to make and implement decisions that affect the policies, procedures, and processes within your company. Avoid the mistake of creating a task team of managers too junior to really make anything fly.

✔ **Determining the overall objectives and goals of the service improvement effort, which include developing a timeline and establishing accountabilities.** Many companies have a vision of serving their customers, but few have articulated a specific strategy to accomplish this goal. By using feedback from surveys, the executive task team can develop an overall strategy for service improvement that includes:

  • Setting specific goals for customer satisfaction — for example, achieving a 90 percent excellent rating on all product review forms.

  • Deciding on specific actions to be taken in each of the key areas involved in creating a customer-centric organization — for example, putting all staff and managers through a training program that improves their basic customer-service skills. (See the section titled "Six Key Strategies for Customer Service" at the beginning of this chapter.)

Phase 2: Education and training

At this stage, your company or department already has recognized the importance of quality service, and the talk in meetings and memos is about the need to take better care of customers. Your senior management team may already have even taken one or two highly visible actions toward this end.

The focus in this phase is on putting a specific structure in place that educates all managers and employees (regardless of department) about how they'll participate in the company's goal of becoming more customer centric. We recommend that at a minimum you:

✔ **Hold an all-company meeting or a series of smaller meetings to introduce an initiative designed to make you and your company more customer-friendly.**

✔ **Implement an organization-wide service training program for staff and managers in all areas of the business.** Long-term service improvements won't happen without providing:

  • Customer-service skills for front-line and backroom staff.

  • Service management skills for all managers.

  • Team-oriented problem-solving skills for all employees.

Phase 3: Process improvement

Companies or departments that are ready for Phase 3 are actively engaged in the process of becoming customer centric and genuinely see providing excellent service as a priority. Even though you still think you have a long way to go, your commitment to service is manifested in everyday policies and behaviors that are noticeable to staff and customers alike. At this point, the goal is to dive into the work of evaluating and redesigning (where needed) the major processes and procedures that affect your customers. We recommend that you:

- ✔ **Implement an employee-centered continuous improvement program that includes such elements as quality groups, task teams, or brainstorming sessions that focus on process improvement within the company.**

    Front-line staff members can provide you with invaluable input about how to make your policies and procedures more customer centric, so be sure to draw on their expert knowledge when reviewing major procedures and design standards.

- ✔ **Review major procedures and processes that impact the customer and redesign the ones that need improvement.**

    Although every company has a multitude of systems, the key systems to examine when striving to become a more customer-centric organization include

    - Sales/ordering systems
    - Supply/logistics systems
    - Accounting/payment systems
    - After-sales service systems
    - Complaint procedures
    - Crisis/contingency systems
    - Telephone/computer systems
    - Web/e-mail interfaces
    - Customer relationship management (CRM) systems

- ✔ **Design and implement standards for service excellence throughout the organization.**

    Standards are specific and measurable. For example:

    - Answering the phone within three rings
    - Responding to all e-mail inquires within 48 hours
    - Returning all customer calls within 24 hours
    - Filling all orders within one day of receipt

Taking a kaizen approach

Your mind probably has been racing as you read this chapter. If you're like many people, your thoughts have ping-ponged between relief and pride about what your company is doing right and feelings of regret, concern, or guilt about the areas where you and it fall short.

The Japanese word *kaizen* expresses what we think is a good, basic philosophy to keep in mind as you go through this process. Loosely translated, it means "small, continuous improvements." If you continue to focus on the little, everyday ways you can improve service, you'll find that over time, your company will be able to face its competitors and its future with confidence.

The quest for excellent service in your business has to be a way of life because it's a continuing process that never is over and done with.

Phase 4: Organizational infrastructure

If you've reached this phase, your company or department already has achieved a strong customer-centric business culture. In fact, service excellence seems to have taken on a life of its own and has been translated into specific standards and procedures that permeate the daily operations of your company. Quality service has become, for all intents and purposes, a way of life. Because of the groundwork you've already laid, any efforts you put into further building your company infrastructure to improve service will be relatively easy to implement and produce a high return within a reasonable amount of time. Recommended actions in this phase include the following:

- ✔ **Conducting performance evaluations using established service standards.**
- ✔ **Formally recognizing individual and team efforts toward making improvements in service excellence.**
- ✔ **Redesigning the hiring process to screen applicants for customer-friendly orientation.**

Four Critical Questions

Although many companies go through the process of writing strategies for customer service improvement, a surprising number don't seriously consider the resources (people, time, money, and effort) that are required to turn a strategy into a reality. The four big questions that your company needs to consider as part of finalizing your service improvement plan are highlighted in the sections that follow.

Who needs to be on the implementation team?

Because the implementation of your strategy affects your entire company (not just the more obvious customer contact departments such as sales, marketing, and customer service), all areas including accounting, production, and information services need to be represented on the implementation team.

Making sure the top dogs are on board

Keep in mind that the members of this team are the people who will lead your company through its transformation from in-focused to customer-focused. As such, they need to have the authority to design an overall service strategy and the power to implement it.

Occasionally, we've worked with companies in which executives have tried to clone themselves by delegating their position on the service improvement team to middle managers within the company. This scenario is especially common in larger companies where executives consider themselves too busy to sit in yet more meetings.

This procedure almost never works, because although the middle managers often are well-intentioned, intelligent, capable people, they don't have the political weight or authority to actually implement the plan they've created. Not only does this tactic undermine the implementation process, it also undermines the managers' morale. Managers come up with a great idea and get excited about the possibility of change only to have their hopes dashed when they discover that the executives who put them on the team are forming the roadblocks to getting anything done. For this reason, the senior executives of your company need to be the ones who spearhead the process and take their place as the players on the team.

If you're the owner of the company or the president of your organization, show your sincere commitment to quality service by making it a priority to be on the team and show up at every meeting enthusiastic about the process. This kind of top-driven commitment does more than anything else to inspire the rest of your company to get on the service bandwagon.

If you're the owner of a small business, your core team probably will be composed of you and your top two or three people. If you're a manager with a larger company, the team will need to include top key players within your organization. We've found that having too many people on the team makes it cumbersome to schedule meetings. To make the group as efficient and productive as possible, no more than eight people are needed on the team.

Ensuring consistent attendance and participation

After you've assembled your team, consistency becomes the single most important factor in your team's success. To be consistent, the team needs to meet from two to four hours every four to six weeks.

Moreover, each member must make attending the meetings a priority. At the beginning of the process, most team members are excited. However, as time goes by, the functions of the members' jobs can start to dampen their enthusiasm as short-term, everyday concerns tug at them for attention. If you aren't careful, the meetings can become just one more item on a never-ending to do list, and the bigger purpose of what you're trying to accomplish will be lost.

Bear in mind that a key player missing from a meeting can create havoc down the road, because any major decisions that are made can affect the entire company. Think of the process as similar to climbing a mountain. You and your teammates are standing at base camp looking up at the peak you want to reach. You're all attached to one another with ropes and harnesses and off you go, up the mountain. If you're halfway up the mountain and a team member says, "Sorry, but I changed my mind, I don't want to be here anymore," you have a big problem.

You can help ensure consistent attendance by setting the dates for the next six meetings at the initial gathering. Doing so enables all team members to schedule the meetings well in advance so they can make plans to attend.

 You may want to consider using an outside facilitator for these meetings. A good facilitator keeps the meetings on track, provides coaching on how to implement the action items, and acts as the nonpolitical mediator when disagreements arise.

How long will this take and how much will this cost?

Once you've formulated the plan, your task shifts to implementing it. Implementation takes both time and money. How much, you ask? Read on and find out.

Time

The amount of time it takes to improve customer service within your company depends on the size of your company and how much work you've already done to develop service awareness. Here are some estimates of how long it will take in specific situations:

- ✔ A small business (fewer than 250 employees) can expect to implement an entire service program (all six areas) within one year and see positive results within the first three months.

- ✔ A mid-size company (250 to 1,500 employees) needs closer to two years to implement the entire program but should see noticeable results within the first six months.

- ✔ A large organization (over 1,500 employees) requires a minimum of three years to implement the process, and it will take about one year before any significant results are achieved.

Because becoming more customer-focused is a long-term process rather than a quick fix, we strongly recommend that you let your entire company know that huge results won't be seen right away. By giving your staff members a realistic timeline of what will happen when, you give them reasonable expectations and curb their natural desire to see quick results. In general, you see faster and better results when you focus on the critical few things to get done rather than the trivial many.

Money

We have no magic formula for figuring out exactly what implementing your company's service improvement program will cost. We've met owners of small businesses who've created entire service improvement programs for $10,000. Then again, we've run across many Fortune 500 companies that have spent millions.

In general, though, a total service-improvement strategy from soup to nuts will cost you approximately $1,000 to $1,500 per employee, sometimes more, sometimes less. Part of your team's challenge is to come up with a budget that is workable for your company and sufficient for getting the job done.

There is no free lunch! If your main concern is how to manage this type of strategy on the quick and cheap, then you may want to reconsider how committed you really are to the process. Although you can do many things to keep your costs down and under control, this process requires an upfront commitment of time and financial resources. (If you own a small business and find yourself in a cold sweat right about now, relax. In the following chapters, we suggest plenty of lower-cost solutions that you can use to stay within your means and still produce the desired results.)

It costs five times more marketing and sales dollars to gain a new customer than it does to retain a current one. Most companies we talk to think the money they spend in the short term to improve service has actually resulted in long-term savings. If you look closely, you, too, will probably find that the cost of repeated efforts, wasted time, loss of customer goodwill, and actual loss of customers, is far greater than the amount of money you may spend creating a more customer-focused company.

Who's going to get all this stuff done?

By this point, your team may be having nightmares about working 20-plus hours a day to get their regular jobs done, and at the same time, taking on all the actions your team is planning. Well, we have good news for you: You don't have to move a cot into your office — not just yet anyway.

Each member of your team is assigned the ultimate responsibility for ensuring that a specific action item is completed. This assignment doesn't mean that person is the one who has to carry out the task. On the contrary, he or she is free to delegate selected activities to members of the staff.

What's the best way to communicate the strategy?

One of the biggest pitfalls we've encountered in this process is senior management forgetting to communicate the strategy to the rest of the company.

By informing your staff about the strategy, you open their eyes to the big picture. Following are some suggested methods for communicating your strategy.

Hold an all-company meeting

A fast-and-easy way to get the message out to your employees is to conduct an all-company meeting at which the president and/or senior managers introduce the service strategy. This technique is a great way to get everyone fired up and informed at the same time, and is the preferred method for many small businesses that we know, because getting everyone together in one place at the same time usually is relatively easy.

This method works great if you already have a company picnic, meeting, or conference scheduled, because you have an excellent opportunity to make the event even more special by announcing the service strategy.

Put a meeting tree in place

If you have a fairly large group of employees, you can get the word out quickly by creating the company equivalent of a telephone tree — a meeting tree. Your task team begins by meeting with their direct reports, who then meet with their direct reports, who then meet with their direct reports, and so on. Usually within a few days you can cover the entire company.

Be sure to outline the specific content that you want your managers to deliver. Doing so prevents them from interpreting the message to the point where their creativity gets too far away from the original point.

Limit meeting tree groups to between five and ten people, have a set agenda that includes time for questions and answers, and keep the meetings to less than 30 minutes in length.

Create a corporate video presentation

A corporate video featuring the president of your company (you, perhaps) talking about his or her (your) commitment to customer service can be a very powerful tool for spreading the service message. A few important items to keep in mind if you decide to go this route are

- **Hiring a professional to shoot and edit the videotape.** Nobody likes being subjected to a cheesy, poorly put together video, especially when the tape is talking about the importance of service and quality.

- **Making sure that the president of the company has practiced his or her presentation and, if necessary, has received coaching on how to appear lively, sincere, enthusiastic, and interesting on camera.** If your president looks like Dr. Death on camera, nobody will care about what he or she is saying.

- **Keeping it short and sweet.** Don't try to cover all your company issues in one video. Instead, choose one or two clear messages and stick to them.

Use your company newsletter

If your company already has a widely distributed newsletter in place, you may want to use it to detail the specifics of the service strategy. We recommend that you do so after you've made a general announcement using one of the previously described methods. Your company newsletter is a good tool for keeping your company updated on an ongoing basis and recording the progress your team is making on implementing the strategy.

Chapter 4

Better Service through Surveys: Questionnaires, Focus Groups, and Interviews

*H*aving a customer-focused company means you must understand what your customers want and expect from your business and then evaluate how well you're meeting those desires and expectations. An often overlooked yet vital tool for accomplishing those tasks is the survey. Surveying helps you

✔ Gather specific feedback about how satisfied your customers are with the level of service they receive

✔ Provide an initial benchmark against which you can measure future progress

✔ Make changes, based on your research, to the way you do business

In this chapter, we clue you in on whom you need to survey, the type of survey to conduct, who needs to conduct it, the best survey method to use, and what you should do with the results.

To get the most accurate picture of your customers' service experiences as a whole, use a combination of the methods that we explain in this chapter. For example, you can combine focus groups and written questionnaires, or telephone interviews and Web-based surveys. Either combination gives you a mix of general and specific feedback and qualitative and quantitative data.

Surveying Staff and Customers

If you've already decided to survey your customers and you're reading this chapter to find out the next step, don't stop there. The importance of surveying customers is obvious to most companies; however, we believe that a staff survey also is an essential part of the surveying process.

We recommend that you survey your customers and staff simultaneously (or at least not too far apart), because often the issues that come to light in your customer responses directly correlate to situations described by your staff.

For example, in a survey we conducted for a software company, the majority of customers reported dissatisfaction with the way they were treated when they called the technical support department. In the corresponding staff survey, several technical support representatives complained that their call times were so closely monitored that they felt pressured to give incomplete answers to one customer so they could move on to the next caller. By observing both sides of the problem, the company was able to make some immediate changes for the better.

Figuring Out What Type of Survey You Need to Do

The type of survey that your company chooses depends on your purpose for doing the survey. Are you looking for some insight into why you've lost market share? Are you interested in getting a general idea of how your customers feel about your company? Maybe you've been experiencing high staff turnover and want to get to the bottom of the problem. Here we discuss some basic types of surveys that you may want to consider and why they may or may not be right for you.

Random customer survey

The *random customer survey* is a tried-and-true, good old-fashioned, all-around survey that's used by companies that want to measure overall customer satisfaction and highlight any widespread service problems. Random surveys involve selecting a percentage of your customers; contacting them by phone, e-mail, mail, or in person (or a combination of these approaches); and asking them to evaluate the service they receive from your company. If your company has never conducted a survey, or hasn't done one in a long time, a random survey is a good place to start.

In the written customer surveys we've conducted, the response rate usually is between 40 percent and 60 percent. Remember to take these numbers into account when deciding how many customers you need to survey to get back the number of responses you want.

Company-wide attitude survey

The *company-wide attitude survey* helps you assess three areas that are critical to forging strong links in the chain that determines the service your customers receive.

The company-wide attitude survey almost always is implemented through a confidential questionnaire that is sent out to all staff members and managers. If your company has never conducted a staff survey, or has morale problems such as high turnover, we strongly recommend that you do a company attitude survey.

How satisfied are your staff members with their jobs?

Nothing can tarnish the service your customers receive faster than coming face to face with an employee who has a resentful attitude about his job or your company.

This attitude can be caused by many things, but we find the most common are:

- Not feeling listened to or appreciated
- Feeling overwhelmed by an ever-increasing workload
- Inadequate job training or support
- Lack of teamwork between departments
- Poor supervisors or managers

Although none of these situations can be corrected overnight, a survey can help highlight common problem areas and put them on the table for discussion.

Do you have open channels of communication?

We've yet to deal with a company that didn't have communication problems. The question is: How serious are those problems? If, for example, your staff members feel disenfranchised because they have no formal avenues for giving feedback to upper management, then their frustration will be taken out on customers. A staff survey can help you assess how well you're establishing open channels of communication and where room for improvement exists.

Do employees feel a sense of teamwork throughout your company?

Is each person within your company an island unto himself or herself? If the coffee pot runs dry, does the last person using it brew another pot? If a customer calls in and reaches the wrong person, is she treated with care and concern or is she transferred randomly into telephone hyperspace? A staff survey can help a great deal with identifying and correcting teamwork deficiencies throughout your company.

Lost account survey

This type of survey is excellent whenever your company wants to know why it has lost a particular customer or group of customers. Using this survey, interviews are conducted (usually by telephone or in person — rarely e-mail) with customers who no longer do business with your company.

One of the greatest benefits of the lost account survey is that you're often able to discover specific reasons why customers left. You can also let the lost customer know that you're sorry that he's no longer doing business with you and that you're interested in learning from your mistakes. Understanding the customer's reasons for leaving helps you make improvements for future customers.

Because you're catching the customer at a critical moment, you may have an opportunity during the interview to save the account by using *bounce-back initiative,* which means responding to a service problem by doing something extra as a way of apologizing to the customer (see Chapter 16).

Depending on your industry, isolating the customer's actual moment of departure isn't always easy, and without that information, recovering a customer before it's too late can be difficult, because you may miss your window of opportunity to take timely and effective actions. If you're able to catch the customer in time, we recommend that you prevent the person who originally was responsible from contacting the customer. To maintain objectivity, you can instead have someone who has no previous contact with the customer conduct the interview.

Target account survey

Rather than doing a random survey of your customer base, you may want to do a more targeted and focused survey of a particular group of customers. For example, if 80 to 90 percent of your business comes from ten customers, you may want to create a survey that is specifically targeted toward them. The advantage of a targeted survey is that it is limited in scope, precisely focused, and can be specifically designed for a particular group.

We recommend this type of survey especially when you want to improve service for a particular segment of your customer base.

Customer exit survey

On-the-spot interviews conducted with customers as they exit from your place of business are great for assessing their immediate opinion of the service they've just received. For example, at one time or another, you've probably been stopped by someone with a clipboard in hand as you left the supermarket. That person probably asked whether you had a moment to answer a few questions about the service you received at the store that day. These *customer exit surveys* are a cousin of random customer surveys (see section by the same name earlier in the chapter), with one important exception: They catch the customer immediately after he or she receives the service. Doing so provides you with specific, accurate, and immediate feedback while the experience is still fresh in the customer's mind.

We recommend this type of survey whenever your customers physically visit your place of business to use services or purchase products.

Determining Who Needs to Conduct Your Survey

Should you use an outside resource or conduct the survey using in-house talent? That *is* the question! And the answer is not unlike deciding whether you should fix your own car.

The main advantages of doing it yourself are that you can save money and learn from the experience. The main disadvantage is that because you're probably not an expert, you may encounter unexpected problems that can cost you additional time and money to fix.

Many companies choose to use an outside resource — a consulting company or market research firm — to conduct their surveys, because they have the expertise on hand to deliver top-notch survey results in the most efficient way.

In either case, conducting a survey requires varying amounts of resources (mostly time and money) depending on the scope of your project. You need to consider three things when deciding whether you conduct the survey using in-house talent or whether you employ the services of an outside agency that specializes in service surveys. We discuss those things in this section.

Assessing the size and makeup of your customer base

If your customer base runs into the thousands and you have various groups (based on buying patterns, geographic location, or type of industry) requiring separate review and analysis, then you probably need to consider using an outside company to conduct your survey.

For example, suppose your customer base is made up of 3,000 accounts that break down into two distinct groups. Accounts in one group buy your services or products in small quantities, yet they buy frequently, and accounts in a second group buy infrequently but purchase large amounts. In this case, you may want to ask each group different questions and then compare the responses. One of our clients discovered that their infrequent customers who purchased large amounts generally preferred a personal call from a company representative once a year rather than receiving monthly newsletters or more frequent follow-ups. On the other hand, their frequent, small purchasers generally wanted monthly updates via e-mail. By adjusting how they contacted each group of customers, they saved money and kept both types of customer happier.

The openness and honesty of your staff

When conducting your staff survey, you should consider how easy — or difficult — getting honest feedback will be. We find that most employees are reluctant to write down what they really think when they know the results are going to be scrutinized in-house. Even if you insist that they fill out the survey anonymously, they may still worry that their answers will somehow be recognized and used against them! Issues about confidentiality (and paranoia) can undermine in-house staff surveys even when they're conducted with the best of intentions.

We once conducted a survey for a company that long ago had forgotten to treat members of its staff like customers. Not surprisingly, low staff morale was taking its toll on the service customers were receiving. After we mailed staff questionnaires, we received several personal phone calls from various staff members wanting to know whether the survey was truly confidential and whether we really could be trusted not to leak their identities to their bosses. Because we were an outside consulting company and had no axe to grind, we were able to reassure staff and get some insightful feedback. This feedback, we are sure, would not have been forthcoming had the company collected the information itself.

Figuring Out Which Survey Method to Use

Survey methods are simply different ways that you can use to collect feedback from your customers and staff. In this section, we talk about the seven main survey methods and why each may or may not be the best method for you to use.

Web-based surveys

A Web-based survey is an easy, effective, and relatively inexpensive way to measure your customers' online service experience. You can hire professional companies to design your survey and evaluate the results, or if you have the time and resources, you can design and evaluate a survey in-house. The three basic types of Web-based surveys are

- **E-mail invitation:** Start by sending out an e-mail invitation to a designated group of customers, asking them to participate in a survey. Embed a link for customers to click if they decide they want to complete the survey. Upon clicking this link, they're electronically whisked away to your survey.

- **Pop-up window:** A pop-up window survey counts the number of visitors who come to your site. At a predetermined number of visits to a company's Web site (for example, every 200 visitors), a pop-up window opens asking that user whether she's willing to fill out a short online survey. If the visitor chooses not to complete the survey, she can click "No." The pop-up window disappears, and she can go on her merry way. Clicking "Yes" takes her to the online survey.

Many people are so tired of pop-up windows that they close them without thinking. If you choose this survey type, be sure to make it clear that the survey is legitimate and part of your Web site rather than an unauthorized intruder piggybacking your page.

- **Feedback or survey buttons:** Similar to the "tell us what you think" survey cards found in most hotel rooms, feedback buttons tend to draw feedback from extreme customers — either extremely satisfied or extremely upset ones. For that reason, we recommend that you try to avoid using feedback or survey buttons. Feedback buttons likewise don't provide representative samplings of your customer population, and response rates for feedback buttons tend to be low (less than 1 percent), so your survey results aren't statistically valid.

Written questionnaires

The Internet has made surveying much easier and more cost-effective than it used to be. Today you can e-mail a questionnaire to your employees and customers on the other side of the world — instantly! Whether they respond as quickly is another matter.

Regardless of whether you go paper or digital, always limit your surveys to one or two pages, because any more can tax the short attention span that most of us have for answering questions. Give good thought to the questions, making sure they address the specific concerns of the customer or staff group that you're surveying. The questions you ask in the survey usually need to be phrased in one of following three ways.

Yes-or-no questions

Yes-or-no questions are *closed-ended questions,* meaning that they're phrased in such a way that they prompt simple *yes* or *no* answers. These questions commonly are used to gather general information. The *respondent* (the person answering) simply circles or clicks the appropriate responses. For example:

Do you have a living will?	Yes	No
Is your current life insurance sufficient?	Yes	No
Do you own your own home?	Yes	No

Poor-to-excellent questions

Poor-to-excellent questions usually begin with the words "how" or "what" and ask respondents to rank their responses on a scale from poor to excellent. Respondents simply answer the questions by clicking the word or number that best reflects their opinions. For example:

How would you rate the overall service you received from our technical support staff? (Circle one.)

Poor   Fair   Good   Excellent

What is your overall evaluation of our technical support group? (Circle one.)

(Poor) 1   2   3   4   5   6 (Excellent)

Degree questions

Degree questions usually start with the words "did," "does," "do," or "to what degree." They usually refer to specific experiences or events and ask respondents to rate their responses by choosing one of four specific descriptive phrases. For example:

To what degree did our Web site answer your questions about our company? (Select one.)

___ To a large degree

___ To a moderate degree

___ To a small degree

___ Not at all

Similarly, you can present statements that offer a scale of possible answers that range from "strongly agree" to "strongly disagree." Respondents simply receive an instruction, such as: "Choose the phrase that best reflects your opinions." For example:

Our accounting department provides you with accurate and timely billing. (Select one.)

___ Strongly agree

___ Agree

___ Disagree

___ Strongly disagree

The salesperson I deal with is very knowledgeable about the product. (Select one.)

(Strongly agree) 1   2   3   4   5   6 (Strongly disagree)

If you're using a numbering format and want to avoid middle-of-the-road answers, use a series of numbers that ends with an even number, such as 1 to 6, rather than a series of numbers that ends with an odd number, such as 1 to 5. By using an even amount of numbers, you remove the middle-number option, and thus the respondent must get off the fence and express a preference in one direction or the other.

Sample questionnaires and memos

Here are samples of a customer questionnaire and a staff questionnaire that you can use as guidelines for developing your own surveys. In addition to the sample questionnaires, we include some sample e-mail memos to customers and staff members inviting them to participate in the surveying process.

These memos give you an idea of the flavor and content you may want to include in your own e-mails to your customers and staff. Make sure that you let your customers and staff members know how much you appreciate their participation in the survey.

Sample Customer Questionnaire General Survey

Please circle one rating for each of the following questions. (A space is provided after each question for you to write down any responses or comments you have that relate to the question.)

1. **How do you rate the overall service that you receive from us?**

   (Poor) 1   2   3   4   5   6 (Excellent)

   Comments:

2. **How do you rate our overall systems capabilities?**

   (Poor) 1   2   3   4   5   6 (Excellent)

   Comments:

3. **How do you rate the overall quality of our sales representative?**

   (Poor) 1   2   3   4   5   6 (Excellent)

   Comments:

4. **How do you rate the consistency of service among our different offices?**

   (Poor) 1   2   3   4   5   6 (Excellent)

   Comments:

5. **Generally speaking, does our company (check one):**

   ❏ exceed your expectations

   ❏ satisfy your expectations

   ❏ not live up to your expectations

   Comments:

6. **What are your recommendations for improving the quality of service/ services we offer you?**

   Comments:

7. **Given your business and industry, how do we need to change to be able to continue to be your partner five years from now?**

   Comments:

8. **How do you rate our overall computer capabilities?**

   (Poor) 1   2   3   4   5   6 (Excellent)

   Comments:

   NAME AND ADDRESS (Optional):

   Thank you.

Sample Staff Questionnaire

On a scale of 1 to 4, with 1 being "strongly disagree" and 4 being "strongly agree," please indicate your response by circling the number that most accurately reflects your feelings about the following statements. (A space is provided after each question for you to write down any examples, suggestions, or comments you have that relate to the question.)

1. **The management of our company genuinely believes in the importance of providing an excellent level of service to customers.**

   1   2   3   4

   Comments:

2. **My manager sets a good example of satisfying customer needs by his/her actions at work.**

   1   2   3   4

   Comments:

3. **When I go out of my way to help a customer, I am usually supported and acknowledged by my manager for doing so.**

   1   2   3   4

   Comments:

4. **I have been provided with the training, support, and equipment that I need to perform my job effectively.**

   1   2   3   4

   Comments:

5. **I understand the policies and procedures of my company and have flexibility to alter them as necessary to get my job done to the best degree.**

   1   2   3   4

   Comments:

6. **My manager gives me regular, constructive feedback on both the positive and negative aspects of how I am performing my job.**

   1   2   3   4

   Comments:

7. **Our company does a good job of recognizing and rewarding staff for excellence in job performance.**

   1   2   3   4

   Comments:

8. **My manager supports and encourages us to create teamwork between our department and other departments within the company.**

   1   2   3   4

   Comments:

9. **My manager makes a habit of asking me and my co-workers what support we need and/or what suggestions we have to do our jobs with the highest degree of excellence.**

   1   2   3   4

   Comments:

10. **In my opinion, our company's strongest points are:**

    Comments:

11. **In my opinion, our company's weakest points are:**

    Comments:

Sample cover e-mail — customer, written questionnaire

Dear Customer:

We are committed to serving you, our customer, to the best of our ability. To this end, we have asked an independent consulting company to assess our customer orientation and commitment to providing quality service.

Obviously, such a study requires that we measure the perceptions of our customers. We would very much appreciate your taking a few moments to complete and return the attached questionnaire by Wednesday, November 8, 2006.

Thank you very much for your participation. We look forward to receiving your response.

Sincerely,

Sample cover e-mail — staff, written questionnaire

To: Company XYZ Staff

From: Bob Smith, President

Date: November 1, 2006

Re: Survey Questionnaires

```
Dear Company XYZ Staff Member:

In the near future, we will conduct a confidential
survey for the purpose of getting recommendations on
how Company XYZ can improve the level of service we
offer to our customers and enhance teamwork within the
company. We have hired an outside consulting firm,
Company ABC, to conduct the survey. Company ABC is a
management consulting company that specializes in help-
ing companies improve teamwork and customer service.

We are asking you and all other employees to complete
the attached questionnaire and return it by November 8,
2006. Thank you in advance for taking the time and
effort to complete this questionnaire. We look forward
to receiving your feedback.

Sincerely,

Bob Smith
President
Company XYZ
```

Telephone surveys

Sometimes geographic distance, time constraints, or other factors make a telephone survey the ideal way to go. Telephone surveys come in two basic styles: ask-and-answer and discussion.

Ask-and-answer surveys

Ask-and-answer surveys follow a predesigned set of questions that are meant neither for improvisation nor embellishment. The interviewer, after explaining the type of rating scale she is using, reads each question to the respondent and makes a note of the answers. Because ask-and-answer telephone surveys are basically written questionnaires that are spoken, they don't necessarily require an interviewer who has any familiarity with the industry that is being surveyed. For example, an interviewer who has no knowledge of cars can ask the following question as easily as a seasoned mechanic could: "Using a scale of one to six, where one means poor and six means excellent, please rate the following question: How would you rate the courtesy of the service technician who checked in your car?"

Discussion

Discussion telephone surveys ask more spontaneous and exploratory questions and can be effectively conducted only by an interviewer who has a good understanding of the nature of the business being surveyed. A good interviewer in this situation picks up on part of an answer and then probes the respondent for more details. The discussion format enables you to conduct surveys in greater depth that often lead to the discovery of issues that weren't identified prior to speaking with the customer. For example:

Interviewer: What was your impression of the service technician who checked in your car?

Customer: He was okay.

Interviewer: Was there something that he could have done better?

Customer: He seemed to be in a bad mood.

Interviewer: Was it something he said?

Customer: Not exactly, it was more the way he said, "Good morning." He sounded kind of gruff, as if he'd just had a fight with his boss.

Focus groups

Focus groups are groups of eight to ten of your customers who come together, at your invitation, to answer service-related questions that are prepared by you and then presented by your moderator. Because of the group dynamic, focus groups usually provide plenty of rich feedback in a relatively short period of time. The average focus group usually lasts for an hour to an hour and a half.

Customers are invited by letter (usually followed with a confirmation phone call) to participate in a focus group. Breakfast or lunch often is served as a courtesy whenever meetings take place during the workday. Some companies invite their customers to participate during the evening and serve light refreshments.

The success of any focus group depends largely on the moderator's skill. The moderator can be an external consultant or someone from inside your company. Armed with a few predesigned questions, the moderator's main role is

✔ Ensuring that everyone around the table has an opportunity to speak.

✔ Keeping the group on track.

✔ Probing for the most in-depth information possible.

✔ Taking detailed notes that will be transcribed later.

Initial questions asked by the moderator usually are simple conversation starters such as:

- ✔ How is the overall level of service of this company?
- ✔ What is one thing you'd like to see this company improve or change?
- ✔ How is the company's response when you have problems?

Invite 50 percent more customers than you want to attend. Doing so allows for about a one-third no-show rate, which is fairly normal. You can choose from several different venues in which to conduct your focus groups. The three main locations or facilities are market research companies that often have specially equipped rooms you can rent, hotel meeting rooms, or a private and quiet onsite meeting room.

Face-to-face interviews

When you want to get the most anecdotal information from your customers in the most personal format, use the face-to-face interview method. These are one-on-one meetings that are useful when dealing with issues such as:

- ✔ Finding out why a customer has stopped doing business with you.
- ✔ Getting feedback from customers who deal with competing companies.
- ✔ Approaching senior executives for whom a group setting would be inappropriate.

We recommend that you don't use tape recorders or video cameras when you're in face-to-face meetings. This equipment is far too obtrusive. The only acceptable method of recording your customer's feedback in this type of setting is by taking notes.

Customer panels

Of all the survey methods we use with our clients, we find that customer panels make the greatest impact on our clients. Something about hearing the information straight from the horse's mouth (if you'll excuse the expression) is both powerful and undeniable. One disadvantage to customer panels is the amount of time they take. Nonetheless, we think the results they produce make the effort well worth it. The sections that follow are suggestions for making the most of a customer panel.

Before the panel

Personally call a small number of your customers (usually no more than three to six people) and invite them to participate on a customer panel. Carefully consider the customers you choose to be on the panel by selecting people who are willing and able to give you balanced feedback. Establish a date, location, and time for your panel to meet (plan for 60 to 90 minutes) and reiterate that you're looking for balanced feedback on both the positive and negative aspects of the service your company provides. In addition, explain to your customers that approximately 10 to 25 of your company's managers and staff members will attend to hear what the panel has to say.

During the panel

Set up the room in a U-shape with a table upfront where members of the panel will sit. Make sure that each participant has a nametag, pen, paper, and water. The moderator asks a single question and gives each participant five minutes or so to answer, then moves on to the next question. Some general questions may include

- What, in your perception, is Company X's biggest strength? Biggest weakness?
- How well does Company X keep you informed?
- How easy is it to do business with Company X?
- Compared to expectations that you have, how do Company X's products and services perform?
- How well does Company X meet its commitments? Does it deliver what it promises?
- What would Company X need to do to exceed your expectations?

Enable the audience to address a limited number of questions to your panelists, so that the audience can be perfectly clear on what the panelists are saying. It's critical that the audience doesn't:

- Argue with the panelists' comments
- Try to explain something the panelist has misunderstood
- Try to fix the problem then and there
- Become defensive in any way

The idea is to *listen* and learn what your customers have to say. Address any issues that arise during the panel's discussion after the panel is adjourned.

After the panel

Personally call and thank each panelist for participating. If issues arose during the panel relating to that particular panelist, set up a follow-up meeting to discuss the specifics of the problem or to outline the steps you're taking to resolve the problem. Although not necessary, some companies send a thank-you gift to panel participants.

Mystery shoppers

Mystery shopping uses detective work to measure your company's service performance. The first thing to do is contract with a professional market research firm that offers mystery shopping. The company then sends employees to your store to pose as your customers. After observing your company's service in action, your contractor puts together a report that offers feedback on your service performance, using a combination of quantitative scoring and anecdotal information.

You can also apply the mystery-shopping method to evaluate your online service.

Communicating the Results

The benefits of gathering feedback can be negated if you don't follow through with the results. After your company takes the initiative to actively invite feedback, you must take actions to correct at least some, if not all, of the problem areas highlighted. Doing so is vital.

Going to the effort of gathering the information and then not doing anything about the problems that are identified not only is a waste of time and money, but it can also increase the likelihood that future service improvement efforts will be viewed with skepticism.

That's why you must close the loop on the surveys you've conducted by getting back to the people — usually via e-mail — who provided you with the feedback. Doing so benefits your relationship with your staff and customers, because you not only confirm that you heard what they said but also that you're making changes accordingly.

After conducting an extensive company attitude survey, one of our clients condensed the report findings, which were some 50 pages long, into a four-page synopsis that was sent out to every staff member. This action was taken several weeks before the beginning of a large customer-service training program was launched. As a result, participants entering the workshops were more aware of current service issues and the reasons for the training program. Forwarding the survey results also helped confirm that employee feedback was being heard and taken seriously by senior management.

Chapter 5

Company-Wide Training as a Catalyst for Change

· ·

In This Chapter

▶ Getting everyone involved with customer service

▶ Looking at different types and methods of training

▶ Preparing your staff for training

▶ Following up after training

· ·

Ask executives from any company that has achieved consistent improvements in customer service and they'll tell you that they could not have done it without a comprehensive and well-executed training program. At the same time a training program enhances the service your customers receive, it also benefits your company by increasing teamwork between departments, improving the customer-service skills of staff, and helping managers understand their roles in making service shine.

After you've created an overall service strategy and surveyed your customers and staff, training is a natural next step because it reinforces your commitment to service excellence. By bringing training into the picture early, you can comfortably ease your staff into the ideas, concepts, and language of customer focus. In creating your training program, you need to consider these questions:

  ✔ Who needs to receive training?

  ✔ What types of training are needed?

  ✔ What training methods will work best?

  ✔ How can you prepare your staff for the training program?

  ✔ How will you follow up after the training?

Service Is Everyone's Business from CEO to Secretary

A big mistake that we've seen many companies make is training only a small percentage of their staffs — usually the people who work directly with customers, such as the customer-service, technical-support, and help-desk departments. Limiting training in that manner is ineffective and dangerous, because it promotes the message that customer service is the specific responsibility of only a limited number of people within the organization rather than everyone's responsibility.

To achieve a true customer focus, service needs to be a way of life for everyone in your company. As soon as you try to confine it to a single department, it's dead. By providing training at all levels — from your part-time help to the president — you promote the important message that service is everyone's business.

Seven Core Types of Training

A comprehensive training program includes different types of workshops on a variety of subjects. The type of training you decide to provide depends on the feedback you receive from your staff and customers.

Too much technology

We find that many companies have a higher comfort level with hard technical training than they do with soft interpersonal training. Although technical training is important, planning for customer-service training must be part of your overall strategy if you want to achieve excellent customer service.

A client of ours spent a few million dollars upgrading its technology. The company installed new systems that enabled its customer-service reps to locate a customer's goods — anywhere in the world — within nanoseconds. Technologically, the company was the leader in its industry, and its customers were impressed with the speedy response times. In spite of this success, and much to the bewilderment of the company, it was receiving an excessive number of complaints from customers using its new super-duper system.

After conducting several customer focus groups, we found that the cause of the problem had little to do with the new technology and everything to do with the way the customers were being treated. Apparently, the customer-service reps had been through technical training on how to work with the new system, but they'd received no interpersonal training on good customer-service skills.

In this section, we discuss seven core types of training and how they impact the quality of service your company delivers.

Awareness building

Training to build awareness serves as a basic introduction to customer service and needs to involve everyone in your company from the top down. This training program is often the first one to be conducted, because it deals with the general principles of customer service (rather than specific skills), emphasizes the concepts of the internal and external customer, and helps build teamwork between departments.

Core customer-service skills

Training focused on improving core customer-service skills is aimed specifically at staff members whose jobs involve frequent contact with customers, whether it's over the telephone or face to face. This training needs to be more in-depth than the awareness-building program and intent on helping front-line staff identify and strengthen the interpersonal and problem-solving skills they need to be able to provide their customers with excellent service.

Members of your staff are less likely to open up and talk frankly about important issues when they're sitting in this training session with their managers. We recommend that you think about group dynamics when planning a training session and exercise care so as not to unwittingly create an uncomfortable situation that can stifle participation.

When providing core customer-service skills training, don't forget to include the members of your staff who perform internal customer-service functions with their co-workers in other departments (human resources, information technology, and so on). Training for internal service staff needs to address these three main issues:

- ✔ Helping staff members understand how the backroom tasks they perform have an indirect yet critical bearing on the quality of service the paying customer receives

- ✔ Identifying who the key internal customers are and clarifying their expectations

- ✔ Teaching employees the problem-solving and interpersonal skills they need to effectively fulfill the expectations of their internal customers

E-mail training

Although e-mail is a staple of the customer-service environment, its remote nature, which eliminates tone of voice and body language (see Chapter 20), presents a huge potential for misunderstanding and misinterpretation with customers. This type of training needs to be provided to anyone in the company who uses e-mail. Topics to be covered in the course can include the following:

- ✔ E-mail etiquette
- ✔ Inbox management
- ✔ The ethics and legality of e-mail
- ✔ Building online rapport

Team building

Team-building training reinforces the message that customer service is a team sport. Specifically, team-building training helps the members of your staff see how they can improve the way they work with each other to provide better service.

For example: Your customer survey showed a consistent problem with on-time delivery. The root of the problem, you discover, is that the different departments involved in the process don't communicate or relate to one another very well. For whatever reason, each department operates in a vacuum and is unaware of (and to tell the truth uninterested in) what other departments are doing. You can use team-building training to dramatically improve the situation by focusing on how each person's job and each department is part of a chain of events that eventually leads to the customer's satisfaction, and of course, on how the chain is only as strong as its weakest link.

Critical to the success of team-building training is that open and honest feedback between the different departments must be encouraged during the training program. You can take three different approaches toward team-building training:

- ✔ **Integrating:** This approach involves integrating the general principles of team building with any existing customer-service training.
- ✔ **Solving a problem:** Use the training session as a forum for brainstorming and discussing a specific problem. Participants who have a stake in solving a particular problem naturally go through the process of becoming a stronger team.

✓ **Simulating team situations:** This approach is probably the most effective way to begin team-building training, because it highlights and isolates specific behaviors that foster or hinder teamwork.

This kind of training uses a simulated situation in which the training group is divided into teams of four or five and then given a prepared scenario (available from training companies) that describes the specific circumstances of their predicament. Each team is provided with a number of different tasks to perform, and then the training group as a whole must come to a consensus on how to complete them. Although the situation is not real, most participants become so engrossed in the problem that they behave exactly the way they would if they were at work dealing with a real problem. After the exercise, the teams analyze the quality of their answers and how well they listened to and communicated with other people on their team.

Problem-solving

Problem-solving training provides a foundation for continuous process improvement and needs to involve everyone in the company from senior management to front-line staff. The purpose of problem-solving training is to help participants understand various models of problem-solving, discover specific techniques for analyzing problems, and use a variety of tools for solving problems on the job. For more information about a specific problem-solving process that we recommend, see Chapter 9.

Consider mixing and matching a variety of employees from different departments when forming the groups that will attend the same training classes. Employees from different departments and geographic locations then have an opportunity to get to know each other during exercises and breaks. A training class is a wonderful way for people who talk to one another over the phone and with e-mail every day to meet each other for the first time.

Service management

Training all front-line staff in core customer-service skills and attitudes is an essential part of sustaining long-term improvements in customer satisfaction. Managers must likewise demonstrate a commitment to being customer-centric through their own management styles and actions. Service-management training provides managers and team leaders with an opportunity to evaluate their current level of customer focus, find a specific process for becoming more customer-focused, and plan key strategies and actions that will enhance the overall service focus of their work groups.

All the managers in your company (including the president and top executives) need to attend some type of service management training that focuses on these three areas:

- ✔ Improving your managers' awareness of and ability to be a role model for service

- ✔ Enhancing your managers' skills and understanding of how to empower and coach members of the staff to provide the best possible service

- ✔ Rewarding staff for customer-service excellence

We recommend that you use an outside consultant or trainer to lead your service-management training sessions. An outside specialist usually is perceived as a more credible source of information, because the specialist has no political ties to your company. Because of this lack of political ties, the specialist is free to challenge the ideas and assumptions of the group without fear of repercussion.

Although other types of training, such as time management, sales, negotiating skills, and so on, aren't basic to customer service, you need to consider them a valuable part of enhancing overall excellence within your company and plan to incorporate them into your training curriculum.

Executive education

Ultimately the success of any customer-service improvement effort within your company rests on the support it receives from the executives and senior managers.

This type of training helps your company's senior managers deepen their insights into the customer focus of the organization, and most importantly, helps foster support and buy-in for the other training programs and initiatives to come. The specific areas to be covered in this program include:

- ✔ Assessing long-range customer-centric issues of the organization/department and highlighting areas of strength and weakness

- ✔ Understanding the positive impact that a clear customer-satisfaction focus will have on teamwork, productivity, and morale

- ✔ Developing specific strategies and tactics for instituting a culture of customer service, satisfaction, and loyalty that is integrated with the current company structure and goals

- ✔ Recognizing the role of training in the overall process and understanding how to maximize the impact of that training

- ✔ Effecting the presentation of any relevant customer or staff survey data

Choosing a Training Method That Works for You

Depending on the size of your company and the resources you have available for training, you can take three major paths toward implementing the types of training you decide to use: classroom training, online Web-based training, and other media-based training.

Classroom training

Classroom training is conducted in person by a professional trainer. Training must be upbeat, highly participative, and include group discussions, team exercises, written exercises, and role-playing, so that participants remain attentive. The following supplies are recommended when conducting a classroom training session:

- ✔ Workbook/materials for each participant
- ✔ Pen or pencil for each participant
- ✔ Notepaper for each participant
- ✔ Nametags or name cards for each participant
- ✔ Two flip charts
- ✔ Four black markers and two red markers
- ✔ Podium for the speaker's notes
- ✔ Bar stool or chair for the speaker
- ✔ Water jugs and glasses (optional)

Figure 5-1 provides you with a diagram that you can use as a guideline for setting up your training room.

As far as how to conduct your company's classroom training, you can choose between in-house programs and public courses.

In-house programs

If you want a training program that is customized specifically for your company, your best bet is to develop and conduct your own in-house training program by using your human-resources or training department. If your company doesn't have the resources, time, or expertise to offer this type of training, you may want to hire an outside consulting or training firm to do the job for you.

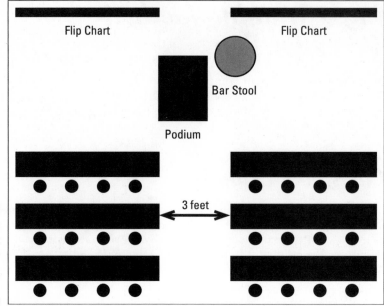

Figure 5-1:
How to set
up your
training
room.

Most established consulting firms work with you to develop and customize a program that fits the specific needs, circumstances, and culture of your company. After the training is developed, selected members of your staff can go through a train-the-trainer program, conducted by the consulting company, where they find out about the content of the program and how to effectively present it.

If you choose this route, the outside training company will charge you a purchase price for using its training program. In some cases this price is a flat fee, and in others, the rate is based on the number of participants.

If a train-the-trainer program isn't right for you, then you can have the outside firm develop and deliver the training program. Although doing so can become expensive, especially when you have large numbers of staff to train, some companies prefer this route because the outside trainer has expertise, credibility, and objectivity that can be difficult to find in-house. Before hiring a consulting firm — if that's the direction you decide to take — you need to ask the different consulting-firm candidates you interview questions like the ones we tell you about in the sidebar "Ten questions to ask a consulting company."

Public courses

If your company is a small business and cost is a major consideration, you may want to send your staff to one of the many public customer-service seminars that are offered. Universities and public seminar companies send out billions and billions of mailings announcing such programs. In fact, flyers for these seminars probably land on your desk every day and end up unread in the circular file. Public seminars are a good option for smaller businesses, because tuition usually is a manageable $99 to $200 per person.

Public seminars have these three disadvantages:

✔ They're large with up to 200 attendees, compared with the usual 20 in-house, and you have precious little time to ask *your* specific questions.

✔ They're generic and need to address a diverse audience, so the training won't be specifically tailored to your company or industry.

✔ They're delivered to the lowest common denominator of attendees, so if your staff members are more experienced, sophisticated, or more highly trained, they may be bored or think their time is being wasted.

Online Web-based training

If you aren't using it already, you need to plan to make online training a part of your overall plan for education. Online training has several distinct advantages, because it:

✔ Provides employees with 24/7 access to training materials, so they can learn on their own schedule

✔ Allows management to track the participant's progress

✔ Less expensive than classroom training because no venue, instructor, or materials are required

✔ Enables staff members from various geographic locations to take the training during a set time period without the time or expense of travel

Beyond just offering one or two programs, many companies and organizations now offer virtual online campuses. A campus is essentially a menu of different training courses that can be viewed online by your staff at the time of their choosing. Some companies even offer certificate programs for employees who complete a prescribed set of courses.

Ten questions to ask a consulting company

Consulting companies vary greatly in the services they offer and their ability to deliver these services. These ten questions can help you find a firm whose style, methods, and approach fit with your objectives and the culture of your company.

✔ **Do you have any references I can call?** Ask the consulting company for a selection of references from a variety of its clients, including a specific contact person with each company. Asking the consultant candidate to contact the persons to whom they're referring you, just to let them know you'll be calling, also is a good idea.

✔ **What makes your firm expert in the area of quality service?** Because the topic of quality service has become so popular in the last few years, many consulting companies have added a customer-service training module to their existing programs. This addition doesn't make them experts and doesn't mean they can help you implement an entire service-improvement program from soup to nuts. Make sure that the consultants you hire are experts in customer-service improvement by asking them whether, for example, they:

- Conduct customer/staff surveys

- Help set up a quality group program

- Coach senior executives

Our admittedly biased experience shows the best customer-service consulting companies are the ones that offer a comprehensive program in customer-service improvement and not just a one- or two-day training program.

✔ **What's your company's background?** Gather as much general information about the consulting company as possible. Some questions to ask include:

- How long have you been in business?

- What industries have you worked with?

- Who are your clients?

- What's your company philosophy?

- How many people work for you?

Don't base your decision to hire a consulting company solely on the convenience of its geographic location. Although we realize that is a consideration, don't sell yourself short and hire the wrong company for the job just because it operates in the same city that you do.

✔ **Do you customize the training programs and materials to match your client's needs?** For a training program to be truly effective for members of your staff, it must include examples, demonstrations, and content to which they can relate. Generic training programs usually miss the mark, because they rely on universal examples that don't hit home. Ask what specific steps the consultants will take to customize their programs and materials for your company.

✔ **Who delivers the training?** Larger consulting companies usually have one group of people sell their product and a different group delivering the training and consultation. Some businesses complain about hiring a consulting company because they were impressed with the salesperson but disappointed with the consultant or trainer who subsequently worked with them. Although nothing is wrong with having one person sell and another deliver the programs, you need to make sure that you can talk to the actual person(s) who will work directly with you.

✔ **Can you put together a proposal for me?** Many ideas get tossed around during initial meetings with a consulting firm. At the conclusion of your first meeting, however, ask for a written proposal that outlines the major points of your discussion and provides specifics, such as:

- How long the program will take to implement

- How soon the program can start

- Fees

- Travel and material costs

- Maximum number of attendees allowed in each workshop

The quality of the proposal says a lot about the consulting company. Is it neat, correctly spelled, and well laid out? Or does it look haphazardly slapped together? Does it reflect the conversation you had — or some other meeting that you don't remember attending?

✔ **How will we keep the program going in the future?** You don't want to spend the rest of your life depending on an outside consultant to keep service training alive and well in your company, so ask how the consulting firm plans to empower you to maintain the changes after its representatives have finished their work and left the scene.

Continuing the process of service improvement is mostly your responsibility and not that of the consultants. After the consulting firm finishes its part, leaving you with the knowledge, tools, and training you need, keeping the program going is up to you.

✔ **How do you deal with managers who aren't behind the program?** A reality of implementing a company-wide service-improvement program is that some managers will be more gung-ho about it than others. Because managers are so important to the process, finding out just what approach the consulting company plans to take toward convincing resistant managers to support its program is a good idea.

✔ **How will we get new hires up to speed?** If your company is a small business, you may want to hire the consulting company to come back once or twice a year and deliver the program for your new hires. If your company is larger, conducting the customer-service training in-house may be more cost-effective. Find out whether the consulting company has a train-the-trainer program or video-based training for bringing new hires up to speed.

✔ **What do you think the most difficult part of this project will be?** At the end of the interview, ask the consultants to give you their impressions (based on what's been discussed so far) of what they anticipate will be the most difficult part of the project. Make sure they explain their strategy for overcoming this difficulty.

Asking these questions should give you an insight into how well the consultants understand your company's issues.

Is live better than online?

Clients often ask us whether we think live training is better than online training. Our answer is that each has its benefits and place in an overall education program. Live training, particularly when it comes to soft skills (management skills, teambuilding, sales, customer service, and so on), has the added benefit of group interaction and live demonstrations that can be experienced and seen. On the other hand, online training has the benefit of being cost-effective and requires no travel. In addition, people can take online training at their own rate of speed. Many companies choose a combination of live and online to get the best results overall.

However, just like any other form of training, the quality of Web-based training can vary greatly, so be sure to take a test ride before making any financial commitments.

If you're in the market for online training from an outside vendor, be sure to look for the following:

- ✔ **Make sure the company that created the training has expertise in the online programs it offers or has hired experts to create the content.** Don't go with the generic online training mills. The quality of the information they provide often is too simple and outdated, and they lack the knowledge required to make a good training program.

- ✔ **One measure of an effective online training program is that it's interactive, not passive.** The more the viewer interacts with the program, the higher retention of the information presented. Look for programs that are interactive with and involve the viewer as much as possible, meaning the viewer can type in answers to questions, do exercises online, and so on.

- ✔ **Avoid programs that are only text based.** Instead look for programs that have *flash technology* and audio built into them. Flash (moving, animated graphics) and audio make a program more interesting to use. Video clips on the other hand can be problematic because the system the viewer is using can affect quality and download speed.

- ✔ **Make sure the program has a tracking system built in that allows you to track who has completed it.** A quiz at the end the program is a plus for testing knowledge.

 Our company, Sterling Consulting Group, offers two popular online training programs: *The Service Advantage,* a comprehensive customer-service-skills program, and *Essential Email,* an e-mail communications course. You can check out both of these programs at our Web site: www.scgtraining.com.

Other media-based training

The advantage of media-based training is that it doesn't rely on a trainer's expertise to get the point across. These methods, which we discuss in the upcoming sections, are particularly effective as a means of enhancing classroom training and implementing a follow-up program.

Video

A wide range of video programs are available on the market today. The differences in quality of those programs are just as wide. Many of them are overly simplistic, poorly produced, and, the worst crime of all, boring! The result is a tape that doesn't teach, enlighten, or entertain. For that reason, always preview a videotape before you buy it so you're sure of what you're getting. Many of the better video programs come with a leader's guide so that a member of your company can facilitate the program while participants watch the tape.

You have the option of hiring a consulting company to custom design video training for you. Although far more expensive than buying an off-the-shelf product, the custom-designed video option has the advantage providing you with a highly specialized product that reflects your company's specific needs and style. A good, customized video-training program can be used for several years and pays for itself over time.

Audiotapes and CDs

Almost every author who has written a book on customer service offers some kind of audiotape or CD based on either a book or a recording of an actual seminar he or she has written or led. Audiotapes and CDs are less expensive than videotapes and offer a greater selection of topics, and you can easily listen wherever and whenever it's convenient — even on the way to work.

Books

Many good books also are available on the topic of customer service. They fall into two categories:

- **Books written by researchers and academics:** Although these books usually provide a good, solid, theoretical framework on what being customer-focused means, they often lack real-world, practical, down-to-earth suggestions about what to do and how to do it.

- **Books full of anecdotal stories and practical tips:** These tomes are written by business people or management consultants that have plenty of hands-on experience in customer service. They're often light on theory, but they contain plenty of useful ideas and examples of how to make your company more customer-focused.

Both types of books are useful and have their places. If you're looking for additional books on the topic of customer service, we recommend that you peruse your local bookstore and take some time to flip through the various titles that are available.

CD-ROMs

Today, many large companies are using CD-ROM technology to train their staff. CD-ROM programs usually are chock-full of information and can contain the following:

- ✔ Video clips
- ✔ Audio
- ✔ Animated charts and graphics

If the CD-ROM program is well developed, it'll be responsive to the learning curve of the individual operating the program. For example, if a staff person is moving through a program at a fast pace, the program automatically takes him or her to a more advanced level of content. However, if the staff person in the next cubicle runs the same program and is moving at a much slower pace, the program focuses him or her toward the basics.

The clear advantage of using the CD-ROM approach is that it enables employees to take training at their own pace, in the comfort of their own work stations; it also is cost-effective and efficient when you have to train a large number of people in a short period of time — especially if they're in different locations.

Don't allow limited resources to keep you from training your staff. If you can't hire an external person and you don't have an inside person to deliver training, use audiotapes, videotapes, and books. Review the tapes or read sections of a book with members of your staff and then discuss how they can apply what they're learning.

Preparing Your Staff for a Good Experience

Believe us when we say nothing is worse than standing in front of a roomful of trainees who either think they've been sent to a training program to be "fixed" or, worse yet, have no idea why they're there. Too often, managers neglect to prepare their staffs for the training they attend. Training is more of a positive experience and has greater impact when participants see it as part of the overall service plan — and not just a day spent away from the office. You can prepare your staff for training in two ways.

Sending a memo regarding the training

Send each person who will participate in training a memo at least two weeks before he or she is scheduled to attend. The memo needs to provide the following information (see Figure 5-2 for an example):

- The date and time of the program
- The location of the program, including directions on how to get there, if appropriate
- The purpose of the program and the main topics to be covered
- The dress code for the program (business, casual, or black tie!)
- Any preparation required before attending
- The instructor's name and a brief bio, if appropriate

Some managers make a mistake of sending members of their staff to training at the last minute without preparation. After wandering through the hallways, they take a seat in the workshop, apologize for being late, and explain: "My manager just told me this morning to show up. I'm not even sure why I'm here." Such short notice and obvious lack of preparation undermines the importance of the training program and creates an attitude that the training is an interruption of the staff person's real job.

Helping your staff set training goals

A week or so before members of your staff go to training, sit down with them and discuss what they want to achieve. Doing so helps them clarify their goals for the training program and provides the basis for a follow-up conversation.

Don't use training as a punishment. Training should never be seen as a vehicle to "fix" a broken employee. This tactic is demeaning to the staff and can create a difficult situation for the trainer. The only effective context for sending an employee to training is a positive one.

Sample Memo

September 14, 1995

Dear Staff Member:

As an expression of our continued commitment to quality service, Company XYZ is undertaking a comprehensive customer service improvement program beginning in November.

We are pleased to inform you that we will be assisted by ABC Consulting Group, a San Francisco-based consulting firm, which specializes in customer service improvement. Its clients include such well-known companies as Friendly Airlines, Pine Box Productions, and the United States Postal Service.

ABC Consulting Group will be conducting a customer relations course that will help us all provide better customer service. Reducing stress, working with angry customers, and using proper telephone etiquette are among the topics that will be covered.

The workshop you will be attending is scheduled for:

Friday, November 3, 1995
9:00 am to 4:00 pm
Room 2C

Comfortable, casual clothing is recommended.

We are looking forward to working with you in continuing to make Company XYZ an outstanding example of service excellence.

Thank you in advance for your participation.

Bob Cress
President

Figure 5-2:
An example of a memo you can send to staff members before training.

Practice Makes Perfect

How many times have you sat through a training program only to have it turn into a distant memory soon afterward? A year later, as you're cleaning out your office, you run across the course workbook that has been sitting on your shelf gathering dust, and you think:

> *Oh yeah, I remember when they sent me to that training program . . . what was that about anyway?*

About a month of practice is needed to turn a new skill into a habit. So now that the formal training is over, be sure to go the distance and help members of your staff put the skills they've learned into practice. By following up and reinforcing the lessons taught in the training program, you reap the greatest rewards for the time, money, and energy you put into training your staff.

Once is not enough. Don't make the mistake of thinking that by sending members of your staff to one customer-service training class they'll be set for life. Repeated exposure to the ideas and techniques of customer service helps make good habits that last a lifetime. Most of our clients do some kind of follow-up customer-service training about once a year.

Following up immediately after training

As a manager, you need to meet with each staff member two weeks after he or she completes a training course. During the meetings, ask your employees for their feedback on the training. Include the following questions:

- How did you like the training program?
- What did you learn?
- Did you achieve your objectives?
- What would you like to see in future training programs?
- How can I support you in practicing what you learned?

Providing ongoing coaching

Another way to reinforce what members of your staff learn from the training is to design a plan for ongoing or continuing education. People have different ways of learning, and what works best for one person may not work well for another.

Find out what types of learning each member of your staff prefers. The basic ways people learn are

- ✔ Hearing about the subject by going to lectures or listening to audiotapes
- ✔ Having a direct experience through role-playing or on-the-job practice
- ✔ Reading about the topic in books, magazines, or manuals
- ✔ Practical demonstration by watching an expert or videotape
- ✔ Talking about the subject in one-on-one or small-group situations

After you grasp the learning preferences of your individual staff members, co-create with each person a plan for enhancing and reinforcing the concepts and techniques that person discovered in the initial training program.

Thinking that the way you learn is the way others learn is a natural tendency; however, that way of thinking isn't necessarily true. Make a point of finding out the best way to approach each of your staff members before you do any coaching.

Creating a training library

Support members of your staff in self-education by creating a training library. One of our clients did so by emptying a large closet, installing book shelves, and then filling them with audiotapes, videotapes, and books on all kinds of subjects related to training. Some of the usual topics included in a customer-service training library are

- ✔ Communication
- ✔ Conflict resolution
- ✔ Customer service
- ✔ Dealing with difficult people
- ✔ Giving effective presentations
- ✔ Management skills
- ✔ Managing diversity
- ✔ Negotiation
- ✔ Problem-solving
- ✔ Running effective meetings
- ✔ Time management
- ✔ Total quality management

After you have your inventory in place, the logistics of operating the training library are easy. Simply set up a sign-in sheet (name, department, title of item, date removed) and place a time limit on how long materials can be checked out (two weeks is standard). After the library is set up, it takes little work to maintain and provides the staff and managers with easy access to learning resources.

Part II
Take It from the Top: Service Management

"I was giving them a rousing motivational speech from my college football days, at the end of which everyone jumped up and butted heads."

In this part . . .

*I*f you're a manager, stop dead in your tracks, grab a pen and paper, a cup of coffee (regular or decaf), and get ready. Filled with real-world suggestions and solutions, this part of the book helps you make excellent service a habit at your company.

In this part, you get real insights into how to replace the corporate gremlins that hamper change with effective methods for building teamwork, morale, and accountability at all levels of your company.

By following the specific exercises and assignments in this part of the book, you're guided in taking a step back to create a working blueprint for service improvement within your department. Using the principles and practices in this part assists you in creating a foundation upon which you and your staff can grow, with distinction, in service excellence.

Chapter 6

Coaching Service Excellence

*E*ven though this book is packed with ideas you can use to rapidly and dramatically improve the quality of service you offer your customers, the truth of the matter is that for long-term and consistently high levels of service, your staff needs ongoing support. We've seen many worthy service improvement initiatives bite the dust through lack of follow-up. Quick fixes are great, but they have a much longer shelf life when they're reinforced by coaching that provides members of your staff with feedback and keeps them involved in the service-improvement process.

In this chapter, we look at different methods for coaching your staff, and give you suggestions for setting up meetings that inspire participation rather than yawns! We've found that service keeps getting better in companies where managers and supervisors take on the role of a coach, so we've included the know-how you need to hone this vital skill.

Meeting Up to Improve Service

Countless are the ways to get your staff excited about and participating in service improvement. However, some of the most stellar results we've witnessed came from short staff meetings, which were usually (though not necessarily) set up by the manager. These kinds of meetings give everyone involved an opportunity to express their thoughts and ideas about specific service-oriented subjects. You can use any or all of the five meeting themes discussed in this section to get yourself and your team into gear.

Meeting 1: Brainstorming

Most people have been involved in some kind of formal or informal brainstorming session, the kind where everyone gets to contribute their ideas on the subject at hand. However, when planning a brainstorming session about service improvement for your staff, we recommend that you take the following actions beforehand, so your meeting is more beneficial and fun for everyone:

- ✓ **Select a subject to which everyone in the room can relate.** Nothing is less inspiring for members of your staff than attending a meeting where they have nothing to contribute because they aren't familiar with the issues. Pick a subject that impacts everybody's ability to provide excellent service.

- ✓ **Don't fall into the trap of judging what people say.** For people to offer input freely, they need to know that whatever they say will be accepted openly, rather than being evaluated as to its merit. In fact, what makes brainstorming so unique is its methodology of putting all possible ideas on the table and *not* deciding whether they're good or bad ideas until the end of the session. If ideas are prematurely rejected, then don't expect people who contributed those ideas to continue contributing. They won't.

  Many managers complain that nobody ever wants to say or contribute anything when they get together with members of their staffs. The reason usually is that their previous contributions have been ignored or shot down.

- ✓ **Invite less talkative members of the group to share their thoughts.** In any meeting, some people who attend are bound to be less talkative than others, or they just don't do well in groups. When brainstorming, or with any collaborative meeting, the facilitator needs to make a point of having everyone say something. Asking a question like, "Jeff, we haven't heard from you yet, what are your thoughts on the subject?" is usually enough to prime the pump.

- ✓ **Manage more talkative members.** Facilitating a meeting is more than just sitting and listening — it's also about intervening when circumstances demand it. When a member of the audience has a strong personality or is forceful in his or her opinions, others in the group may be uncomfortable about speaking up. We find that saying something like, "Joe, I want to hear what you have to say, but I want a few other people to have a chance to speak," works well.

Brainstorming primer

Brainstorming is a technique designed to express as many different ideas about a specific subject as possible. The focus isn't on the quality of ideas but rather on the quantity. Criticism or evaluation is the enemy of brainstorming, because it can stop people from thinking creatively and speaking freely.

By giving people free reign to express their ideas, brainstorming taps into less traditional and more innovative ideas. Guidelines for brainstorming include the following:

✔ Accepting only one thought at a time. Some groups do better taking turns, others prefer to be more random.

✔ Never criticizing ideas.

✔ Never discussing ideas — except for clarification.

✔ Encouraging people to build on the ideas of others in the group.

✔ Recording ideas on a flip chart and displaying full pages so they're visible to everyone in the group.

Meeting 2: Problem-solving

The problem-solving meeting is an effective way of working with your staff on a service problem that just won't seem to go away. Getting input from all participants not only heightens the possibility of a great solution, it also motivates them to successfully implement that solution. The steps of a problem-solving meeting are:

1. **Defining the problem.**

   This part of the process may sound like a waste of time, but it's actually one of the most important parts of the problem-solving process. By accurately defining the problem so that it precisely states the issue that needs to be fixed, you can be more exact when focusing on possible solutions.

2. **Brainstorming possible solutions (see the previous section).**

3. **Evaluating possible solutions.**

   Some of the solutions the team devises are better than others and must be evaluated for how feasible they are to implement. This step helps you eliminate solutions that look good on paper but won't work in reality.

You can count on different degrees of agreement and enthusiasm from group members as you go through this step. For example, members who are detail-oriented may want to dwell on certain issues while others who see a bigger picture won't want to dwell on details that they find boring and insignificant. These two different perspectives can create a synergy where the whole is greater than the sum of its parts. Remember that your job as facilitator is to respect each person's point of view, ask questions that reveal assumptions, and help your group move forward.

4. Coming up with an implementation plan.

Once a solution (or solutions) has been agreed upon, create a checklist of who is going to do what and by when that work is to be done. As the coach (and manager) you probably need to follow up and make sure that those tasks are fulfilled by the time promised.

If you don't follow up on the implementation plan, you send a message that nobody is responsible and that it doesn't really matter, one way or the other, whether the solution is implemented.

Meeting 3: Creating service enhancers

Service enhancers are specific *moments of truth* (see Chapter 2) that you select and then enhance to create a positive impression with your customers. For example, if new customers contact you mostly by phone, you may need to work on enhancing their first impression when they call. Doing so may involve how you greet them, how you put them on hold, and so on. By working on service enhancers in a group meeting, the diverse opinions of different members can help you discover overlooked or less obvious ways of making your service shine.

We've discovered that the following steps make the process of creating service enhancers easy for everyone to follow:

1. Choosing a cycle of service.

A *cycle of service* is a phase in the service delivery cycle, somewhat like a chapter in a book. Say, for example, that you operate a bicycle repair shop. Your cycles of service (excuse the pun) may be:

1. Customer contacting you about a repair

2. Booking the repair

3. Completing the repair

4. Customer picking up repaired bicycle

2. **Breaking down the cycle you've chosen into specific moments of truth.**

   Within each cycle are specific moments of truth when you have an opportunity to make a positive impression with the customer. For example, if you decided to work on the cycle when the customer picks up the repaired bicycle in this example, you can break it down into the following moments of truth:

   1. Notifying the customer when the bike is ready

   2. Customer picking up the repaired bike

   3. Customer paying for the repairs

3. **Selecting one moment of truth.**

   Ask the group which moment of truth has the most potential for improvement. Doing so may lead to a discussion in which you end up with more than one possible moment. When that happens, choose one to work on now and save the other(s) for future service-improvement sessions. At this point, assume that the group chose "Customer paying for the repairs" from the list above.

4. **Enhancing the selected moment of truth.**

   Now ask members of the group for ideas for enhancing this experience for the customer. Possible enhancers may include:

   - Giving clients a discount card for 10 percent off any additional items purchased within the next two weeks

   - Presenting clients with small laminated cards with recommended weekly bicycle maintenance tips

   - Asking clients whether they'd like a courtesy call the next time their bike is due for a service

5. **Devising an action plan.**

   This final step takes the results from the meeting and turns them into a workable reality. People volunteer their expertise and know-how to take on specific tasks associated with the chosen enhancer.

Meeting 4: Planning service recovery

If your business is prone to frequent service breakdowns — for example, deadlines that are frequently not met because of the unpredictability of a supplier — then this meeting is a great way to involve the members of your team in service improvement, challenging them to come up with ideas for service recovery.

As we mention in Chapter 16, an important aspect of service recovery is offering a care token. A *care token* is something you do to let the customer know that you're sorry for the problem and are committed to keeping her business.

When you experience frequent service breakdowns that are similar in nature, coming up with a standard and uniform way of dealing with them makes sense. Doing so makes the situation less stressful for your staff by providing an agreed upon procedure and creating consistency for staff and customers.

Here's an idea of what we're talking about: Coauthor Keith Bailey recently sent an overnight package to an associate on the East Coast. When the package didn't arrive, Keith called up the express shipping company to trace it. The agent answering the phone politely explained that the package had been held up because of a large snowstorm. She apologized but couldn't predict when it would be delivered given the weather conditions. The agent had been well trained in handling regular winter service breakdowns. That was obvious, because she knew exactly what to say and exactly how to say it, which made Keith feel taken care of even though she couldn't resolve the issue.

Meeting 5: Listen and learn sessions

This meeting has one purpose: A manager listens to the feedback from his staff. We have facilitated many of these meetings, and you'd be surprised how difficult just listening to what staff members have to say — without responding, explaining, defending, or refuting — can be for a manager.

Choose a subject about which you want to gain some insight. For example, if you're the manager of a help desk, you may want to discover what your department can do better to speed up response time to customer requests.

Informing people about the subject of the meeting is a good idea, because they then have time to think about their feedback. At the start of the meeting, explain that your job is just to listen, because you really want to know what they have to say.

Don't be tempted to talk back except for purposes of clarification. If someone either states as fact something you know to be untrue, offers an opinion about you that is negative, or presents an idea that you find preposterous, don't react. Bite your tongue and keep on listening.

After the meeting, it's important to use the feedback for positive improvement. If nothing happens, the listen and learn sessions were a waste of time, and your staff will be less likely to contribute next time. We recommend creating a steering committee, or group of interested volunteers, to sift through all the feedback, classify it into broad headings, and then prioritize what should be worked on first. A memo outlining this information should be sent to all those who contributed their time and opinion.

Taking a Three-Stage Coaching Approach

Although meetings outlined in the previous section are effective ways of getting everyone involved in the service-improvement process, coaching often requires a more personal, one-on-one approach. For that reason, each manager needs to know how to prepare and facilitate such coaching sessions. *Coaching* means working with members of your staff in a collaborative way. By asking questions that give rise to discussion or suggesting alternative approaches, managers and their staffs share the discovery of new ways of improving service delivery. If you live in fear of leading a coaching session — or have tried but failed in the past — read on. In this section, we break down the coaching process into three stages that remove the mystery and increase your mastery.

Stage 1: Preparing yourself for coaching

If you volunteered to coach the junior soccer league, you'd probably do some preparation before arriving at the field. If you were asked to make a presentation at your firm's annual conference, you might stay up all night making sure you were ready and well prepared. Coaching your staff is no different, and because it's a skill that most of us have to learn, preparation is the first step toward mastery. Preparing to coach service excellence means two things:

- Knowing your strengths and weaknesses so you're better prepared
- Knowing how members of your staff learn so you can coach them in the most effective ways

Determining your strengths and weaknesses

You can determine your coaching strengths and weaknesses by rating your responses to the ten statements in the survey that follows. These statements are designed to show you — and get you thinking about — where you may need to place extra emphasis when conducting your coaching sessions. As you read each statement ask yourself, "How would my staff rate me?" and resist the urge to look good and score the right answer. Use the questionnaire as an opportunity to assess your strengths and to find out where you can use some improvement.

To analyze your coaching strengths and weaknesses:

Rate how frequently you make use of the techniques described by each of the following ten statements about coaching according to these values: 1 = Rarely, 2 = Sometimes, 3 = Frequently. Place your score in the blank provided after each statement, and then add them together to get your score. Be honest with yourself.

When coaching (or working with my staff) I:

1. Solicit their input and listen to their ideas. _____

2. Take time to develop an environment of trust. _____

3. Make my expectations and priorities clear. _____

4. Look for positives rather than negatives. _____

5. Give credit when it's deserved. _____

6. Know how to be direct without being personal. _____

7. Hold employees accountable for their results. _____

8. Rarely give up on an employee. _____

9. Always start by reviewing the "big picture." _____

10. Know what results I want to accomplish. _____

Total of all scores = _____

Evaluating your score

Scoring this survey highlights areas where you have strong skills and shows you weaker areas of which you need to be mindful when conducting the coaching session. If you scored:

25–30: You have excellent coaching skills — or terrible math skills. This score signifies that you have a collaborative working style, and coaching probably comes easy to you. Look at the one or two areas where you scored less than 3 and focus on honing those skills.

15–24: You have above-average coaching skills, but you can use some refinement. Look at the values you gave each statement and determine in which one or two areas you scored low and then work on them. However, if you want to score more 3s, you can use this chapter to brush up all your skills.

Less than 15: Read this chapter twice! You probably have had little exposure to effective coaching, so the skills and techniques we describe in this chapter can have a positive impact on how you relate to your staff — and your levels of service.

Anyone can dance — it just takes time

Until two years ago, coauthor Keith Bailey believed he couldn't dance. He attended a beginner's class and, unable to follow the teacher's instructions, grew frustrated and embarrassed and ran out of the studio as fast as his two left feet would carry him. Then a friend suggested that he may be learning dance the wrong way; that he may need a teacher who enables him to experience the movements slowly rather than relying on observing a role model — the dance teacher — showing him the steps. Keith took the friend's advice and found a beginner's class that taught the same basic steps every week. After a few weeks and several jokes about the Groundhog Day dance class, Keith could salsa alongside the best of them.

Think of coaching as an approach rather than a series of techniques. For example, coaching is usually more effective when the approach is collaborative, where you and your staff members have partnerships based on mutual understanding and trust. If you adopt this approach when working with your staff to improve service, the techniques you use will be that much more effective.

The next part of preparing yourself is gaining an understanding that not everyone learns in the same way.

Knowing how members of your staff learn

Different people learn in different ways. For example, when you're handed a new project, you may be the kind of person who thrives by being left alone to figure out what and how you're going to accomplish the task. Someone else who's just as competent as you may struggle needlessly if you incorrectly assume that he or she also likes the same hands-off approach. Spending a little time thinking about the people you're about to coach can expedite the learning process and minimize everyone's frustration.

In the following example, Judy is a customer-service manager who is coaching Jim, one of her customer-service reps, to better deal with angry customers. Judy must first reflect on how Jim learns, and then she must coach him using one or more of these methods:

- ✔ **Learning by experience.** This type of learning takes place by trial and error. The individual tries something, corrects any failures, and celebrates the successes.

  For example: Judy suggests that Jim learn by experience and then report back to her to talk about what worked well — and what didn't.

This technique is *not* the same as the sink-or-swim approach that is all too rampant in organizations that throw people in the deep end but don't offer them a life preserver when the waters get choppy. In experiential learning, the employee feels supported at all times by a structure that makes sure his head never goes under the waterline.

✔ **Observing role models.** Many people learn best by watching others around them who have developed skills in the area they want to improve.

For example: Judy suggests Jim work alongside Alice — the department's bomb defuser — who can calm the most irate of customers. By observing what Alice says, and how she says it, Jim picks up valuable information.

✔ **Taking passive instruction.** This type of learning is accomplished by reading a book, listening to an instructor or a CD, or watching a DVD.

For example: Judy suggests that Jim read Chapter 16 of this book. To maximize Jim's learning experience, Judy sets up another meeting so they can discuss what Jim learned and any questions he may have, after he reads the chapter.

✔ **Relying on reflection and discussion.** Some people learn best by having discussions that present new ideas or different viewpoints either in groups or one-on-one.

For example: Judy meets with Jim and a few colleagues and invites people to share their experiences — both good and bad — about dealing with upset customers. She asks Jim to share what he has learned so far.

Stage 2: Preparing the coaching session

After you prepare yourself to coach, you're ready to prepare the session. This process consists of the three steps that are discussed in the following sections.

Step 1: Notifying and preparing participants

Some people hear the word "coaching" and think "Oh-oh, I'm going to be reprimanded." Banish this thought from the minds of your staff members by giving them plenty of notice that you plan to conduct a coaching session — at least a week's advance notice. If you notify them by e-mail, we recommend:

✔ **Telling them what you want to accomplish in the session.** Word the e-mail in a positive and collaborative way. For example, if you're meeting with your staff members to reduce customer complaints, explain that you'd like their input and feedback regarding customer complaints and their ideas for improving the way they're addressed.

✔ **Asking them to prepare for the meeting ahead of time by bringing written suggestions or ideas to discuss.**

✔ **Asking everyone to think about times when they were a customer with a complaint and received exceptional treatment from another company.** What did the customer-service representative do or say that made it so memorable?

✔ **Noting the date, time, duration, and location of the session.** Ask everyone to arrive five minutes early so the meeting can start promptly.

Step 2: Setting up the physical location

The location of the meeting needs to be:

✔ **Private.** As we've already mentioned, success in coaching is partly a function of trust. The location can enhance this feeling by being away from high-traffic areas and free from distractions.

✔ **Interruption free.** If the room in which you plan to meet has telephones, make sure to forward any incoming calls to those phones somewhere else during your meeting. Nothing is more disturbing than a constantly ringing phone. Have all who attend turn off their cellphones or switch them to vibrate, and tape a notice to the door asking not to be disturbed.

✔ **Organized.** Make sure you have the correct number of chairs facing forward (or in a circle). Neatly place any other debris, such as computer terminals, unwanted overhead projectors, extra chairs, telephones, and so on, against a far wall out of the way.

Likewise, prepare any materials you may need and have them ready to go. Handouts need to be copied, collated, and ready to be distributed; overhead presentations need to be in order and ready; and computer projectors need to be humming along and ready to rip. If your participants need pens, pencils, and notepaper, have them ready to hand out.

We know from years of working with people in rooms of varying sizes (little-to-large) all around the world that the more attention and awareness that's given to the physical surroundings, the more members of your group (usually without realizing it) will feel supported and safe.

Step 3: Creating an agenda

Even though coaching is a dynamic process that usually doesn't follow a straight course, setting down a series of steps that you plan to follow nevertheless is important during any service-improvement meeting. The basic parts of an agenda are included (start-to-finish) in the list that follows. They are the same regardless of whether you're planning a one-on-one or a group session. Use each agenda item as a guideline and feel free to elaborate on each of them, depending on the needs of your session. Allow time for the following:

1. **Greeting and thanking everyone for attending.**

   Let them know that you appreciate their time.

2. **Stating the purpose of the meeting and what you'd like to accomplish.**

3. **Eliciting feedback and opinions about the topic.**

4. **Discussing and clarifying the issues.**

5. **Summarizing the feedback from Steps 3 and 4 and asking for ideas for improving the situation.**

   Be encouraging no matter how outlandish the suggestions.

6. **Agreeing on what needs to be done.**

   Hint: This step often takes the biggest chunk of time.

7. **Writing down all agreed upon action steps while noting who you're expecting to get the jobs done and when they need to be finished.**

8. **Concluding and summarizing the meeting.**

Stage 3: Conducting the coaching session

The make-it-or-break-it part of a service-improvement coaching session is how well you give and receive feedback. More times than not, you end up having to tell someone about a behavior or an attitude that is counterproductive and far from customer friendly. Giving this kind of feedback is difficult for many managers, and if it comes out wrong or is misconstrued, the people you're meeting with may become upset and defensive.

The list that follows includes five tips — using the example of a rental-car agency supervisor coaching one of her counter agents — for delivering feedback that ensures your coaching sessions have an excellent chance of being received in the spirit of appreciation and growth rather than anger and blame. When giving feedback, you must:

✔ **Get the conversation off on the right foot by starting with open-ended questions.**

For example: "Rose, I wanted to meet with you to discuss some ways we can improve check-in wait times. What have you noticed that slows down the process?"

Open-ended questions usually begin with words like what, where, when, how, and why. By asking Rose the open-ended question, "What have you noticed that slows down the process?" the supervisor opens the door for a two-way dialogue. Because coaching is a collaborative process, getting people involved in the conversation early on creates trust.

Imagine how different the conversation would be if the supervisor asked a closed-ended question (beginning with do, will, can, and so on) such as: "Rose, I need to improve check-in wait times. Do you have any ideas?" Closed-ended questions tend to illicit one-word answers, and in this case, if Rose answers "No," the conversation may be over.

✔ **Sandwich small bits of criticism between large pieces of praise.**

For example: "Rose, I really appreciate all the extra care you take with customers and your ability to deal so well with all sorts of different personalities. Yesterday you seemed a little more stressed than usual; I noticed you lost your temper with one customer. What was going on? Usually you're so calm."

By sincerely accentuating strengths, the supervisor boosts the staff person's morale and makes it clear that what she brings to her job is far greater than yesterday's incident. The staff person is left feeling bigger rather than smaller.

✔ **Start with general feedback and then move to specific behaviors.**

For example: "Rose, as you know, we all tend to go a little nuts around the holidays when rental activity is at its peak. I've been doing this job for three years, and I still get caught up in the frenzy. I wanted to talk with you a little bit about making sure you don't pass that feeling on to the customers and give him or her the impression that we're being sloppy or rushed. Specifically, I noticed that several of your lease agreements had some key information missing, and that's unusual for you."

In this scenario the supervisor softened the feedback by including her own shortcomings in the general situation and then transitioned into how the holiday rush may be affecting Rose's work. Rose's behavior was normalized while still needing to be corrected.

✔ **Use more "I" statements than "you" statements to reduce defensiveness.**

For example: "Rose, I think it's important that we wear our nametags — even during breaks. I'd like you to keep yours on when you're in this building."

Compare the above statement with the following version, which accentuates the "you" more than the "I."

"Rose, you haven't been wearing your nametag when you're on a break. You have to wear it any time you're in this building."

In the first interaction, the supervisor talks from her own point-of-view about the situation, which focuses less attention on Rose's behavior and consequently produces less defensiveness. Likewise, speaking from an "I" rather than a "you" perspective makes maintaining a calm tone of voice much easier for the supervisor.

✔ **Mutually agree on any action items.**

For example: "Just to recap, Rose, you will give me your list of recommendations by 4 p.m. Tuesday, and I will set up a meeting to discuss them with you by the end of the following day."

Agreeing on the action items at the end of the session makes everyone responsible for the promises they have made and stops any misunderstandings about who is going to do what by when.

Do's and Don'ts for Dealing with Difficult Coaching Situations

From time to time you may be in a situation in which someone becomes angry and hostile. Whenever that happens, the following guidelines can help you respond:

✔ **Do empathize/don't defend.** Often the easiest and most effective way to avoid a confrontation is to let the person (or persons, if it's a group) know that you understand and sincerely appreciate her frustration or point-of-view.

✔ **Do admit when you don't know/don't pretend to know.** If you're asked a question and you don't know the answer, please don't pretend that you do and make something up. You experience no shame in saying you don't know and offering to find the answer. If someone in the group knows the answer, redirect the question to that person.

✔ **Do make eye contact/don't stare them down.** Making eye contact with an upset group member lets that person know that you can deal with the interruption and that you're interested in (rather than intimidated by) what he or she is saying. However, breaking eye contact when you answer the individual and redirecting your attention to the others in the room is a good idea. Doing so enables you to include everyone in the interaction and to avoid a stare down that usually results in an escalation of hostility.

✔ **Do listen to the intent/don't just hear the words.** When someone asks a challenging question, hearing only the words and the tone of voice may lead you to think that the confrontation is with you personally. Usually it isn't. By listening to the intent behind the words, you can avoid the trap of becoming defensive or argumentative and thereby address what they're really reacting to.

Chapter 7

What You Can Measure, You Can Manage: Service Standards

A company we once worked with balked at the idea of having everyone in the company answer the phone with the same greeting. "Won't this make us sound like robots to our customers?" the staff moaned. We assured them that customers see standards as evidence of service consistency and reliability, so they didn't need to worry about sounding artificial to customers. A few months later, we conducted a survey for the same company, and many customers had positive comments about the new phone standards and praised the company for its efforts.

Service standards serve two purposes. They're a powerful way of shaping the image that your customers have of you and a great management tool for measuring how well each person in your company meets the levels of service to which you aspire. In our view, too few companies have meaningful standards, simply because they don't know how to translate a general service quality into a specific service standard.

In this chapter, we show you how to create and implement measurable service standards.

You Can't Measure Friendly

General service qualities can be defined by adjectives that describe the basic ways you want your staff (and managers) to treat your customers, including:

- ✔ Friendly
- ✔ Courteous
- ✔ Efficient
- ✔ Pleasant
- ✔ Responsive
- ✔ Helpful
- ✔ Caring
- ✔ Prompt

Companies often write policies proclaiming how members of your staff need to exhibit these qualities. For example:

> When greeting customers, act in a friendly way.
>
> Be prompt in responding to customers' requests.
>
> When dealing with upset customers, show them that you care.

Although these goals all are worthy, they mean different things to different people. If you ask ten staff members to define being friendly to a customer, you get ten different answers. General service qualities, such as friendliness, are not specific or measurable, and they therefore are open to individual interpretation.

Service qualities are important because they provide your staff with general guidelines to follow in unpredictable situations for which no specific service standards have been set. However, if these qualities are going to be consistently put into practice, they must be made measurable.

You Can Measure Smiles

Service standards go one step further by turning general service qualities into specific, measurable actions that you expect your staff to take in given situations. For your staff to understand what you mean by friendly service, you must break the definition down into the components that make up friendly, such as:

- ✔ Smiling at customers as they approach
- ✔ Making direct eye contact while explaining the situation
- ✔ Greeting customers by saying "Good morning" or "Good afternoon"
- ✔ Using the customer's name at least twice during the conversation

By taking these observable actions, members of your staff convey friendliness to your customers. Table 7-1 lists some examples of how general service qualities can be turned into specific service standards. The measurable aspect of each standard is in bold type.

Table 7-1	From General Service Qualities to Specific Service Standards
Service Quality	*Service Standard*
Answer the phone promptly.	Answer the phone **within three rings.**
Return customer calls in a timely fashion.	Return all customer calls **within 24 hours.**
Be attentive to the customer.	Make eye contact with customers **within 5 seconds of their approaching you.**
Be empathetic with an upset customer.	**Always apologize if a customer is upset.**
Take personal responsibility for helping the customer.	**Always give the customer your name, phone number, and extension.**
Dress appropriately for work.	**Wear your uniform at all times including the cap and tie.**

Criteria for Effective Service Standards

Seven criteria make a service standard effective. We recommend that you review your current standards against this list and revamp the ones that need it. Effective standards need to be

- ✔ **Specific:** Standards tell service people precisely and exactly what is expected of them. Customers don't have to guess about your expectations or make anything up.

- ✔ **Concise:** Standards don't explain the philosophy behind the action. Instead, they get right to the point and spell out who needs to do what by when.

- ✔ **Measurable:** Because actions in a standard are all specific criteria, they are observable and objective, which makes them easy to quantify.

- ✔ **Based on customer requirements:** Standards need to be based on customer requirements and not just your industry's standards. Fulfilling your customers' expectations gives you an advantage over competitors that do not.

✔ **Written into job descriptions and performance reviews:** If you want employees to adhere to the standards, then write them down and make them part of each employee's job description and performance review. Using standards as a management tool gives them more credibility.

✔ **Jointly created with your staff:** The best standards are created by management and staff together based on their mutual understanding of customer needs. You may want to consider using quality groups (see Chapter 9) as a vehicle for having members of your staff come up with service standards.

✔ **Fairly enforced:** Standards that are enforced with some people and not with others quickly erode. Company-wide standards require everybody to conform to them, including the top brass. Department-specific standards apply to everyone within that department, including the manager.

Acing the Invisible Score Card

How do customers judge the service they receive from you? Customers, it seems, have an invisible mental score card on which they continually judge your service. Based on our research, your company is being evaluated in three basic areas:

✔ Product quality

✔ Ease of procedures

✔ Personal contact quality

Because these qualities are fundamental to your customers' experiences while doing business with you, we strongly recommend that you develop service standards in all three areas.

Exploring product quality

Product quality refers to the physical quality of the product you produce. In a service business, the product is only one aspect of the customer's overall experience. When eating out, for example, the product is the food you're served. You evaluate the restaurant based on the way the food is cooked, how it tastes, and the way it's presented. Examples of product quality standards at a restaurant may include:

✔ All vegetables must be purchased and served fresh daily.

✔ Two ounces of bay shrimp accompany each house salad.

✔ All entree dishes must have a fresh-fruit garnish.

The Malcolm Baldrige Quality Award

The Malcolm Baldrige Quality Award was created by an act of Congress in 1987. According to the application guidelines, the award is designed to promote:

✔ Awareness of quality as an increasingly important element in competitiveness

✔ Understanding of the requirements for quality excellence

✔ Sharing of information on successful quality strategies

Every year, hundreds of large and small businesses alike complete an application, hoping to win this award, which is one of the most prestigious that a business can receive. Past winners include such companies as Xerox, Motorola, Federal Express, and Cadillac.

The award is based on seven categories of criteria with customer satisfaction leading the pack. Fewer than 30 percent of the companies that apply are service businesses. For the service companies that do apply, standards is an area in which they typically receive the lowest ratings, because they're too general, not measurable, and not based on customer requirements. Service businesses, in general, seem to focus on communicating general service qualities to their staff but not specific service standards.

If you're interested in reviewing the criteria for the Malcolm Baldrige Quality Award, go to the National Institute of Standards and Technology (NIST) Web site at www.quality.nist.gov.

Making procedures easy

Ease-of-procedure standards make doing business with you and your company easy, fast, and efficient for your customer. In a restaurant, excellent food is only part of the picture. Customers also expect not to have to wait too long for their meals or their checks. Some typical procedural standards in a restaurant may include:

✔ Bringing all food to the table within three minutes of it being prepared.

✔ Setting up a baby seat before escorting a party with a small child to their table.

✔ Picking up a check within two minutes of payment being placed on the table by the customer.

Enriching personal contact

Standards for the quality of personal contact include the attitudes, actions, and behaviors that you expect your staff to show your customers. Your restaurant experience — no matter how mouthwateringly delicious the food — can be ruined entirely by a rude server. Some personal contact standards that can make this experience positive include:

- ✔ Greeting customers with a smile and saying, "Good evening. Welcome to The Feedbag."
- ✔ Asking whether customers have any questions about the menu before taking their order.
- ✔ Saying, "Thank you for dining with us tonight. We look forward to seeing you again," as you hand the customer the check.

Developing Service Standards in Four Simple Steps

The key to developing service standards is organizing the process into bite-sized pieces. We discuss each of the four steps for developing standards in this section.

Step 1: Defining your service sequences

Viewing your business as a series of separate but connected interactions can help you define and understand what we call *service sequences*.

Service sequences are to your business what chapters are to a book. They're a way of conveniently subdividing the aspects of your service so you can discover specific customer encounters that require standards. For example, if you're in the hotel business, your basic service sequence may go something like this:

Reservations

Check in

Use the room

Check out

Viewing your service sequences from your customer's perspective is important. If customers look at your business as separate chunks, what do they see? Not all of the services you provide follow precisely one after the other, so the important thing to do is to subdivide your business into the different aspects of the services you provide.

Step 2: Mapping out the steps

After you break your business services up into various chapters, choose one area that needs improvement (as indicated by customer feedback). You need to map out the major steps that make up that particular customer encounter chronologically (like the paragraphs within a chapter). For example, the check-in sequence for a hotel includes the following steps:

1. **Guest approaches the front desk.**
2. **Desk clerk asks for the guest's name.**
3. **Desk clerk pulls the guest's reservation from the file (hopefully).**
4. **Desk clerk asks what form of payment the guest will use.**
5. **Guest is given a room key and directions to the elevator.**

In this encounter, no value is added to the basic interaction. It simply is an accurate, step-by-step process that probably reflects how every hotel in the world checks in a guest. Thus to be able to add value to the guest's experience of staying at this particular hotel, you need to define key experience enhancers.

As in life, basic service sequences don't always go as planned. Our hotel guest may have made a reservation, but the desk clerk may not be able to find it in the system. In that situation, the clerk deviates from the normal sequence of events and goes off onto a new branch of the service sequence. Regardless of how many twists and turns there are, the basic process for developing standards is the same.

Step 3: Determining your experience enhancers

For each individual step of your service sequences, ask yourself:

What general service qualities will enhance the customer's experience of doing business with my company during this step?

As your "guest approaches the front desk" in the first step of the check-in sequence, your actions are critical, because they make an immediate first impression on the guest. Two of the most important general service qualities at this point are being friendly and attentive to the guest.

Make sure you carry out this same procedure for each step of each service sequence you want to improve until you determine the key experience-enhancing qualities for each step.

Step 4: Converting your experience enhancers into standards

After discovering how you can enhance the quality of service in a given sequence, you can then rewrite the step-by-step interaction by converting your general service qualities into the three types of service standards: personal, product, and procedural (see the earlier section on "Acing the Invisible Score Card"). In the hotel example, you can rewrite the sequence for checking in a guest to reflect these important standards:

- **Promptness:** When more than three people are waiting in line, call the desk supervisor for assistance.

- **Friendliness:** Smile at the customer as he or she approaches the front desk, make direct eye contact, and say "Good morning," "Good afternoon," or "Good evening."

- **Recognition and attentiveness:** Use the guest's name as soon as you know it.

- **Initiative:** Ask the guest whether he or she would like a wake-up call in the morning.

- **Quality assurance:** Call the guest within 15 minutes of checking in to make sure that everything in the room is satisfactory.

As your business grows and changes, remember to periodically update your standards. Don't get stuck defining one set of standards and keeping them for life. You need to review your standards at least once a year and update them as necessary to reflect changes in your market and your business.

Chapter 8

Beyond Employee of the Month: Reward and Recognition

In This Chapter

▶ Informally recognizing and praising your staff, even on a budget

▶ Exploring five ways to formally reward members of your staff

*A*ll people have a natural need to feel good about the jobs they do. According to a recent Gallup survey of more than 80,000 employees, reward and recognition ranked as key factors in customer satisfaction, employee retention, productivity, and profitability. By regularly rewarding and recognizing members of your staff when they do something right, rather than noticing and commenting only when they do something wrong, you help motivate them to keep up the good work. You can let your staff know they've done a good job in two ways:

> ✔ **Informal recognition:** This spontaneous, everyday type of recognition lets members of your staff know that you appreciate the jobs they're doing, and best of all, it takes little time, money, or planning to execute.

> ✔ **Formal reward program:** This preplanned, company-wide program rewards individuals, departments, and teams for achieving outstanding results in customer service. In general, these programs take time, money, and a good deal of planning to implement.

An outdated, yet not uncommon attitude that we often come across in our work is that if you're paying employees for the work they do, why do you need to reward or recognize them further? Some managers and supervisors believe that their staffs shouldn't need many strokes or *attaboys,* because they receive financial compensation for doing their jobs well. That simply is not true. Research and experience show that people thrive when they receive personal recognition for the work they do. Although a paycheck is important, it never replaces the need for genuine appreciation for the efforts your staff members put in. Although everyone is, of course, expected to do their jobs well, recognition encourages and motivates staff members to exceed what is expected of them.

Informal Recognition

Studies show that regularly giving informal recognition to an employee is a stronger motivator than providing him or her with formal rewards. Simple praise is remembered long after the event, because it tells your employees that you noticed their efforts and took the time to personally thank them.

If your heart is in the right place and you follow these recommendations, we promise that your praise will be warmly appreciated by others.

Basic praise primer

Although informal recognition is effective, inexpensive, and convenient, many managers don't give members of their staffs as many pats on the back as they could. Consequently, when they praise their staffs, the managers' inexperience (and often awkwardness) can be interpreted as a lack of genuine appreciation.

We set matters straight in this section by cluing you in to a few basic skills that can complement your compliments.

Always reward the behavior that you want repeated. When members of your staff receive positive feedback, they look for ways to repeat the behavior. Sincere praise is the best way to ensure that good service habits stick.

Don't do it in the hallway

Before you praise someone, always make sure that you have his or her full attention. Don't try to give your staff a compliment when they (or you) are scurrying down the corridor, rushing to a meeting, or trying to meet a dead-line. Instead, set up a time and place that is convenient for them. If you're acknowledging a team of people for their efforts, set up a time when you can meet with all of them in one place so you can praise them as a group.

Go to them

Talk to your members of your staff on their own turf or in a place where they feel comfortable and relaxed, such as at their desks or in the lunchroom. Don't ask them to come to your office because they may mistakenly think that something is wrong.

Maintain eye contact

Because people can perceive lack of eye contact to mean insincerity, deceit, or dishonesty, looking at your employees when you recognize them is criti-cal. On the other hand, your employees probably are going to look away from you, because they haven't likely had much practice at accepting honest, straightforward praise.

You don't want to be standing up and looking down on your staff when you praise them. The trick is to stay level with them, perhaps by taking a seat next to them.

Don't delay

You need to recognize your staff as quickly as possible after the achievement has occurred to have the biggest impact. Don't wait until the holiday party to praise the heroes of last spring. The further away you get from the event, the less impact the acknowledgment has.

The most heartfelt praise misses its mark whenever your tone of voice does not convey genuine enthusiasm. Your level of excitement, in addition to your words, tells your staff how you really feel.

Recognition thought starters

Although you may like nothing better than to show your appreciation to service heroes by sending them to Hawaii, you have many other avenues of recognition to pursue without them costing an arm and a leg. The simplest, most spontaneous ideas often yield the best results and the most fun. You can use the following checklists to find a form of recognition that fits the employee, your budget, and the occasion. The checklists are divided into three price categories.

Ideas that cost less than $25

When your gut's telling you to praise your employees, but your budget cries out, "I don't have the money," there's still hope. Here are a few suggestions that'll cost you little or nothing to try:

- ✔ **Send a thank-you note.** You can personally hand the note to your staff person, leave it for him to find on his desk, or tape it to the door of his office. Make sure the employee knows the specific actions for which you are thanking him.

  We know it's tempting to send an e-mail rather than a letter — but it isn't recommended. E-mails are too casual and run-of-the-mill and often aren't read. If you really want your thank-you to count, do it the old-fashioned way.

- ✔ **Have a senior executive personally thank the employee.** This form of praise always is special, because members of your staff know that an executive's time is a precious commodity, and they'll know that you've passed on the positive feedback. If possible, have the employee and executive meet face to face. If you can't work out such an arrangement, then a telephone call will do. In addition, make sure the executive is well briefed on what the service person did and why his or her action deserves special recognition. Be sure to ask the senior executive in charge of your department to recognize your employee.

✔ **Send a letter of praise from a senior executive.** This alternative to a personal visit or a phone call has an added advantage, because the letter can be placed in the employee's personnel file. This option differs slightly from a thank-you note, because it comes from a senior executive, not the immediate supervisor or manager.

✔ **Create a hall of fame for service heroes.** Use a lunchroom wall or another area that is routinely seen by everyone and put up postcard-size photos of your service heroes. We recommend that you update the photographs with new service heroes every month or two. Include a short caption beneath each picture about what the person did to earn a place on the wall.

✔ **Display customers' letters of praise.** Similar to the hall of fame, pick a common area that is traveled by everyone to show off framed letters of praise that customers send to staff.

✔ **Highlight service heroes in the company newsletter.** Regularly dedicate a part of your company newsletter to recognizing service heroes. Include a brief description of their achievements in the article.

Create an award for people who aren't usually in the limelight. This award can be any form of recognition that you choose, but it needs to have a specific name and be given to people whose work is usually out of sight or low profile. Call it something like the Backroom Award, make a big deal about it, and present it on a regular basis (once a month or quarter).

Ideas that cost less than $50

Getting accounting to let the purse strings out slightly enables a little more creativity in terms of the type of recognition you can give to members of your staff. Here are a few great ways to recognize hard-working employees for fewer than 50 bucks:

✔ **Lunchtime pizza party.** Send out for pizzas and soft drinks and have them waiting in the lunchroom for your team or department — do this on a Friday so you can end the week on a high note. Be sure to make a brief speech about how the food is just your way of saying thank you to everyone for a week of great results.

✔ **Take employees to lunch.** If you have an employee or a few employees who really went the distance for a customer, thank them by inviting them to join you at a restaurant for lunch. The cost is kept down by making the meal a lunch rather than a dinner. Be sure to allow yourself enough time to recognize all the participants for their contributions without being rushed.

✔ **Surprise employees with balloons.** For the biggest impact, deliver the balloons to the employees' desks while they are away from their work area. The balloons will be a pleasant surprise when the employee returns. Be sure to attach a personal thank-you note to the balloons recognizing each person's achievement.

✔ **Send flowers.** A simple bouquet of fresh-cut flowers always brightens a person's day. If they're delivered, the cost will be a little bit higher, but the recognition will be even more special.

✔ **Buy a plant.** Because cut flowers have a limited life, try recognizing a staff person for something special by giving him or her a potted plant, such as an orchid, which stays in bloom for several weeks.

✔ **Give away tickets to a sporting event.** We know many companies that get discount tickets for their local sports teams. Have tickets available for different sports and always give them in pairs so that the staff member can take a friend or family member along.

✔ **Let the employee come to work an hour late (with pay).** This thank-you always seems to work well. The time can be increased to fit the deed. We recommend a maximum of two hours, because rewarding any more than that may require extra planning to cover the person's job. An alternative to this idea is letting the employee leave work an hour early.

✔ **Buy a magazine subscription.** Most monthly magazines cost less than $30 a year for a subscription. Select magazines that reflect employees' interests or let them select their own. Magazines take a while to be delivered after an order is placed, so include this lag time into your timing. You can present the award by giving the employees a card or letter informing them about the magazine. Recipients will be reminded of their achievements every month when they receive their magazines.

✔ **Give a gift certificate.** You can find gift certificates these days for just about any product or service. Gift certificates to bookstores, record stores, restaurants, and movie theaters are particularly popular.

Ideas that cost less than $100

You can come up with some nice ways to recognize an employee who provides excellent customer service when your spending limit increases. If you can swing a budget of around $100, then you can treat your top performers to some top rewards including:

✔ **Treating an employee to dinner for two.** Select a good restaurant and arrange for a gift certificate. Determine a dollar limit ahead of time that covers dinner, dessert, and beverages for two.

✔ **Giving the employee a day off.** When one of your staff members does something really special, consider giving her an extra day off with pay. In most businesses, Friday is a good day to choose, because it often is the least busy day of the week, so the interruption at work is minimized, and the employee gets a three-day weekend.

✓ **Sending the employee to an outside training program.** Show your appreciation for members of your staff by investing in their education. Let them choose a training course that supports their personal or professional interests and have the company pay. This course can be anything from a cooking class to a time-management workshop.

Formal Rewards

Although they don't have the same everyday impact as informal recognition, formal awards nevertheless are an important part of your strategy for service improvement. Annual or semi-annual award presentations need to be highly publicized and must send a clear message about what values and behaviors your company holds in high esteem. Managers and supervisors also benefit from a formal reward program, because it lends credibility to the values and behaviors that they've been informally recognizing.

Formal reward programs require time and planning, because your service improvement strategy must include a simple and practical way to measure who wins. Attention must be given to every department and group so that those people who have little or no customer contact have as much chance of winning as those with front-line service jobs.

Two essential aspects of leveraging the success of any rewards program are

✓ **Fairness:** Make sure programs are neither political nor relationship biased. Everyone needs to have an equal chance at recognition.

✓ **Consistency:** Use the same or comparable criteria for selecting reward candidates. If your staff members perceive inconsistencies with the program, it will rapidly lose support.

Keeping the rewards interesting

Formal reward programs that stay the same year after year eventually stop being special. Winners begin to think that their rewards are just routine, and other employees lose interest in winning. You can keep your reward program dynamic and alive by updating it from year to year, altering the ceremony, the prizes, and the criteria for winning.

Varying the rewards to suit the person

Taking the one-size-fits-all approach is a big mistake when dealing with formal reward programs. Having a variety of awards available ensures that the prizes you offer have meaning to the individuals who receive them. So if you have a winner who hates sports but loves music, give him tickets to the symphony — not the ball game. Prizes are most often given at a special event, such as an all-company meeting, picnic, or, if appropriate, a company dinner. Awards can range from personalized mementos to family vacations, depending on the size of your company, your budget, and the achievement. The sections that follow describe five awards that you may want to consider for a formal reward program.

A fancy dinner

A special meal is a wonderful way to celebrate a winning team's achievement. The team becomes your guest at a fancy restaurant, and you play host to the evening on the company. During the dinner, you can highlight your team's accomplishments and invite other team members to speak. If your group is larger than six people, hearing each other in a crowded restaurant can become difficult, so consider going to one that offers private dining facilities. The dinner also needs to be highly publicized by memo, bulletin board, or newsletter, so that other staff members are aware of the achievement.

Customized gifts

Customized gifts are available from catalogs or companies that specialize in incentive and motivational products. Some items that are easily personalized and readily available are

- Pen-and-pencil sets
- Notepads
- T-shirts
- Paperweights
- Award pins

Some incentive companies have Web-based programs that offer managers a way of designing, tracking, and administering all aspects of an employee reward program. With different levels of sophistication available, managers can create a custom designed, soup-to-nuts incentive program or a simple reward catalog that is e-mailed to service winners to choose their own prizes ranging from clocks to chainsaws.

Customized trophies

Plaques, silver cups, desk awards, and other trophies can be engraved with the employee's name, the date, and a brief description of the achievement.

Travel

Travel awards range from weekend getaways at a nearby bed-and-breakfast to a week-long vacation trip to a resort. These awards always include travel and lodging expenses for two and sometimes an allowance for meals and incidentals. If the vacation is a week long, don't forget to make arrangements for the winner's work to be handled during his or her absence; otherwise, vacation memories will quickly sour on the first day back on the job.

Cash

Two schools of thought exist about giving cash awards to staff. Some companies don't give monetary awards because they think that the money will be used to pay bills and provide no lasting memory. Other companies think that their employees appreciate extra money more than anything else, and cash awards are the best motivators. One suggestion: Develop an award program that incorporates both cash and prizes.

Making the award appropriate to the achievement

Be careful not to cheapen or lessen the value of an award by making it less significant than the achievement calls for. For example, giving a personalized pencil cup to the service hero whose initiative saved your largest account probably isn't the best idea.

The most successful and well-designed formal reward programs are simple to administer. They give everyone in every position a chance to win, and have simple, easy-to-understand rules and goals that everyone considers attainable.

Making it fun

We urge you to make your rewards and recognition programs fun! We've discovered through the years that an environment of good humor helps everyone learn more, work harder, and show added interest in whatever task is at hand.

Chapter 9

It Takes a Team: Problem-Solving with a Twist

A large number of policies and procedures at many of the companies with which we've worked were designed with the company's convenience in mind, rather than that of the customer. Reinventing these processes to make them more customer-oriented is not unlike cleaning out your clothes closet. As you remove each item and give it a closer look in the bright light of day, you can't believe the number of outdated things (wide ties, neon prom dresses, platform shoes, and so on) you've kept.

Your company probably has a number of outdated processes, procedures, and policies that are of limited value to you and an annoyance to your customers. Many of these outfits have been hanging around your corporate closet for so long they've just become "the way we do business" without much careful consideration about their current usefulness or effectiveness. If you suspect that these types of outdated policies and procedures exist in your company, but you haven't tackled them yet, it may be because you're afraid of opening a Pandora's box.

However, for your customer service to continually improve and flourish over the long term, you must be willing not only to take a close and honest look at the current customer focus of your policies and procedures but also to implement a structure for solving ongoing service problems and making your existing processes and procedures more customer focused. This structure must address two issues:

✔ Getting your staff involved in the process of change.

✔ Providing a specific method for improving your processes, procedures, and policies.

Problem-Solving with Quality Groups: Killing Two Birds with One Stone

The best structure we know for addressing both of the preceding issues is the implementation of quality groups, or process improvement teams, as they're sometimes called.

Just what exactly is a quality group?

Quality groups provide a step-by-step method for using your staff's talents and knowledge to solve ongoing quality and service problems. A quality group is made up of a group of staff members who are temporarily brought together either in meetings (usually once a week, for about an hour) or cyberspace to solve a specific problem. The quality group is disbanded after the problem is solved. The entire process usually takes anywhere from a couple of weeks to a few months, depending on the scope and complexity of the problem.

Traits of successful quality groups

Companies that have had the best results with quality groups or process improvement teams understand the essential elements necessary to ensure success. In the following sections, we discuss each of these elements.

ANECDOTE

Repairing customer service in an auto repair shop

An auto repair shop decided it wanted to improve its customer service. By using a simple, written questionnaire, the staff of the auto repair shop discovered that most customers were very happy with the work the shop performed, but they hated to wait in a small, grimy office until someone in the back garage happened to come in and notice them. The repair shop owner set up a small quality group to address the problem. The members of the group came up with a solution that involved painting the office, installing a small coffee maker, and wiring up a buzzer that sounded in the back when the office door was opened. Each day a different person was responsible for replenishing the coffee, and a standard was set that required the customer to be attended to within one minute of the buzzer sounding. This simple yet elegant example demonstrates how a small company used the powerful resources of a quality group to improve its service.

A user-friendly process

Quality groups originally were started within manufacturing companies to decrease defects and improve the physical quality of their products. This type of engineering-driven environment not surprisingly gave birth to a problem-solving process that was heavy on graphs, charts, and statistics.

Many of our clients, being service companies, were not passionate about using Pareto charts or histograms (in fact, one staff member thought the latter term was a surgical procedure), so we went searching for a much simpler and user-friendly process that better fit the needs of a service business.

We became so disenchanted with how non-user-friendly these processes were that we decided to create our own. What we outline for you in the next few pages is a user-friendly twist on the typical quality group process. In our opinion, a quality-group process is user-friendly when it has

- ✔ Short and simple steps for identifying, evaluating, and resolving service problems.
- ✔ Language that is easily understood and not loaded down with tons of jargon.
- ✔ Problem-solving techniques that are based on simple models rather than complex matrices.

A strong quality-group facilitator

A quality group is made up of four to eight staff members who are guided through the process by an in-house facilitator either face to face in live meetings or in cyberspace via e-mail. The facilitator needs to be someone who has strong communications skills and has been trained in the problem-solving process your company has decided to use.

Most facilitators are staff members who have attended special training to find out how to be a group facilitator. Because the duties of a facilitator usually only take about an hour a week, they shouldn't interfere with other job responsibilities.

Training in-house staff to be facilitators gives them an opportunity for professional development and provides you with a group of employees who are experts at solving problems. The facilitator makes the job of the group members easier by

- ✔ Encouraging full participation.
- ✔ Guiding the team through problem-solving methods.
- ✔ Finding outside resources that can shed light on the problem.

> ✔ Educating group members about each step of the process.
>
> ✔ Providing a liaison between the quality group and management.

The facilitator doesn't necessarily have to be familiar with the particular problem on which the quality group is working. Sometimes a lack of hands-on involvement can actually help the facilitator remain impartial and objective.

Support from management

When quality groups fail, it's most often because they weren't supported by management. We've found the main questions that managers have about quality groups are

> ✔ Will I lose control of my department or staff?
>
> ✔ Will my input on the problem be ignored?
>
> ✔ What if the quality group comes up with an innovative solution to a problem that I've been trying to solve for years?

In most cases, these fears are unfounded, and for that reason, we recommend that prior to the first quality group meeting, the facilitator meet with or e-mail every manager whose staff will be participating in the quality group. Use the meeting to quell management fears by explaining how a quality group works. Topics to cover include

> ✔ An overview of the specific process to be used (see the section, "Using a Step-By-Step Problem-Solving Method in Your Quality Group").
>
> ✔ How the manager, although not a member of the group, can address the team from time to time and offer his or her input.
>
> ✔ Ways the manager can support the quality group, including how the manager plans for times when the department is short-staffed and he or she cannot afford to let staff attend a scheduled quality group meeting.

The sooner managers are brought into the information loop, the better, although some managers balk at the idea of involving staff in the process of changing policies or procedures. As one unenlightened vice president put it: "You mean you want me to turn over the asylum to the inmates?" Our experience has consistently been that when they're given guidance and support, staff members will come up with innovative ideas that benefit the customer and the company.

Starting off with the right problem

In most cases, management determines which specific problem a particular quality group is going to work on. We recommend that you begin with a small problem that's relatively easy to solve. An initial success creates momentum and positive press that you can then use as a springboard for taking on bigger, more complex problems. Try to choose initial problems that are

✔ Simple rather than complex.

✔ Local and specific rather than widespread and general.

✔ Free of heavy political implications.

✔ Beneficial to both customers and staff.

The right mix of staff

The staff members who participate in the quality group must have a hands-on relationship with the problem they're going to solve. Including group members from different departments is a good idea, whenever appropriate. Doing so ensures that the solution the group comes up with addresses how the problem impacts different departments.

By setting up your quality group only after you've selected the problem, you ensure that the members you select for any given team are the right people for the right problem.

Using a Step-by-Step Problem-Solving Method in Your Quality Group

Although very similar, the process you use with a quality group in meetings is somewhat different than the process you use for virtual online quality groups.

For a real-time, face-to-face quality groups that meet each week, use the five-step problem-solving process that we discuss in this section.

To make it easy for your company or department to follow this process, we've created a guide that describes, in detail, what takes place every step of the way. We've also included a special facilitator's checklist at the end of each step to provide your facilitator with some valuable tools.

Step 1: Introduce the basics

The first quality group meeting is critical because it introduces the members to an overview of the six steps and gives them the opportunity to ask questions. In addition, the first meeting agenda needs to do the following.

Explain the nature of a quality group

Many companies live by this misguided rule: *There's never enough time to do it right but always enough time to do it over.* Being *service-focused* means taking the time to prevent future problems — instead of merely reacting to current ones.

On more than one occasion the president of a company has said to us: "Quality groups are a good idea, but we just can't afford to take the time to do this right now." Our response: "How can you afford not to take the time?"

Everyone knows a problem exists, but the culture of *deadline thinking* doesn't give your staff or managers the opportunity, or time, to actually sit down and come up with a thorough and well-thought-out solution that fixes the problem in the long term. Quality groups give your company a short period each week when *deadline thinking* is put on the back burner and thorough thinking takes the spotlight. *Thorough thinking* is different from the everyday work mode, because it requires the group to approach problem-solving by

 ✔ Sorting out the facts of the situation from the assumptions.

 ✔ Looking at all the possible solutions — not just the obvious ones.

 ✔ Gaining widespread acceptability for the solution rather than imposing a solution on others.

 ✔ Looking at long-term impact and short-term gains.

After members of your staff get a taste of this way of working, you'll find that they take the habits back to work with them and, even when under time pressure, bring a new level of quality to their everyday decisions.

Establish ground rules

As a group, you must decide on and agree to adhere to specific ground rules — or rules of conduct. On the quality group ground rules worksheet shown in Figure 9-1, we provide you with what most groups consider the essential items for running smooth quality groups. Before the first meeting, make copies of the list for each member, and then after a group discussion, delete or add items accordingly.

Confirm dates and locations

Because the meeting day and times aren't always fixed and may be different from week to week to suit the schedules of group members, make sure that your meeting room is available for all the scheduled dates and double-check to make sure that all members are confirmed for the correct dates and times.

Clarify individual responsibilities

Nothing is more annoying than a meeting that's slowed because one or more group members didn't do what they were supposed to do. This problem frustrates other members of the group and hurts the credibility of the persons who didn't deliver. Each group member is responsible for showing up on time and bringing the results of any assignment he or she agreed to take on.

Quality Group Ground Rules Worksheet

As a group, add any extra ground rules in the spaces at the bottom. Delete those ground rules that you do not agree with.

- Be open and honest.
- Attend every meeting.
- Be punctual.
- Evaluate ideas – not people.
- Stay open – even if you disagree.
- Participate.
- Question.
- Don't complain.
- Listen for the positives, not the negatives.
- Show respect for each individual.
- _____
- _____
- _____
- _____

Figure 9-1:
The quality group ground rules worksheet.

Facilitator's checklist

If you're a facilitator of a quality group, this section is especially for you. It contains tips, techniques, and ideas about how to make your quality group meetings a roaring success. Your level of enthusiasm and excitement at the first meeting is especially critical because it sets the stage for a great quality group and creates rapport between the team members.

As facilitator at the first quality group meeting, try to accomplish the following:

❑ **Make everyone feel welcome.**

After everyone is seated, have each person introduce himself or herself. If everyone already knows one another, you can ask each of them to explain why he or she is in the quality group and what he or she expects to gain personally by participating.

❑ **Write the problem on the flip chart.**

Ask whether anyone in the group has any questions about the problem — what it means, is it stated clearly, and so on.

❑ **Talk about the importance of teamwork in the quality group.**

Explain that good teamwork in the quality group is achieved by combining effective interpersonal skills (listening, supporting each other, and offering constructive ideas) with creative problem-solving (brainstorming, looking for realistic solutions, and not making assumptions).

❑ **Answer any questions that group members have.**

Some common questions may include: Are the meetings approved by upper management? Will the group be meeting in the same place each week? Will you always be this group's facilitator?

If you don't know the answer to a question, don't make something up. Nobody expects you to have all the answers, and you'll develop trust by telling it the way it is. Please don't try to snow the group with your infinite wisdom.

❑ **Be sure that the next meeting is set up and ready to go.**

Because each group member's attendance is key to the success of the quality group, verify that everyone knows the date, time, and location of the next meeting and that all members are able to attend. In addition, make sure that you have a room reserved for the next meeting and all necessary supplies, including:

• A flip chart with markers and masking tape or thumb tacks

• Any blank forms that are needed

• A blank minutes sheet for the note taker

❑ **Use the action plan worksheet.**

Any agreed-upon actions need to be written down on an action plan worksheet like the one shown in Figure 9-2 and brought to the next meeting.

❑ **Arrange the note taker for the next meeting.**

Before the end of the first meeting, decide who will serve as note taker for the next session. Be sure to have that person make a copy of the minutes worksheet (see Figure 9-3) and bring it to the next session. Because the note taker is focusing on recording what is said, he or she probably won't participate as much in the discussion as other members. For that reason, every member of the group eventually needs to take a turn as note taker.

Action Plan **Worksheet**

Quality group name: _____ Date: _____ Page: ____ of ____

TASK/PROJECT	ASSIGNED TO	DUE DATE	STATUS/REMARKS

Figure 9-2:
The action plan worksheet.

Quality Group
Name:

_____

Quality Group
Minutes
Worksheet

Quality Group
Facilitator:

_____

Number of quality group members in this meeting: _____

Quality group members **not** present:
_____
_____
_____

Guests present:
_____
_____
_____

Activities, actions, and so on:
_____
_____
_____
_____
_____
_____
_____
_____
_____
_____

Notetaker: _____

Figure 9-3:
The quality
group
minutes
worksheet.

Step 2: Find the cause of the problem

Unlike the first step, finding the actual cause of the problem usually takes more than one meeting because it involves listing and then evaluating all the possible causes.

Listing all possible causes of the problem

Determining a problem's causes is a brainstorming activity (flip back to Chapter 6 for tips and rules about brainstorming). As the group brainstorms, each member indicates what he or she thinks are the possible causes of the problem. The facilitator lists the causes on a flip chart. After each group member has spoken and all possible causes are listed, the group is ready to discuss and evaluate them.

Evaluating the various causes

Now that all the various causes are laid out on the flip charts, the group can discuss and evaluate them. First, the group needs to eliminate the causes they see as having only a minor impact on the problem. After this task is complete, the group must come to a consensus decision (see the sidebar titled "Consensus decision-making") on the causes of the problem they think are most significant.

At this point, further investigation and fact gathering about the supposed causes often is necessary; however, because this investigation usually occurs between meetings, you probably will have several different actions that need to be carried out by several different group members. Use the action plan worksheet in Figure 9-2 to keep track of who will do what and by when.

Consensus decision-making

In the normal course of work, groups use many different methods for making decisions, including:

✔ Voting

✔ Assigning a leader who makes the ultimate decision

✔ Doing nothing and letting circumstances decide

✔ Letting the customer make the decision

In a quality group, however, many discussions are aimed at helping the team reach a *consensus decision,* or one that's supported by all the members of the team. Reaching a consensus decision doesn't mean that all group members are head-over-heels in love with the decision, just that they will be able to genuinely support it.

For example, a group member who has participated actively in the discussion may at some point say, "This option would not be my first choice, and it wasn't what I originally thought we would do, but I can live with the decision." Chances are this team member thinks that his or her point of view has been heard and appreciated and thus will continue to participate wholeheartedly in future meetings.

On the other hand, consensus decision-making is not forcing group members to acquiesce by ignoring their opinions or intimidating them. For example, if a group member thinks that his concerns have not been addressed, he may say in frustration, "Okay, go ahead, if that's what you've decided to do. I won't get in your way." The tone of his voice and his body language obviously show you that he doesn't really support the decision and is just going along because he feels too frustrated to do anything else. When that happens, this group member probably will participate less in discussions and then bring up unresolved issues in later meetings — much to the chagrin of other members — and may be the first to undermine the decision when problems with implementation crop up along the way. Without a true consensus in decision-making, the quality group will have a hard time moving on to the next steps.

When team members are familiar with a problem or the problem has been around for a long time, you need to avoid the common tendency toward quickly developing a solution without stopping to understand why the problem exists. This often misdirected inclination is why looking beyond the symptoms of the problem to the root causes is so important.

Facilitator's checklist

Because your group will be using brainstorming and consensus decision-making techniques for the first time during this step, make sure that you manage the process so that everyone feels that he or she is making a positive contribution to the group. Some tips that can help you make this step smooth as silk include

❑ **Writing all brainstorming ideas on a flip chart.**

After you've filled up a page, tear it off and stick it to the wall with masking tape or thumb tacks so that everyone in the room can see it. Having all the ideas clearly visible to all members of the group stimulates creativity.

❑ **Asking members of your group the following questions to help them cover all the bases:**

- What percentage of the problem is eliminated if this cause is fixed?

- Is this cause of the problem constant or intermittent?

- Are we overlooking another cause that leads to this cause?

- Are we making any assumptions about this cause?

- Do we need any extra information about this cause?

❑ **Concluding meetings at ideal stopping points.**

Avoid taking up the entire time slot just because you have scheduled a certain amount of time. If you find that you're 15 minutes away from the meeting's allotted time and you think the next discussion will require more than 15 minutes to complete, feel free to stop. You can begin the next session with the tabled or postponed topic.

Step 3: Brainstorm solutions to the problem

Now that your team members have identified the major causes of the problem, they're ready to brainstorm possible solutions. Because you've already done the groundwork and identified the real causes of the problem, the group is better equipped to come up with more targeted solutions during this session.

At this point, your team is in the middle of the quality group process. The potential danger here is that team members may become embroiled in their differing points of view about the right way to solve the problem. Some of the actions you can take as a facilitator to make sure this step is as productive as possible are:

✔ **Being aware of any change in a group member's behavior.**

Pay attention to any normally active member who suddenly begins behaving in an uncharacteristically quiet manner. This behavior may mean that the member thinks the group isn't paying attention to his or her ideas and opinions.

✔ **Remaining sensitive to the fact that some group members may be overwhelmed.**

In this part of the process, you're dealing with large amounts of information and some members may begin to feel buried by details and may want to either throw in the towel or simply go along with the team members who are the most persistent and forceful. Show your sensitivity to this situation by explaining that feeling overwhelmed isn't uncommon and that the group soon will be out of the woods.

Part of your job as facilitator is to ensure that everyone participates regardless of their differences or inhibitions. You can use several of the following techniques to accomplish that goal:

❑ **Ask group questions.**

These questions enable everyone to participate, and they're a good way to begin a brainstorming session. In general, open-ended questions (questions that begin with what, where, when, and why) work best for brainstorming. For example, you may ask the whole group, "What do you think are some of the main solutions to this problem?"

❑ **Ask an individual a question.**

These questions help involve group members who aren't yet participating because they may be quieter or a little bit shy. For example, you may say "Jose, how do you feel about this option?"

❑ **Gather specific information.**

Whenever group members present information that's too general, you can use closed-ended questions (questions that begin with did, does, do, and can) to get more specific information from them. For example, "Can you be more specific?" or "Do you have an example?"

❑ **Acknowledge what group members say.**

When group members speak, you need to let them know that you understand and are interested in what they're saying and that their comments are important. For example, nod your head, lean forward, and say, "I see," "Okay," "Yes," or "Uh-huh" to encourage the person to continue.

❑ **Practice active listening.**

This technique is also called *paraphrasing*. You repeat back the main points of what a group member has said to you. For example, if a team member thinks the only solution to the problem is buying a new computer system, you'd say back to him, "Let me see if I understand. You don't think updating the old computer system will fix the problem. You think we need to invest in a new one. Is that correct?" This technique clarifies what the person has said, lets him know that you have heard and understood him, and provides him with an opportunity to make corrections as needed.

❑ **Remain silent.**

Often, you won't want to speak or initiate conversation. Your not speaking enables the team to think about the topic on the table. This time to think is especially important when you start a brainstorming session because people usually need a minute or two to gather their thoughts.

❑ **Sustain participation.**

If you encounter a lull in the conversation, asking the question, "What else?" helps stimulate the group to take a deeper look at the issue before them. It keeps the discussion going when you know that there is more to be said.

❑ **Conclude.**

When the group has nothing more to say and you think that all the feedback has been given, wrap up the discussion by using the phrase, "Anything else?" Doing so lets group members know that this is the last call for feedback on this part of the discussion.

Step 4: Evaluate possible solutions

Some of the solutions the team comes up with will be better than others and must be evaluated for how feasible it is to implement them. This step helps you eliminate solutions that look good on paper but won't work in reality. The solution evaluation worksheet in Figure 9-4 can help the group evaluate each possible solution against important criteria. Review the form and add anything that your group feels is critical.

Finding the most viable solution

As each box of the form is filled in, the group needs to stop and discuss any pertinent issues. If the group determines that more information is needed, be sure to allow enough time between meetings to gather the information. When each solution has been fully evaluated, total the ratings and the solution with the highest score is the winner — and usually the all-around best solution.

Solution Evaluation **Worksheet**

POTENTIAL SOLUTION	Can team implement?	Short-term impact	Long-term impact	Relatively low cost	Resources readily available	Management commitment level	TOTAL

Rate each of the above criteria on a scale of 1 through 5.
1 = low or unlikely
5 = high or likely

Figure 9-4:
The solution evaluation worksheet.

Facilitator's checklist

At last your group is ready to talk about solutions, but to avoid getting slowed down by personality conflicts and different points of view, keep the group moving toward consensus decision-making by using these strategies:

❑ **Respect differences of opinion in the group.**

You can count on different degrees of agreement and enthusiasm from the group members as you go through this step. For example, members who are detail-oriented may want to dwell on certain issues until they're completely satisfied that every facet has been examined. Others who see a bigger picture won't want to dwell on the small specifics that they find "boring and insignificant." These two different perspectives can create a synergy where the whole is greater than the sum of its parts.

Your job as facilitator is to respect each person's point of view, ask questions that reveal assumptions, and help your group move forward.

❑ **Recognize each team member's unique contribution.**

Each person in your quality group brings unique strengths and talents to the table. Some members may have a natural inclination toward working with numbers, others are better at interviewing, and still others may excel at creating charts, graphs, and diagrams. The success of your team depends largely upon each member appreciating what the others bring to the party.

Step 5: Recommend a solution to management

Effectively presenting the findings and recommendations of the quality group is, in some ways, the moment of truth. It's when all the hard work that's been done during previous weeks comes to fruition.

The more organized and prepared the quality group is, the more confident its members will be when the presentation rolls around. Prepare for the meeting by following the directions in the sections that follow.

Deciding who will make the presentation

Before members of the quality group begin planning the structure of the presentation, they need to decide who will make the presentation. You may want to consider:

- ✔ Having different quality group members present different parts of the presentation, depending on their expertise or the depth of their involvement in a particular area.

- ✔ Having two members of the group give a brief talk on the benefits that they personally received from being involved in the quality group.

- ✔ Having all the team members attend the presentation. To miss it would be like missing the grand finale.

- ✔ Directly involving all team members with some aspect of preparing the presentation even if they cannot attend.

Determining what materials and equipment are needed

Do team members have all the graphs, charts, overheads, handouts, and so on that they need to make the presentation? Is any special audiovisual equipment needed, such as an overhead projector, VCR, computer, television, and so on? Make sure that you have all of the research, evidence, and analysis needed to back up the team's proposals.

Preparing the structure of the presentation

The presentation shouldn't take any longer than an hour. The group needs to prepare the presentation (including who will present what) using the following information:

- An introduction of the members of the quality group and the problem they worked on.

- A discussion of how long the quality group took to resolve the problem.

- A description of the key causes that led to the problem.

- The general direction taken and methods used for arriving at the solution.

- An explanation of the proposed solution and its expected impact.

- A note thanking the people who contributed information and assistance but were not on the team

Reaching Online Consensus in Virtual Quality Groups

Today, it's something of a luxury for a quality group to be able to sit in the same room together. Sit-down meetings are rare not only because of time constraints, but also because companies have *virtual teams* — groups of people who are dedicated to the same project but who live and work in different geographical locations. The technological revolution has made physical location less important than ever before. So how do you problem-solve using the *synergy,* or collective power, of a group, when members of the group are scattered across the country or around the world? E-mail, of course.

E-mail is an effective tool for online quality groups, because it provides a forum for brainstorming, gathering input from others, and agreeing on the best course of action. The online problem-solving process presented in this section provides an alternative to traditional face-to-face quality groups and produces innovative and cost-effective solutions that motivate everyone involved.

Similar to the traditional five-step process for quality groups outlined in the section on "Using a Step-by-Step Problem-Solving Method in Your Quality Group" earlier in this chapter, the following process features a few special twists and turns to make it work online.

Step 1: State the problem and request feedback on possible causes

After team members have been selected (a group of four to twelve people works well), the facilitator begins the process by sending an e-mail to all team members. This message contains

- ✔ A description of the problem to be solved
- ✔ A request for the team's input

The facilitator needs to state the problem as simply and clearly as possible and must be careful not to state the problem as a solution, because doing so preempts the team from coming up with a different — and probably better — solution. For example, "Should we cancel the interoffice Fruitcake Bake-off?" is better stated as, "We don't have enough volunteers for the interoffice Fruitcake Bake-off."

If needed, the facilitator can include a small amount of background information in the e-mail message. Any background information must be kept brief, because most team members already should be familiar with the problem.

Next, the facilitator asks team members to write down what they believe are the possible causes of the problem and explains that they should feel free to write down whatever comes to mind in this brainstorming exercise without too much editing — that will take place later.

The e-mail may look something like the following:

```
Dear Team:

I would like to get your input regarding a problem that we
have every year about this time. We do not have enough
volunteers for the interoffice Fruitcake Bake-off.

Before we deal with the solutions to this problem, I would
like to know what each of you believes is the cause of
this problem. Right now, I am interested in getting all
your ideas. Please write down anything that comes to mind
and e-mail me back before noon on Friday.

I will publish all the results that I receive on the fol-
lowing Monday. Thank you.

Regards, Steve
```

Step 2: Publish possible causes and request cause evaluations

Having received all the e-mails from the group, the facilitator cuts and pastes all the feedback into a new e-mail that is sent to all team members. Each person on the team sees all the ideas submitted by the other people on the team.

This step is the online version of writing ideas on a flip chart at the front of a meeting room. The facilitator needs to remain impartial throughout this process and never edit or paraphrase other people's ideas, because doing so can change the intended meaning. If your organization conducts plenty of online discussions, consider investing in discussion group software.

The second part of the e-mail asks team members to consider all of the possible causes that were contributed and select the one that is the root cause of the problem.

Some root causes are difficult for an organization to change, so try to avoid having the participants agree on a *general* root cause, such as:

- ✔ Company culture
- ✔ Upper management
- ✔ Communication

Obviously, anything goes in online brainstorming, but as the evaluation process begins, facilitators must ensure that any of the general root causes listed above are defined in a more specific manner. The following e-mail shows you how:

```
Dear Team:

Thank you for your timely responses to the Fruitcake prob-
lem. Here are the causes that you came up with. Please
read through them and pick the one that you believe is the
root cause.

People hate anything to do with fruitcake

The 60 Minutes piece on baked goods that can kill has
people worried

People are too busy to spend time volunteering

The word volunteer reminds people of being in the army
```

Bad timing — the world shortage of glazed fruit makes the contest politically incorrect

The event has negative PR — last year the winner got into a fight with the runner-up

People don't want to give up their lunch hours

I need to receive your vote for the root cause by end of business on Tuesday. Thanks.

Regards, Steve

Step 3: Publish root cause and request feedback on possible solutions

After all the evaluations are received, the facilitator counts the number of votes for each possible cause. After tallying all the numbers, the facilitator publishes the cause with the most votes, which thereafter is considered the real cause of the problem.

Make it clear to all team members that they can add potential causes and new information at any point during the process. Often, as more information is transmitted to each member, new ideas emerge that may be more innovative and effective than the original input.

Now that the real cause has been agreed upon — by group consensus — the next job is to brainstorm possible solutions. To request feedback on possible solutions, send an e-mail like the one that follows:

Dear Team:

Here is the most agreed upon root cause to the fruitcake volunteer situation:

People hate anything to do with fruitcake

Now we need to come up with some creative, cost-effective ways of solving this problem. Once again, I need your input. Please send me an e-mail listing all your ideas for solving this problem. I need your responses by Friday at noon.

Thanks, Steve

Step 4: Publish possible solutions and request solution evaluations

Having received all the responses back from the team, the facilitator cuts and pastes the feedback into one e-mail that's sent to all team members.

Be sure the e-mail asks each person in the group to evaluate all the suggested solutions and choose the one that he or she thinks will be the most effective. The criteria for a workable solution will vary with your specific circumstances, but usually these areas are important to consider:

- ✔ Financial cost
- ✔ Resource cost
- ✔ Work interruption
- ✔ Management support
- ✔ Implementation time

The message needs to look something like the following:

```
Dear Team:

Here are the solutions the group came up with. They are
very creative and I believe we are close to a fruitcake
breakthrough!

Use French to disguise the negative fruitcake connotations —
something like "Festival de Gateau Fruit"

Publish a list of famous sports personalities who like
fruitcake

Change the event to the Fruitcake Hurling Contest

Educate our staff about fruitcakes by setting up a
Fruitcake U or an intranet Web page with fruitcake FAQs

Make it a brownie cook-off

Please study this exciting list and vote for the solution
that you believe will best solve this annual problem.
Please have your responses back to me by Wednesday at
noon. Thank you.

Regards, Steve
```

Step 5: Publish consensus solution

The facilitator tallies all the votes and publishes the most popular solution.

```
Dear Team:

Here is the solution that the group unanimously agreed on:

Change the event to the Fruitcake Hurling Contest

There's already an excited buzz about the office. In fact,
several people have already volunteered to bake the fruit-
cakes.

Thank you all for doing an outstanding job. I will contact
you next week to get your ideas about the best cake size
and weight for hurling.

Regards, Steve
```

This process not only helps strengthen teamwork, but it also lets people know that their input is valuable. By using the synergy of a group, you're sure to end up with higher quality solutions than those generated by one person.

Overcoming roadblocks

Sometimes teams get bogged down in the details and come to a roadblock in the decision-making process. When that happens, the facilitator may need to coach the group through the stalemate. Coaching via e-mail often takes the form of asking pertinent questions that create dialogue and mutual understanding to get the team back on track. Here is a list of questions that will get you started:

✔ What are the key issues that are holding up the process?

✔ What have you done to try and break the deadlock?

✔ What happened?

✔ What would be a satisfying outcome?

✔ What team values are needed to guide the final outcome?

✔ What decision best reflects these values?

✔ Can the group live with this decision?

✔ What are the next steps in moving on with this decision?

Part III
Keeping Your Customers: Simple Actions, Significant Payoffs

The 5th Wave   By Rich Tennant

CUSTOMER PHONE SERVICE AT THE WALT DISNEY CO.

In this part . . .

Have you ever called a company and been rudely put on hold before you even gave your name? Have you ever waited at the counter in a department store while the sales clerk chatted with a co-worker? Have you ever been informed in a not-so-friendly tone by the waiter or waitress that "Substituting tomatoes for potatoes is against our policy"?

If you're like most people, you've encountered these situations, and you probably find yourself thinking about how little this person would have to do to turn the situation from a service failure into a service success. In every one of the above situations, some small aspect of the body language, tone of voice, or words used put the customer off.

In this part of the book, we explore those little things, those simple actions that lead to significant payoffs in customer satisfaction and sales. We provide you with time-tested techniques for dealing with people face-to-face and over the telephone, and we cover a variety of important communication skills that you can easily use every day at work and at home.

Chapter 10

A Wink, a Smile, and a Nod: Body Language

*B*ody language is a constant, nonverbal flow of communication. Without saying a word (and sometimes without realizing it), your body language can reveal what you're feeling and thinking. For example, you can guess how the service person feels about you — the customer — in the following situations:

✔ The bank teller whose eyes roll in exasperation when you bring in the loose change you've collected during the past five years

✔ The doctor who ignores you and stares at your chart while you explain your symptoms

✔ The painful expression on the full-service gas station attendant's face when you ask him to put air in your tires (he thought "full service" was Latin for "pay extra for gas")

A few years ago, a major university conducted a study on how people receive messages from other people (see Figure 10-1). It showed that 55 percent of what you learn from others comes from their body language, 33 percent comes from tone of voice, and a mere 7 percent comes from the actual words they speak.

Actions obviously do speak louder than words, and body language conveys what you're truly thinking and feeling, regardless of what you say. Your ability to read your customers' body language and project your own in a way that says, "I'm here to help," are among the least expensive but most powerful skills you have.

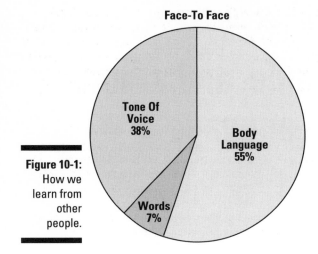

Face-To Face

Tone Of Voice 38%

Body Language 55%

Words 7%

Figure 10-1: How we learn from other people.

The primary aspects of body language are eye contact, facial expressions, body posture and movement, hand gestures, touching, and physical distance. If any of these aspects of body language are overdone or underdone, they can misfire and create a negative impression. Although interpreting body language isn't an exact science, some general rules apply, and that's exactly what we discuss in this chapter.

Seeing Customers Eye to Eye

Eye contact is one of the most powerful of all the body-language skills. It's called an *attending skill,* because it tells customers that you're interested, receptive, and attentive to what they're saying. Eye contact enables you to listen to customers' feelings in addition to their words.

Effective eye contact is achieved by softly focusing on a customer's face. By that we mean the moment a customer walks up to you, regardless of what you are doing, make immediate eye contact by focusing on the customer's entire face, not just the eyes. As the conversation moves on, look away from time to time to avoid giving the impression that you're staring.

Overdone: Students of the Zombie School of Body Language are easy to spot — they stare the customer down with a hard gaze and never take their eyes off him. This I've-got-you-in-my-sights approach gives customers the willies and makes them want to leave before they can zero in on your products for the kill.

Underdone: You walk up to a bank teller and instead of looking up at you, she continues to look down at her paperwork. This lack of eye contact, combined with a clear view of the top of the teller's head, is a negative moment of truth and can be interpreted as lack of interest in helping you. Likewise, when you're talking to someone and he constantly looks around the room and not at you, you get the impression that he has something more important that he'd rather be doing.

Research shows that people stop making eye contact and look away the moment they sense that the other person is showing emotion on his or her face. This natural desire not to be intrusive or embarrass the other person is misplaced when you're dealing with an upset customer. By not looking away from the irate customer, you project a positive impression that shows you really care. So be sure to maintain eye contact and thus give your customers the impression that you want to hear what they're saying. An added benefit: Maintaining eye contact usually makes the customer feel less upset.

In many Asian countries (Japan, Korea, and Thailand, in particular), making strong and continuous eye contact with another person during a conversation is considered rude. In fact, in these cultures, children are taught from a young age to avert their eyes and avoid direct eye contact.

Minding Your Facial Expressions

Your facial expression is like a billboard that tells everyone around you whether you're happy, sad, excited, and so on. Be careful how you allow stress to affect that billboard's appearance. Don't allow the stresses of the day to gather on your brow so that you resemble a scrunched up prune. Customers don't care whether you've had the day from hell; as far as they're concerned, their encounter with you is your first of the day. Simply make sure that your facial expression sets a positive tone before you ever begin to speak. A relaxed or pleasant facial expression most of the time is the ideal; however, when concern or upset enter the picture, you need to adjust your facial expression to suit the customer's state of mind.

Overdone: A client in England told us about a bank that decided to improve its customer service by slapping happy-face stickers (the big, ugly, yellow ones) up behind each teller's counter with the message "Remember to smile at the customer" written underneath. Although not a terrible idea, we thought that this procedure might lead to problems: Imagine how annoyed you'd be if your bank teller informed you that you were $5,000 overdrawn — and he had a big fat grin on his face! Even a positive facial expression, such as smiling, can be overdone.

What's with the wrinkled nose?

We once had a client who worked for a manager who consistently wrinkled his nose whenever our client approached him with a question. To her, his expression conveyed a message of, "Oh, no, not you again with another stupid question!" To this day, our client wonders what her manager was really thinking every time she came into the room. Regardless, his facial expression prevented her from asking him for the information she needed.

Underdone: The daydreaming stare, faraway gaze, and blank look are classic expressions that can creep over your face without your realizing it. When caught with one of those looks on your face, the customer certainly doesn't want to be the one to wake you from your coma.

Using a relaxed and pleasant facial expression with your staff is as important as using that same look with your customers. Using effective facial expressions encourages your staff to seek you out for coaching, guidance, and information. The same is true of your customers. Becoming more aware of your facial expressions is easy; we recommend examining how you look in family snapshots or videos, especially the ones that were taken before you had a chance to say "Cheese!"

From the Waist Up

Body posture — and body movement in particular — shows your energy level and reflects your interest in what the customer is saying. You can tell when people are listening impatiently or want to end the conversation by simple body-language clues you can pick up from the way they move, such as:

- ✔ Leaning back or stepping away
- ✔ Turning their bodies away from you
- ✔ Pushing away from their desks or tables
- ✔ Gathering up papers
- ✔ Closing their briefcases while you're still talking
- ✔ Looking at their watches repeatedly

To show that you are intently listening to and interested in a conversation with your customer, try nodding, facing the customer, or leaning forward.

Nodding

Nodding is one of the best nonverbal ways to show that you're paying attention to what someone is saying. Nodding is particularly useful when you don't want to interrupt a customer who is explaining the details of a situation but you still want her to know that you're following along with what she's saying.

In many parts of the world, a nod up and down means "Yes." However, if you find yourself in Turkey, Iran, or Bulgaria, be forewarned: When you nod your head up and down in those countries, you're saying "No," and when you shake your head back and forth, you're saying "Yes." If you understand what we're saying, say yes with your head, Bulgarian style.

Overdone: Although occasional nodding shows that you're listening, continual nodding communicates impatience. We're talking about the distracting nod-nod-nod that people do when they want to hurry the conversation along. This action translates to the customer as, "Hurry up and finish so that I can say what I want to!"

Nodding during a lull in conversation is a clue that you don't have any connection with what's going on around you.

Underdone: The next time you watch a sci-fi movie, pay close attention to the way aliens are characterized by their body language. Their lack of human qualities is emphasized by their staring straight ahead with arms pinned to their sides and heads locked forward in one position (not to mention their green skin and the one eye sticking out of the middle of their foreheads). Don't let this phenomenon happen to you. Make a conscious effort to show, with your body language, that you are from this planet.

Facing the customer

By turning your whole body (not just your head) toward the customer, you convey the message that she has your full and undivided attention. Facing away from the customer can make her feel that something else is distracting you.

Leaning forward

Although you don't want to end up in the customer's lap, you do want to lean forward slightly to let the customer know that you're interested in what is being said. When a customer is expressing strong emotions or feelings, leaning forward says, "I really want to hear and understand what you're saying to me."

Getting a Handle on Hand Gestures

Using your hands when you talk (even on the phone) is a natural way to express your feelings. When some people talk with their hands, they appear to be conducting an orchestra whenever they speak. Two varieties of hand signals that you need to be aware of are hand-and-object gestures and hands-alone gestures.

The first variety features hand gestures that rely on certain props and can give you clear signals about your customer's state of mind. These gestures can include:

✔ **Placing the cap on a pen and putting it in a pocket:** This action signifies a readiness to conclude the meeting or conversation.

✔ **Tapping fingers on the tabletop:** This gesture signifies impatience or frustration.

✔ **Repeatedly clicking a ball point pen:** This action can mean the customer is either uneasy or deep in thought. Look for other body-language signals to cue you in to which is applicable.

✔ **Rattling loose change in a pocket:** This motion usually means, "I'm anxious and ready to move on."

The second variety of hand gestures doesn't require any props. These gestures can include:

✔ **Open-hand gestures (flat hand, palm up, or palm out):** When used to give directions, they convey an invitation to move or look in a certain direction. Open-hand gestures are a more gracious and softer way to point at a person or object.

✔ **Closed-hand gestures (pointing with index finger straight out):** This hand movement can be construed as a command, rather than an invitation, when used to convey a direction. Closed-hand gestures usually are considered rude and intimidating when directed at another person. Although pointing may be discourteous, pointing a finger in someone's face at close range is even worse. This action definitely communicates hostility or anger to the customer.

✔ **Driving gestures:** You see these gestures in your rear-view mirror when you're stuck in traffic on Friday night. They usually communicate very clearly and need no further explanation.

The key, whether you use your hands a little or a lot, is to be natural in your movements. Hand gestures should never detract from the conversation.

Overdone: To see overdone hand gestures at their best, watch the TV commercials for car dealerships during the late, late movies. Focusing on what the dealers are saying is often difficult because their hands are flying around in big, unnatural, exaggerated, and distracting movements.

Underdone: A noticeable lack of hand gestures can be just as distracting as waving them around like an octopus. Some people are so self-conscious about what they should do with their hands that they clasp them behind their backs, in front of their bodies, or pin them to their sides. This lack of motion can give a customer the impression that the service person feels threatened by — or uncomfortable with — what is being said.

Wherever the hands go, the arms are likely to follow. Some cultures, such as the Italians, naturally tend to use big, sweeping hand and arm motions; others like the Japanese prefer to keep their arm and hand gestures small and infrequent. In fact, moving your hands or arms in big gestures is considered impolite in Japan.

A Touchy Subject

The most acceptable form of touching in the American work environment is the handshake. In some professions, such as healthcare, touch can take on a more important role. Nurses and doctors, for example, use touch partly out of necessity but also to convey a caring and concerned attitude. Regardless of your profession, the least threatening place to touch someone (with whom you don't have a personal relationship) is on the arm between the elbow and the wrist.

You always need to be sensitive to the other person's reactions when touching is involved. If you touch someone in a nonthreatening manner on the hand, wrist, or elbow, and he moves his arm away, he's telling you something. Let this reaction be your clue not to touch him again.

Overdone: We don't recommend the grip of death handshake used by some people. This type of handshake is overly aggressive and can actually hurt the recipient, giving that person the impression that he or she somehow is being used to help you strengthen your tennis grip.

Touching overseas: What to know before you go

As part of his research for *Nonverbal Communication for Business Success (American Management Association),* author Ken Cooper sat in outdoor cafes around the world, observing conversations and counting the number of times the patrons casually touched each other. The results are as follows:

✔ San Juan, Puerto Rico, came in at first with 180 touches per hour.

✔ Paris, France, had 110 touches per hour.

✔ Florida had 2 touches per hour.

✔ London, England, had 0 touches per hour.

Obviously the way we touch, how often we touch, and who we touch vary from one country to the next almost as much as the languages that are spoken in those places.

If you're planning a business trip or vacation to a country you've never visited before, you may want to do some research first. Several excellent books are available that can help you understand cultural differences and customers throughout the world. For more information about body language and other important things to know about a country, try the following resources:

✔ **Culture Shock Series (Times Books International):** This series of books is wonderful. Each book focuses on a specific country within Asia (*Culture Shock! Malaysia,* for instance) and is full of detailed information, covering most business and social situations. The books differ from most other travel books, because they not only tell you rules of behavior, they also explain the thinking and mind-set behind them. We find them extremely useful, especially for doing business in Southeast Asia.

✔ *Gestures,* **by Roger E. Aztell (John Wiley & Sons, Inc.):** This book provides a broad look at how body language is used around the world. One thing we like about this book is its coverage of more than 86 different countries. The tips are well-written, clear, and to the point. Note that this book focuses its attention on the specific do's and don'ts of body language and doesn't go into great detail regarding the psychology of the culture.

Touching can also be overdone by crossing over the nonthreatening boundaries of people with whom you don't have a close relationship. Some common, easily made mistakes include:

✔ Putting an arm around the customer's shoulder (unless he is about to faint)

✔ Slapping the customer on the back (unless she is choking)

✔ Mussing up the customer's hair (unless you're a hairdresser)

✔ Hugging someone and refusing to let go (unless you're married to that person)

Underdone: You go to work for a new company, and you're being shown around the office. Your manager introduces you to a co-worker. You extend your hand with certain confidence, prepared to provide her with a nice, firm grip. In return you are offered a weak, dead fish (uggg!) type of handshake. You shudder all over. Offering your hand in a tentative way is almost guaranteed to create a bad first impression.

Excuse Me, You're Standing in My Space

Personal space is the distance that feels comfortable between you and another person. If someone else approaches you and invades your personal space, you automatically move back without a thought.

Whenever you see customers moving away from you, they may be doing so in attempts to create more space. If that's the case, step back and keep your distance. By maintaining a safe personal zone, you facilitate communication, comfort, and trust. Three distinct spatial zones exist:

- ✔ **Zone 1/Intimate (0–2 feet):** This zone is reserved for romantic partners, family members, close friends, and children. Entering this zone when you don't belong there is embarrassing and can be threatening to the other person. That's why standing close to people in a crowded elevator is so uncomfortable. The small space forces you to be closer to other people than you'd like. Most people deal with this feeling by staring up at the floor numbers as though they hold the meaning of life.

- ✔ **Zone 2/Personal (2–4 feet):** Most of your conversations with customers take place within this range. The personal space creates the privacy necessary for a confidential discussion while a safe and comfortable distance is maintained between you and the customer.

- ✔ **Zone 3/Social (4 feet or more):** This onstage range is mainly used by teachers in the classroom, the boss at a company meeting, or the instructor in a training class. However, in the same way you can get too close for comfort in the intimate zone, it's also possible to be too far away from someone for comfort in the social zone.

Overdone: The personal zone is most commonly overdone when you're waiting in line at customs at the airport, the pharmacy, the checkout stand at the grocery store, and other such places.

Because people usually are impatient in these places, they tend to stand closer to you, hoping that doing so moves them to the front of the line faster.

Shall we dance?

As with touch, personal space is different throughout the world. In general, most Asians, especially the Japanese, tend to stand farther apart than Europeans and North Americans. Latin Americans and Middle Easterners, on the other hand, stand much closer together.

A friend of ours was at an embassy cocktail party where a South American gentleman was talking with a Japanese gentleman. Our friend reported that the two of them never stood still the entire evening. They waltzed around the room as the South American kept moving closer, trying to close the gap between them, and the Japanese gentleman kept backing away, trying to increase the gap.

Underdone: Coauthor Karen Leland once had a meeting with a prospective client. She was shown to his office and asked to take a seat. In the room was a giant desk with a large chair behind it and two very small chairs about six feet away from the big desk. Karen sat in one of the two small chairs and waited. When the client came into the room, she expected him to sit down next to her. Instead, he walked behind his giant desk and sat down in his large chair. The distance between the two of them made it hard for Karen to pay attention to what he was saying. She left the meeting feeling that the physical distance between them had stopped them from having an in-depth conversation.

Neatness Counts

Another part of body language is neatness. Being neat and organized plays an important role in your interactions with customers.

How you look

Personal grooming has a big impact on your customers. Dirty hands and fingernails, messy hair, and body odor may be delicate topics to discuss, but the cost of not dealing with them can mean the loss of otherwise happy customers.

Similarly, incomplete or dirty uniforms create a negative impression. If most employees wear complete uniforms, but one is missing a cap, jacket, or tie, that person sticks out like a sore thumb. This wardrobe oversight is seen by customers as a sign of sloppiness and inconsistency.

Coauthor Keith Bailey once was in a preliminary meeting with a financial planner he was going to hire to help him organize his finances. Toward the end of the meeting, the financial planner crossed his legs, and Keith caught a glimpse of the bottom of his left shoe, which had a hole in the sole. Keith couldn't help but think of this sloppiness as a bad sign for someone whose job was promoting financial sufficiency; he ended up not hiring the man. Whether this decision was fair or not took second place to the impression that the hole in the shoe had left on Keith.

Customers expect you to look appropriate for the job you do. Don't try to have clean hands and fingernails if you're an auto mechanic — customers probably will get the impression that you've never lifted the hood of a car.

How your work area looks

The neatness of your work environment is especially important if your customers have access to it. Customers make decisions about how organized and competent you are by the way your desk or work area looks. If your desk is piled high with papers, files, messages, and memos, making the excuse, "I have a system, I know where everything is . . ." impresses only the gullible and is a negative moment of truth for everyone else.

Customer logic has its own rules. One such rule is that the customer is allowed to make what seem like unreasonable connections between totally different things. A classic example of customer logic at work is the airline executive who once noted that his passengers assumed that if their seat pockets or trays were dirty, they couldn't be sure that the airline did a good job of servicing the airplane's engines.

Small Things Mean a Lot

The information in this chapter can be summarized by an article we read about a university library that wanted to study the effect that simple, interpersonal actions had on students' perceptions of the services they received.

They divided librarians who checked books out to students into two groups. The first group was instructed to be efficient and help the students check the books out without any added interpersonal skills, such as eye contact, smiling, or physical contact. The other group of librarians was instructed to be efficient and to add some interpersonal skills such as looking the customer in the eye, using his or her name (written on the library card), and casually touching the customer on the wrist when giving the book back. Student-customers were interviewed as they left the library and asked to share their feelings about the service they had received.

Not surprisingly, customers who received efficient service and nothing else agreed they received poor to fair service. Customers who received the added interpersonal skills, on the other hand, reported they received good to excellent service. The point: The little things we do with body language often have the biggest impact.

The next time you're a customer in a restaurant, hotel, or bank, take a moment to evaluate how well the service person uses his or her body language. The better you get at observing other people's body language, the more aware you become of your own.

Chapter 11

It's Not What You Say, It's How You Say It: Phone Tone and Etiquette

● ●

In This Chapter

▶ Discovering two keys to good inflection

▶ Controlling your volume

▶ Pacing a customer's rate of speech

▶ Establishing good tone on the phone

● ●

*T*he minute you pick up the phone, body language disappears, and your tone of voice and the words you use become the entire story (see Figure 11-1).

Face-To Face

Over the Phone

Figure 11-1:
Tone of
voice
becomes
important
when
dealing with
customers
over the
phone.

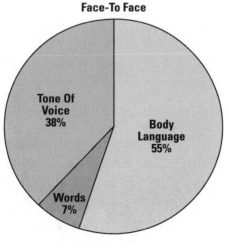

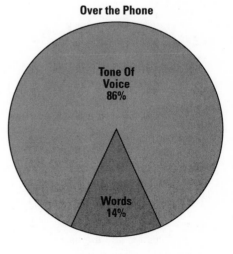

In fact, almost the entire message you project to a customer over the phone is communicated through your tone of voice. For example:

- A monotone and flat voice says to the customer, "I'm bored and have absolutely no interest in what you're talking about."
- Slow speed and low pitch communicate the message, "I'm depressed and want to be left alone."
- A high-pitched and emphatic voice says, "I'm enthusiastic about this subject."
- An abrupt speed and loud tone say, "I'm angry and not open to input!"
- High pitch combined with drawn-out speed conveys, "I don't believe what I'm hearing."

It doesn't take long after a customer hears the tone of your voice to pick up on your attitude. In fact, your customers know within ten seconds of initiating the call whether they're talking to beauty or the beast. Some people you speak to need only say "Hello," before you find yourself thinking, "I don't want to deal with this person." So you hang up and call again, hoping someone with a more compassionate tone picks up the phone.

Developing excellent telephone customer service (in both tone and words) is one of the most valuable business skills you can acquire. In this chapter, we cover five skills that can help you be a winner at using the phone.

Improving Your Inflection

If you've ever read a story to a child, you know that the words of the story are far less interesting than the inflection you put into your voice. In fact, if you get lazy and don't make a ruff, grumbling sound when you say, "I'll huff, and I'll puff, and I'll blow your house down!" your child will more than likely stop you and say, "Read it like you mean it."

If I've said it once, I've said it a hundred times

When you're saying the same thing again and again, slipping into the habit of speaking in a monotone voice is easy. The receptionist who answers the phone by saying, "Good morning, law offices of Smith, Smith, and Smith" a hundred times a day can forget to put any life into that greeting. Even though you've said something a thousand times, your customer may be hearing it for the first time. So remember, using inflection is as important with the first call of the day as it is with the last.

Beware of the disk jockey

Too much inflection is just as bad as too little. Don't scare your customers away by unleashing on them your hidden desire to be a disk jockey. Answering the phone with a resounding have-we-got-a-deal-for-you tone of voice creates instant distrust. These are the people, usually from the we-got-your-number phone-solicitation service or credit-card company, who call as you're sitting down to dinner and excitedly say, "HELLO!" as if you're a long lost friend. This tone, as you know, is your cue to hang up.

Inflection is the wave-like movement of highs and lows in the pitch of your voice. The peaks and valleys in your voice let your customers know how interested (or uninterested) you are in what they're saying. Inflection also reflects how interested you are in what you're saying to the customer. When inflection is missing, your voice can sound monotone (read boring and tedious).

Some people are born with naturally interesting voices, and they seem to effortlessly use inflection to sound warm and friendly. Others, who aren't so fortunate, need practice. If you think that your vocal inflection needs some polish, you can try the four techniques we describe in this section to improve the quality of inflection in your voice.

Smiling when you talk on the phone

One way to positively affect the inflection in your voice is to smile, especially when you first answer the telephone. The reason is not psychological but rather physiological. When you smile, the soft palate at the back of your mouth raises and makes the sound waves more fluid. For those of you who sing in a choir (or in the shower), you know that the wider you open your mouth and the more teeth you show, the better tone you get. The same applies on the telephone. Smiling helps your voice to sound friendly, warm, and receptive.

Some telemarketing companies are so convinced of the value of smiling when talking on the phone that they install mirrors above telemarketers' desks to remind them to smile. These same people, by the way, call you when you're just sitting down to dinner.

Changing the stress on the words

Another way to improve your inflection is to be aware of how stressing certain words changes the feeling of what you're saying. The following sentence, "What would you like us to do about it?" changes in feeling, meaning, and tone when you:

- Say it **defensively** (emphasizing the words "would you").

  "What *would you* like us to do about it?"

- Say it **with curiosity** (emphasizing the words "like us").

  "What would you *like us* to do about it?"

- Say it **with apathy** (not emphasizing any of the words).

  "What would you like us to do about it?"

Breathing

Believe it or not, the inflection in your voice can be greatly increased by learning to take long, slow, deep breaths. Most people become shallow breathers when they're under pressure. The next time you're in a stressful situation, try to notice what happens to your breathing. The more upset you become, the shallower and quicker your breathing will be. When this breathing pattern happens, your vocal cords tend to tighten, making your voice go up and sound strained. By being aware of your breathing, especially in stressful situations, you can slow it down and thereby relax your vocal cords, bringing down your pitch and creating a calmer tone of voice.

Exaggerating your tone

Whenever we're asked to help someone who has a monotone speaking voice improve his inflection, we have him start by practicing exaggerating his tone using the following three steps:

1. **Take a short and uncomplicated sentence like, "Bill isn't here right now," and say it out loud with your normal level of inflection.**

2. **Think of inflection on a scale of one to ten, with one being monotone and ten being a disk jockey. Now say the same sentence again, but this time exaggerate your inflection all the way up to a ten.**

   Sometimes we ask people to visualize themselves as circus barkers under the big top announcing to a noisy crowd of a thousand people, "Bill isn't here right now." Practice this step and stop only when you sound really obnoxious and embarrass yourself and everyone around you.

3. **Say the same sentence again, but this time take your inflection down a couple of notches to a level eight. Finally, say the sentence one more time, taking it down to a level five or six.**

   Level five or six is a good level at which to keep your inflection over the phone. If you find your inflection slipping over time, go back to Step 1 and repeat the process.

Adjusting the Volume

Imagine you're at a party talking to a close friend when she leans toward you and starts to tell you something private. She begins speaking in a soft voice, almost a whisper. Invariably, as soon as your friend's tone lowers, the people standing nearby will strain their heads in your direction trying to hear what is being said. Such is the power and uncanny magnetism of volume control. Some of the most common ways to use volume control to your advantage include the following:

- ✔ If a customer is angry and speaking loudly, don't yell back at the same volume even though your instinctive reaction may be to do so. Instead, behave like a professional and start out by speaking at a somewhat lower volume than the customer, gradually bringing the customer's volume down to yours.

- ✔ With a confused customer, speaking a little louder than usual helps give him something to focus on and helps you control the conversation more easily.

- ✔ Avoid starting out a conversation in too loud a tone of voice as this may signal stress on your part and serve to unwittingly increase the customer's volume and stress level.

Pacing Yourself

Pacing is approximately matching your customer's rate of speech and intensity of feeling. Pacing is the best single tool you have for creating rapport with your customer.

By focusing on the similarities (as opposed to the differences) between you and your customer, you meet the customer at her level and make her feel at ease.

Matching your customer's rate of speech

The average American speaks at a rate of 100 to 150 words per minute. The average American listener, on the other hand, is capable of listening up to a rate of 600 to 650 words per minute. So, some people will speak faster than you do, some slower, and some at the same rate. By pacing a customer's rate of speech, you can close the gap and have more hits than misses in your telephone communication.

One factor that significantly affects a person's rate of speech is where he or she comes from. See the next section for more.

Closing the geographic divide

Geographic location can influence the speed at which you talk. Two extremes are native New Yorkers, who generally talk a mile a minute, and Southerners, who are known for their slow drawl. If you put a Southerner and a New Yorker together (we've seen it happen, and it isn't a pretty story), the New Yorker always is trying to get the Southerner to speed up, and the Southerner always is trying to get the New Yorker to slow down. For any ground to be gained, either the New Yorker or the Southerner must keep pace with the other.

As a service provider, your job is to keep pace with the customer — not the other way around! If you notice that you're thinking bad thoughts about your customer, wondering why he is not slowing down or speeding up to your rate of speech, quickly shift gears and move into a pacing mode. The point is that you need to listen more carefully to your customer, and regardless of whether they're a fast or slow talker, it's your job to adjust the pace you speak at to mirror the speed at which your customer is speaking.

If you're a fast-talking New Yorker on the phone with a customer from Texas, remember to use the conversation as an opportunity to bridge the gap by practicing your pacing skills and slowing way down.

Reflecting your customer's intensity

Intensity is the strength of emotion that is projected along with the words you're saying. Your level of intensity changes with your level of concern. For instance, saying, "I'm not ready yet" has a different level of intensity when you're getting dressed for a party than when you're next in line to jump out of a plane as a first-time skydiver.

The way your customers feel determines their level of vocal intensity. If they're calm and relaxed, their level of intensity probably is fairly low. If they're upset or angry, their level of intensity rises.

Testing your tele-tone

You can improve your tele-tone — the tone that you use on the telephone — by trying the following exercise: Tape record yourself while talking during a telephone call and then listen to your voice on the tape. However, don't record your customers without asking their permission first. (It's impolite — and illegal. Remember Watergate?) If you don't feel comfortable taping a real conversation, try taping yourself as you role play with a co-worker. As you listen, use the following questions to evaluate your tele-tone:

✔ Did I speak with inflection to show interest and concern?

✔ Did I use a level of volume that gained the customer's attention?

✔ Did I pace the customer by adjusting my rate of speech to match his or hers?

✔ Did I pace the customer by adjusting my intensity to match his or hers?

If you're a manager, you can support your staff in improving their tele-tone by periodically listening in on their conversations and coaching them afterward. Be sure to tell your staff when you plan to listen in and why. Tell them that you view this exercise as a positive opportunity for them to improve their skills, not as a way for you to catch them doing something wrong.

Imagine leaving your wallet, keys, or date book at a restaurant. When you call the restaurant, you're probably panicked and want quick action. The hostess, wanting to calm you down and thinking your problem is no big deal (because it happens all the time), may respond to your high intensity by being casual, low key, and calm. The hostess believes this strategy is excellent for keeping the situation under control. She's wrong. This action has the opposite effect, because she isn't reflecting back to you the intensity of your concern. You'll know that you're both on the same wavelength only when she paces you by stating strongly: *I will look for it immediately!*

Telephone Etiquette

Unlike body language, which can vary from culture to culture, telephone etiquette has a universally agreed upon set of rules that paves the way for smoother, faster, telephone calls with customers. Even small things, such as how long it takes for your phone to be answered or the words you use when you answer a call, can create a lasting impression. In many businesses, the telephone is the customer's first contact with a company, so being telephone-friendly is one of the least expensive ways to immediately upgrade your service. Telephone etiquette helps take the guesswork out of what to say and when to say it.

The cursing caller

Once in a while, you get a call from a customer who is so angry that he or she hurls words at you that we can't print. What do you do with the cursing caller? We hear this question in almost every seminar we lead. Telephone etiquette dictates that you handle the situation with the following three steps:

1. **Give the customer the benefit of the doubt and politely say, "I really want to help you, but I'm having trouble with the kind of language you're using. Can you please refrain from using that kind of language?"**

   The customer may be so carried away with emotion that he may not even realize he's cursing. After hearing this polite response, most customers will stop to apologize and will be a little embarrassed, but will be much better-behaved. For the few who are more thick-headed, move on to Step 2.

2. **Give the agitated caller a second warning and restate what you said in Step 1.**

   For example: "As I have said, I really want to help you, but I'm having trouble focusing on the problem because of the language you're using. Would you please stop?" Most people, after the second warning, will refrain from cursing. If the customer does not stop at this point, your only alternative is to catch him off guard by countering with your own barrage of foul language . . . Just kidding, of course. If all else fails, move on to the final step.

3. **Let the customer know that you're no longer the person who can help him, and inform your supervisor of the problem.**

   Say, "As I have said, I really want to help you, but I am having trouble with the language you are using. What I am going to do is have my supervisor call you to discuss the problem." Hang up and immediately inform your supervisor of the situation. You should only have to use this step on very rare occasions.

If a caller starts threatening you physically (he or she is going to come to your office, seek you out, and so on), go immediately to Step 3. Although you're paid to provide service, you're not paid to be abused or threatened.

 Good telephone etiquette is one way that you can help ensure that a customer can call any department within your company, in any city, on any day, and be dealt with in a uniform way. Customers love consistency, and they expect to receive the same level of service that they received today when they call tomorrow, next month, or next year.

Answering the phone

We've found that the way a company answers the phone tells the entire story about the kind of service you can expect to receive. How you answer the phone sets the tone of the entire call. The correct phrases said in the right order can give a positive first impression and convey an immediate message about your company. The basic rules are as follows:

- ✔ **Pick up the phone within three rings.**
- ✔ **Greet the caller.**
- ✔ **Give your name or company name.**
- ✔ **Ask the customer if you can help.**

Using the guidelines outlined above, three typical ways your company may want to answer the phone are

- ✔ **Direct line that goes right to an individual's desk:** "Good morning, this is Andrew, how may I help you?"
- ✔ **Company phone that goes to a receptionist or general incoming area:** "Good afternoon, Pine Box Productions, how may I help you?"
- ✔ **Department phone that goes to a specific work group or department:** "Good morning, Technical Support, this is Andrew, how may I help you?"
- ✔ **Voice mail:** More and more companies are choosing the option of having their main company phone answered by a voice-mail system. While we are still fans of the old-fashioned idea that a "real person" should answer the phone, we are realists. We understand that in some cases, voice mail may be more efficient and provide the customer with faster service if properly set up.

  For more on how to use voice mail effectively see the section titled "Voice-Mail Excellence."

 If you hear a common line (as opposed to someone's personal line) ringing in your department and no one picks it up, make it your business to do so. Remember, a person expecting a prompt response is on the other end. Even if you personally can't help the caller, you can at least take a message and further the cause of good customer relations.

Last name grunt

Some people believe that because they only deal with internal customers, they don't need to use good telephone etiquette, so they answer their phones in a short, curt, or gruff manner. A typical example is the last name grunt, where the caller hears nothing but the quickly blurted last name of the person picking up the phone. Regardless of who is calling you, your phone tone has an impact on how much rapport you create with the caller.

Don't make your greeting too long or over the top. One annoying trend that we're trying to stamp out is the greeting that tells us stuff we really don't want or need to know. This kind of greeting usually goes something like: "Hello. It's a beautiful day here at Spatula Cosmetics. How may I help you?" This greeting is guaranteed to annoy even the most positive of customers and invites mockery and sarcasm (especially in our office).

Call into your own company or department anonymously and see how well you're dealt with. How does your staff rate at answering the telephone, transferring your call, taking a message, and so on? If you think your staff will know your voice, try having your spouse or significant other call.

Putting a customer (or co-worker) on hold

Most of the questions that we get from people attending our seminars about putting customers on hold are about dealing with many different things at one time — several people on hold, people in your face needing your attention, and so on. We've found that the biggest problem is the stress level of the service provider. Without knowing the following steps, you can easily lose control and stop thinking clearly. Using the proper etiquette for putting your customers on hold helps you avoid becoming confused and befuddled, which thereby helps you avoid the many negative moments of truth that customers associate with the telephone.

The main points of telephone etiquette for putting customers on hold are

- ✔ Asking customers if you may put them on hold.
- ✔ Waiting for a response.
- ✔ Telling customers why they're being put on hold.
- ✔ Giving the caller a time frame and explaining how long the caller will be on hold.
- ✔ Thanking customers for holding after returning to the line.

A trend we love

If you're on hold and you've called a company that has installed one of the newer, more-sophisticated, auto-attendant technologies, you're given an approximate wait time and told how many callers are waiting ahead of you. This information, at least gives the customer some control over whether she chooses to wait and helps eliminate the I've-been-forgotten factor you can feel when left on an indefinite hold.

Silence can be golden

In our experience, most customers prefer to have silence or soft music while they're on hold. Our hate list for on-hold strategies is as follows:

✔ **Prerecorded advertising:** Absolutely hands down the worst! Apparently leaving you on hold for an hour or two isn't sufficient for some companies; they want to add insult to injury by subjecting you to endless advertising slogans promoting their entire product line and the superiority of their service.

✔ **Weird computer music:** Some companies take a classical or popular piece of music, usually *Greensleeves,* and play it on something that sounds like an electric hairpin. Then the music is reconfigured for the high-tech world in which we live. This type of music is annoying and serves only to irritate customers even more while they're forced to wait.

✔ **Local radio station tuned in to the heavy-metal retrospective program:** Any music that is loud, aggressive, or hurts the ears isn't what you want to play for customers while they're waiting on hold.

As soon as the customer agrees to hold, be sure to say "thank you" before clicking off the line.

Some confusion exists about the difference between keeping the customer you've placed on hold well-informed with pertinent information and making excuses for poor service. For example, imagine that you receive a call from a customer who has not received a delivery. An informative response would be: "May I put you on hold for a moment while I call the dispatch department?" An excuse response would be: "I don't know why that happened . . . I know that we've had a few people out sick this week and things have been a little backed up, but these circumstances shouldn't have affected your delivery. Let me put you on hold while I call them to see what's going on."

Sometimes being placed on hold is an inconvenience for callers, so don't automatically assume that they'll accept. Whenever a caller responds with a "No," be sure to ask whether you can have someone return the call, take a message, or transfer the caller to someone else.

Transferring the call

We've found that customers have the least telephone tolerance when they're being transferred again and again. Customers may think being shuffled from department to department means that staff members are too overwhelmed to care or that the company just isn't interested in what they need.

Too much information

The best example of the worst explanation for a person's absence was when a secretary informed us that her boss (the person we were trying to reach) wasn't in the office because he and his wife were getting a divorce, and they were at the lawyer's office finalizing the divorce papers. Believe us when we tell you that we didn't want to know that.

The main points of telephone etiquette for transferring a customer are

- ✔ Explaining why the caller is being transferred and to whom.
- ✔ Asking the customer whether he or she minds being transferred.
- ✔ Making sure someone picks up the call before you hang up.
- ✔ Telling the person to whom you're transferring the call the caller's name and the nature of the call.

In the event the caller doesn't want to be transferred, offer to take a message and assure the customer that you'll personally see to it that the message gets into the hands of the right person. Then, after you hang up, see that the message gets safely to its destination.

Taking a message

If you've ever received a hastily scribbled message with the caller's name misspelled and the phone number missing an area code, you know how frustrated you can feel as a service provider. As a customer, you likewise know how you feel when you leave a message with someone whose sloppy attitude leaves you feeling as if your message never will see the light of day. Poorly taken messages produce uncertainty and worry for the customer and put the person receiving the message at a disadvantage when she calls the customer back. You can take messages that provide the customer with a sense of confidence and empower your co-workers by incorporating the following steps in your message-taking routine:

- ✔ Explaining your co-worker's absence in a positive light.
- ✔ Informing the caller of the general availability of the person to whom he wants to talk before asking for the caller's name.

✔ Giving the caller an estimated time of your co-worker's return.

✔ Offering to help the caller yourself, take a message, or transfer the call to another capable party.

✔ Writing down all of the caller's important information and attaching any pertinent files.

You can always explain a co-worker's absence in a positive light by using general phrases that convey the message, but don't reveal too much personal information, such as:

✔ "Nan isn't available at the moment."

✔ "Nan stepped away from her desk."

✔ "Nan is out of the office today."

✔ "Nan is in a meeting."

Ending the call

Even if you practice letter-perfect telephone etiquette throughout a call, don't underestimate the importance of ending the call on a positive note. Some key actions for ending calls this way include:

✔ **Repeating any action steps you're going to take to ensure that you and the customer agree on what's going to be done.**

✔ **Asking the caller whether you can do anything else for him or her.**

   Doing so gives the customer a final chance to tie up any loose ends that may not have been discussed during the call.

✔ **Thanking the customer for calling and letting him know that you appreciate his bringing the problem (if there was one) to your attention.**

✔ **Allowing the caller to hang up first so that she doesn't accidentally get cut off in the middle of a sentence.**

✔ **Writing down any important information as soon as you get off the phone.**

   Doing so prevents you from getting caught up in other things and forgetting pertinent information.

What's in a name?

When sorting through all of the possibilities for addressing callers, you're bound to ask, "What salutation shall I use with my customers?" The short list includes Mr., Mrs., Ms., Bill, (if that's his name), sir, madame, Your highness, and so on. The possibilities are endless, and negotiating the shark-infested waters of remaining service oriented and politically correct at the same time can be difficult. Here are some tips that can help you form a roadmap to addressing your callers the way they like:

✔ **Listen to your customers; they'll tell you how they like to be addressed.**

"This is Dr. Smith." (Call him Doctor.)

"This is Mrs. Simon." (Call her Mrs.)

"This is Carol Cransbee." (Call her Carol or Ms. Cransbee, to be safe)

✔ **When in doubt, play it safe and address your female customers as Ms. rather than Mrs. or Miss.**

If she wants to be called something else, she'll let you know.

✔ **Ask permission to use your caller's first name.**

"May I call you Bob, Carol, Ted, or Alice?"

Good luck, and remember that if customers don't like what you call them, apologize and address them the way they prefer.

Voice-Mail Excellence

No chapter on telephone skills is complete without a discussion of voice mail. We find two opposing points of view on the subject of voice mail, and no other topic, save for e-mail, can divide a room faster. Basically, some people see voice mail as a great timesaver, but others view it as a customer-relations killer.

Voice-mail adversaries

The main objections raised by service providers who dislike voice mail center around their customers' reactions to its use. Issues that we've heard expressed, include the following:

✔ Will our customers object to talking to a machine?

✔ Won't it remove the personal touch that we've always considered so important?

✔ What if people don't return their voice-mail messages promptly?

From the customers' point of view, the negatives of using voice mail include the following:

✔ **Being given a choice of eight different numbers to press, choosing one, and then finding out that it was the wrong choice.**

Some ill-designed voice-mail systems can trap you in a loop with no way of reaching a live receptionist. You sometimes get caught in this trap when you press *0* (zero) and get a recorded voice telling you: *This is not a valid option.* The only way out is to hang up and call back.

✔ **Leaving several voice messages and never getting a call back.**

This problem has convinced some customers that voice mail is just another obstacle in the way of getting the service they need.

 Always give your customers a way out of voice mail so they have the option of talking to a real person.

Voice-mail advocates

Undoubtedly, voice mail has a big upside. Three important benefits voiced by service providers who are voice-mail fans are

✔ **Voice mail saves time.** The customer can leave detailed information that the service person can act upon before calling the customer back.

✔ **Voice mail provides better messages.** Service providers who check their voice mail regularly get messages faster than when they have to depend on getting them from a co-worker who may not be readily available or who may be available but takes incomplete messages.

✔ **Voice mail increases productivity by enabling you to switch it on when you're in a meeting or discussion in your office.** Using voice mail this way means that you're not interrupted during your meeting and that you can give your undivided attention to the customer when you return his or her call.

Ten paths to voice-mail excellence

When used effectively, voice mail can enhance service by giving your customers the quick answers they demand in today's fast-paced world. The following ten suggestions can help you enhance your voice-mail communications.

Talking to a real person?!

Last year, coauthor Keith Bailey received a call from his car lease company. Apparently, he'd been sending his payments to an incorrect address. When Keith picked up the phone, the person on the other end asked whether she was speaking to Mr. Bailey. After Keith confirmed that she was, she said, "I have a very important message for you." Keith listened and after a few seconds, a recorded message stated that his payment had not been received and asked if he was planning to send it right away. Keith just wasn't in the mood to have a conversation with a machine, so he hung up. A week or so later, he received another call — same company, same person, same important message. This time, determined not to be trapped in a one-sided conversation, Keith said that he didn't want to talk to a machine. The line went silent while the service agent regrouped after such an impudent request. She then continued, "You have to listen to the recording!" Keith politely refused again. She retorted, "If you don't listen to the recording, you're going to have to talk to a real person!" Keith found himself wondering . . . Is it me or is something very wrong with this picture? Keith, like most customers, wanted the option of dealing with a real live person.

No. 1: Don't hide behind your voice mail

Whenever possible and practical, answer your own phone or take calls that are forwarded to you by your assistant. Remember that although many people don't mind using voice mail, most prefer to speak with you directly. Don't sit at your desk, day after day, and let your voice-mail system intercept all callers. We ran across one company where people almost never answered their own phones, regardless of whether they were at their desks. The culture of this company viewed phone calls from customers and co-workers as interruptions (instead of the essence). Good customer care requires that you answer your phone most of the times that it rings — at least. When you do, you send a positive message to your customers that you're available and want to help.

No. 2: Update your greeting regularly

How many times have you called someone only to be greeted by an out-of-date voice-mail message? Say that it's Wednesday, January 17. You hear a greeting that goes something like this: "Hi. This is Ed. Today is Monday, January 15, and I'll be out of the office until Tuesday, January 16." Besides the fact that this error is annoying, what impression do you get of Ed? Do you think that Ed is well organized and on top of his work? Probably not.

You always need to update your greetings to reflect your schedule and provide callers with the best time to reach you. Your callers need to be able to figure out an expected time frame for a return call by the greeting you leave. Additionally, if you're going to be out of the office, away on vacation, or otherwise away from your phone for a prolonged period of time, you need to let your callers know when you'll return and provide the name and number of a co-worker who can assist them in your absence.

Record all greetings in a noise-free environment. Background conversation, honking horns, barking dogs, and the like, create negative impressions and communicate to your listener that you're unprofessional. If your work environment is noisy, try arriving at work early or staying late to record your message — when less noise is likely.

No. 3: Respond to messages promptly

One common complaint that customers have about voice mail is the potential for a delayed response. If your callers don't receive a response from you within a reasonable period of time (usually a day or two), they begin thinking that voice mail is an ineffective way of communicating with you. Remember that callers will feel secure and comfortable leaving you voice-mail messages only if you consistently get back to them in a timely fashion.

Get in the habit of checking for messages at least three times a day, including every time you return to your office from lunch or a meeting. After you receive a message, you need to act immediately. Choose one of these options:

- Reply immediately.
- Forward the message to someone else for action.
- Save or write down the message for reply at a later date.
- Delete the message.

When forwarding a voice-mail message to another user, be sure to add an introduction that explains when the message was originally left, why you're forwarding it, and what actions, if any, you want the other person to take.

No. 4: Encourage your callers to leave effective messages

The more specific the information that callers leave, the better the chances are that you'll be able to get back to them with a response or take the action they need and desire. Encourage your callers to leave more effective messages. Craft your voice-mail greeting so that you ask for:

- The reason for the call and any specific information that you need to know.
- An e-mail, if necessary, that conveys any additional, helpful details.

✔ The caller's phone number. Many people, in the rush to leave a detailed message, forget to leave their number. Consider incorporating into your greeting a statement like, "Please leave your phone number, even if you think I already have it."

No. 5: Give callers the option of skipping your voice-mail greeting

Nothing is more frustrating than being forced to listen to a voice-mail greeting that you've already heard at least ten times. You can set up most phone systems so that your caller can bypass your greeting by pressing the pound (#) key. The caller then goes straight to leaving a message. Although you may need or want to leave a lengthy greeting to provide important information, enable frequent callers (who presumably already know the information that you put in your greeting) to skip it. Likewise, if your system permits, give your callers the option of pressing *0* (zero) to reach a company operator.

No. 6: Plan and prepare your return calls

You can save time and effort by carefully planning your return calls. Making specific notes on what you want to cover — rather than relying on memory — can reduce the amount of time you spend on the phone when you return a call.

You can also make your calls more efficient by stating a time frame, for example, "Bob, I wanted to get back to you with this information, but I only have about five minutes to talk."

The best times of day to return phone calls are ½ hour before lunch and ½ hour before the end of the day. People have less time to chat at these times and are more focused on getting the job done so that they can leave for lunch or go home.

No. 7: Provide a context for your call

Breakdowns in voice-mail communication that lead to *telephone tag*, or unnecessary back-and-forth phone calls, and frustration most often occur because of three mistaken assumptions on the caller's part. You can instantly improve your voice-mail messages by never assuming that the person you're calling:

✔ **Recognizes your voice.** No matter how well you think he knows you or how many times you've spoken with him on the phone, assuming that the person you're calling on business will recognize your voice is a mistake. Always state your name at the beginning of your message. Doing so keeps the receiver from having to listen to your message a dozen times to figure out who the heck called.

✔ **Has your phone number handy.** Make it easy for the person you're calling to respond to your call by including your phone number in your message. Don't make him do the extra work of looking up your phone number.

Remember that he may be checking his messages away from the office and may not have your number with him (or may have lost your number).

✔ **Knows what you're talking about.** When responding to a voice message, don't assume that the person you're calling knows which message you're referring to. Instead, introduce your response with an opening that explains why you're calling. For example, say something like, "Hi, Cheshta. This is Ginger. I'm getting back to you on the message you left me regarding your billing problem."

No. 8: Keep your outgoing messages short and to the point

Americans who work in corporations receive an average of 175 fax, e-mail, telephone, and voice-mail messages per day. Don't add to this burden by leaving rambling messages. Limit the length of your voice messages to between 20 seconds and two minutes. After a couple of minutes, you risk annoying or even losing your listener. Likewise, you want to avoid unfocused messages that obscure the purpose of your call.

Before you leave a message (albeit before ever making a call), know the points you want to cover and focus on one topic per message. If you group several topics together into one message, the person you're calling may wait until she can address all the topics before taking action or responding. In addition, single-topic messages are easier to forward.

If you're calling to ask a question, ask it directly. Rather than saying, "Hi. This is Cynthia. I have a question. Call me back." leave your actual question on the voice mail. By doing so, the recipient can prepare an answer before calling you back, thus saving both of you time and effort.

No. 9: Specify the response you expect

Giving the people you call some guidance on how you'd like for them to respond makes things easy on them. If your call is simply an FYI and you don't expect a response, say so. If you want them to take action, be specific:

✔ Please let me know that you received this message.

✔ Please call or e-mail me back with your response.

✔ Please take care of this immediately.

✔ I need this item by next Tuesday; please let me know if you can do this.

Many voice-mail systems give you the option of marking a message as urgent. Use this feature sparingly! You don't want to run the risk of becoming the voice-mail equivalent of the boy who cried, "Wolf!" Marking too many voice mails as urgent can lead to a situation in which you send a message that *really* needs immediate attention, but based on your frequent use of the urgent feature, it's automatically sent to the bottom of the return pile.

No. 10: Take security measures

Unauthorized entry into your voice mail can potentially cause anything from embarrassment to disaster for you and your company. Take the following measures to increase your mailbox security:

- **Use five to ten digits for your security code.** The more numbers you use, the harder it is for someone to figure out the code.

- **Avoid overly simple or obvious codes.** Obvious numbers, such as your birth date, anniversary, or repetitious numbers such as 2222, are too easy to figure out. To reduce the risk of your mail being broken into, choose a code that's not so obvious.

- **Memorize your code.** Don't keep your code written in the phone directory of your time management system or on a slip of paper you carry in your wallet. Instead, take some time to commit it to memory.

- **Change your code.** Just to be safe, occasionally change the access code that you use for voice mail. Doing so is especially important if an employee who knew the code has left the company or if you think the code has been compromised in any way.

Chapter 12

It Takes Two to Tango: Getting in Step with Your Customer

In This Chapter

▶ Defining your working style

▶ Getting acquainted with four distinct working styles

▶ Working in step with different working styles

*Y*our customers fall into two general categories: the ones who think and behave similar to the way you do and the ones who don't. With the first group, you often seem to know what they're going to say (even before they say it), how they respond, and what it takes to satisfy them. The second group of customers is obviously harder to relate to. You're often surprised by what they say, puzzled by how they react, and uncertain about how to satisfy them.

The most successful service providers have discovered how to work with both groups of customers, especially the ones who think and act differently. We call these differences *working styles,* and they reflect the various ways that people behave at work. Understanding your working style and the styles of those around you dramatically improves your communication with customers, co-workers, and even your boss. Think of getting to know these styles as the customer service equivalent of learning a new language. When you can speak another person's language, it becomes easier to understand — and be understood by — that person. You start by identifying your own individual working style. Then, you need to figure out how to get in step with your customers' styles.

What's My Style?

Consider each of the questions that follow separately and circle the letter (a, b, c, or d) that corresponds with the description that best fits you. If you have trouble selecting only one answer, ask yourself which response would be the most natural or likely for you to make at work.

Self-evaluation questionnaire

The answers to these questions are neither right nor wrong, so base your responses on how you are today, not how you think you need to be or want to be in the future.

1. **When talking to a customer or co-worker . . .**

    a. I maintain eye contact the whole time.

    b. I alternate between looking at the person and looking down.

    c. I look around the room a good deal of the time.

    d. I try to maintain eye contact but look away from time to time.

2. **If I have an important decision to make . . .**

    a. I think it through completely before deciding.

    b. I go with my gut instincts.

    c. I consider the impact it will have on other people before deciding.

    d. I run it by someone whose opinion I respect before deciding.

3. **My office or work area mostly has . . .**

    a. Family photos and sentimental items displayed.

    b. Inspirational posters, awards, and art displayed.

    c. Graphs and charts displayed.

    d. Calendars and project outlines displayed.

4. **If I am having a conflict with a co-worker or customer . . .**

    a. I try to help the situation along by focusing on the positive.

    b. I stay calm and try to understand the cause of the conflict.

    c. I try to avoid discussing the issue causing the conflict.

    d. I confront it right away so that it can get resolved as soon as possible.

5. **When I talk on the phone at work . . .**

    a. I keep the conversation focused on the purpose of the call.

    b. I spend a few minutes chatting before getting down to business.

    c. I am in no hurry to get off the phone and don't mind chatting about personal things, the weather, and so on.

    d. I try to keep the conversation as brief as possible.

6. If a co-worker is upset . . .

   a. I ask if I can do anything to help.

   b. I leave him alone because I don't want to intrude on his privacy.

   c. I try to cheer him up and help him to see the bright side.

   d. I feel uncomfortable and hope he gets over it soon.

7. When I attend meetings at work . . .

   a. I sit back and think about what is being said before offering my opinion.

   b. I put all my cards on the table so my opinion is well known.

   c. I express my opinion enthusiastically, but listen to other's ideas as well.

   d. I try to support the ideas of the other people in the meeting.

8. When I make a presentation in front of a group . . .

   a. I am entertaining and often humorous.

   b. I am clear and concise.

   c. I speak relatively quietly.

   d. I am direct, specific, and sometimes loud.

9. When a customer is explaining a problem to me . . .

   a. I try to understand and empathize with how she is feeling.

   b. I look for the specific facts pertaining to the situation.

   c. I listen carefully for the main issue so that I can find a solution.

   d. I use my body language and tone of voice to show her that I understand.

10. When I attend training programs or presentations . . .

   a. I get bored if the person moves too slowly.

   b. I try to be supportive of the speaker, knowing how hard the job is.

   c. I want it to be entertaining and informative.

   d. I look for the logic behind what the speaker is saying.

11. When I want to get my point across to customers or co-workers . . .

   a. I listen to their point of view first and then express my ideas gently.

   b. I strongly state my opinion so that they know where I stand.

    c. I try to persuade them without being too forceful.

    d. I explain the thinking and logic behind what I am saying.

12. **When I am late for a meeting or appointment . . .**

    a. I don't panic, and I call ahead to say that I'll be a few minutes late.

    b. I feel bad about keeping the other person waiting.

    c. I get very upset and rush to get there as soon as possible.

    d. I apologize profusely after I arrive.

13. **I set goals and objectives at work that . . .**

    a. I think I can realistically attain.

    b. I feel are challenging and would be exciting to achieve.

    c. I need to achieve as part of a bigger objective.

    d. Will make me feel good when I achieve them.

14. **When explaining a problem to a co-worker whom I need help from . . .**

    a. I explain the problem in as much detail as possible.

    b. I sometimes exaggerate to make my point.

    c. I try to explain how the problem makes me feel.

    d. I explain how I would like the problem to be solved.

15. **If customers or co-workers are late for a meeting with me in my office . . .**

    a. I keep myself busy by making phone calls or working until they arrive.

    b. I assume they were delayed a bit and don't get upset.

    c. I call to make sure that I have the correct information (date, time, and so on).

    d. I get upset that the person is wasting my time.

16. **When I am behind on a project and feel pressure to get it done . . .**

    a. I make a list of everything I need to do, in what order, by when.

    b. I block out everything else and focus 100 percent on the work I need to do.

    c. I become anxious and have a hard time focusing on my work.

    d. I set a date to get the project done by and go for it.

17. **When I feel verbally attacked by a customer or a co-worker . . .**

    a. I tell her to stop it.

    b. I feel hurt but usually don't say anything about it to her.

    c. I ignore her anger and try to focus on the facts of the situation.

    d. I let her know in strong terms that I don't like her behavior.

18. **When I see a co-worker or customer whom I like and haven't seen recently . . .**

    a. I give him a friendly hug.

    b. I greet him but don't shake his hand.

    c. I give him a firm but quick handshake.

    d. I give him an enthusiastic handshake that lasts a few moments.

Scoring the questionnaire

After you finish the questionnaire, review the following scoring sheet (shown in Figure 12-1). You can score yourself on these four specific working styles:

- ✔ Driver (DR)
- ✔ Expressive (EX)
- ✔ Amiable (AM)
- ✔ Analytical (AY)

Later in this chapter, we explain each style in detail, but first transfer your answers from the questionnaire to the scoring sheet and then count up the number of times you circled each style. Enter these scores at the bottom of the scoring sheet. The style where you scored the most points is your primary working style.

What does working style measure?

Research on the general concept of individual styles goes back to the work of Carl Jung, the famous psychiatrist. Since Jung's day, many researchers, psychologists, and consultants have studied and further developed the concept of styles. One thing that all the researchers agree on is that these styles measure two important aspects of a person's behavior: how emotionally expressive you are and the degree to which you assert yourself.

Scoring Form

1	7	13
a Driver	**a** Analytical	**a** Analytical
b Amiable	**b** Driver	**b** Expressive
c Analytical	**c** Expressive	**c** Driver
d Expressive	**d** Amiable	**d** Amiable
2	**8**	**14**
a Analytical	**a** Expressive	**a** Analytical
b Driver	**b** Analytical	**b** Expressive
c Amiable	**c** Amiable	**c** Amiable
d Expressive	**d** Driver	**d** Driver
3	**9**	**15**
a Amiable	**a** Amiable	**a** Expressive
b Expressive	**b** Analytical	**b** Amiable
c Analytical	**c** Driver	**c** Analytical
d Driver	**d** Expressive	**d** Driver
4	**10**	**16**
a Expressive	**a** Driver	**a** Analytical
b Amiable	**b** Amiable	**b** Driver
c Analytical	**c** Expressive	**c** Amiable
d Driver	**d** Analytical	**d** Expressive
5	**11**	**17**
a Driver	**a** Amiable	**a** Driver
b Expressive	**b** Driver	**b** Amiable
c Amiable	**c** Expressive	**c** Analytical
d Analytical	**d** Analytical	**d** Expressive
6	**12**	**18**
a Amiable	**a** Analytical	**a** Amiable
b Analytica	**b** Amiable	**b** Analytical
c Expressive	**c** Driver	**c** Driver
d Driver	**d** Expressive	**d** Expressive

Total Driver Score _____
Total Analytical Score _____
Total Amiable Score _____
Total Expressive Score _____

Figure 12-1:
The working
styles
scoring
form.

Gauging emotional expression

The degree to which you show or hold back your emotions helps determine your style. In particular, emotions are expressed in these four ways:

- ✔ **Verbally:** What type of language do you use? Are your discussions filled with colorful metaphors and larger-than-life phrases, or do you tend to say things in an understated way? The types of words you use and the way you use them is a direct reflection of your working style.

- ✔ **Vocally:** Are you a fast talker or do you go at a slow and easy pace? Do you use a great deal of intensity and excitement in your voice, or do you usually sound calm and relaxed? The tone you use communicates as much about your working style as the words themselves.

- ✔ **Through body language:** Do you talk with your hands or hold them by your side when you speak? Do you walk at a brisk pace, or do you prefer a leisurely stroll? Your body movements tell a story about which working style is the most natural to you.

- ✔ **Through your environment:** Do you have a neat and tidy office with charts and graphs, or do you prefer posters and motivational sayings plastered on your walls? Your office environment provides a clue to the type of working style you have.

Examining the levels of assertiveness

Assertiveness relates to how much or how little you try to influence and control the actions and opinions of the people around you. If your working style reflects a high degree of assertiveness, others probably see you as forceful and direct. A lower degree usually signifies being more reserved and easygoing.

Don't make the mistake of thinking that one style is better or more desirable than another. Everyone expresses himself or herself differently, and each style adds to the richness of your working environment. Wanting to trade your style for the one that you've always yearned for is as fruitless as wanting another personality. Appreciate the way you are and read on to discover ways that you can adapt your style to better communicate with the people around you.

Looking for more information?

The four work-style terms (driver, expressive, amiable, and analytical) originally were coined by Dr. David Merrill, founder of Tracom Consulting Group. If you're interested in reading more about the research done by Dr. Merrill and his associates, read *Personal Styles and Effective Performance: Make Your Style Work for You,* by David Merrill and Roger Reid (Chilton, 1981).

Understanding Your Working Style

Your working style describes how you primarily approach and deal with people and situations at work, although many of our clients tell us that they see similarities that carry over into their personal lives.

If you have two scores that are the same and you're uncertain about which style is yours, you need to be able to pinpoint where you fit in by reading through the descriptions of each of the four primary styles presented later in this chapter. If that doesn't work, ask a co-worker, spouse, or close friend which working style they think you have — they usually know.

You can gain a better understand your working style, by plotting your scores on a working-styles grid like the one shown in Figure 12-2) and by reading and sorting through the descriptions of the working styles in the sections that follow.

We recommend that you read through all four of the working style descriptions because understanding the other three styles can help you become more sensitive and flexible with customers and co-workers who have a style different from your own.

The analytical working style

The analytical working style, found in the top-left corner of the grid in Figure 12-2, has a low degree of assertiveness and a low degree of emotional expression. People with this style focus on facts more than feelings. They evaluate situations objectively and gather plenty of data before making a decision. They prefer an organized work environment where they know exactly what is expected of them. Words that describe this style include the following:

✔ Serious

✔ Well-organized

✔ Systematic

✔ Logical

✔ Factual

✔ Reserved

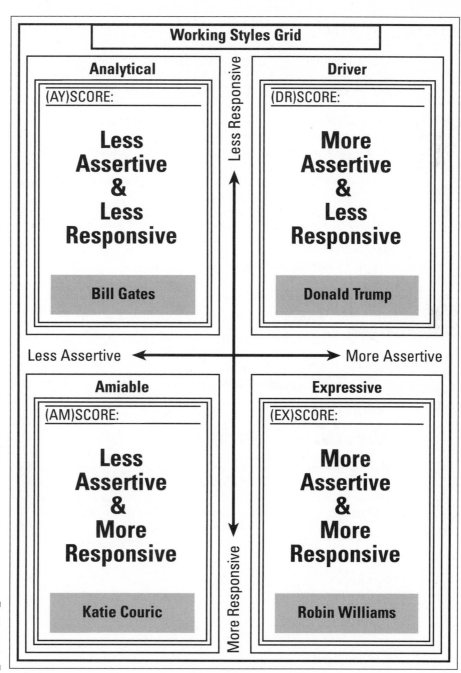

Figure 12-2:
The working
styles grid.

Strengths of the analytical style

Their natural inclination toward fact-finding makes *analyticals* good problem solvers who have the patience to examine the details and come up with a logical solution. They can work independently, and as such, they are well-suited for the finance, science, and computer fields. Bill Gates is the perfect example of this working style.

Weaknesses of the analytical style

Analyticals place facts and accuracy ahead of feelings, and they sometimes are seen by others as emotionally distant. Under stress, they have a tendency to overanalyze to avoid making a decision. Because analyticals are uncomfortable with feelings — their own and others' — they may avoid expressing feelings even when doing so would be the best thing to do.

Key analytical behaviors

People with the analytical working style tend to

- Show little facial expression
- Have controlled body movement with slow gestures
- Have little inflection in their voice and may tend toward monotone
- Use language that is precise and focuses on specific details
- Have charts, graphs, and statistics displayed in their office

The driver working style

The driver working style, found in the top-right corner of the Figure 12-2 grid, has a high degree of assertiveness and a low degree of emotional expression. People with this style know where they want to go and how they are going to get there. They are good at managing tasks and are results-oriented. Drivers like competition, especially when they win. Words that describe this style include:

- Decisive
- Independent
- Efficient
- Intense
- Deliberate
- Achieving

Strengths of the driver style

The ability to take charge of situations and make quick decisions are what often make drivers high achievers. They put a single-minded focus on the goals they want and are not afraid to take risks to accomplish them. They do well in positions of authority, can work independently, and are well-suited for being lawyers, surgeons, and CEOs. Donald Trump is a good example of someone with the driver working style.

Weaknesses of the driver style

When feeling stressed, drivers can be so focused on getting things done quickly that they can overlook details and make mistakes. They may push aside their own and other's feelings to get the job done, which can create tense situations with co-workers. Because of their hard-driving, competitive nature, drivers can sometimes become workaholics.

Key driver behaviors

People with the driver working style tend to

✔ Make direct eye contact

✔ Move quickly and briskly with purpose

✔ Speak forcefully and fast-paced

✔ Use direct, bottom-line language

✔ Have planning calendars and project outlines displayed in their offices

The amiable working style

The amiable working style, found in the bottom-left corner of the Figure 12-2 grid, has a low degree of assertiveness and a high degree of emotional expression. People with this style are responsive and friendly — but not necessarily forceful or direct. Words that describe this working style include:

✔ Cooperative

✔ Friendly

✔ Supportive

✔ Patient

✔ Relaxed

Strengths of the amiable style

Amiables are generally good listeners to whom others come for support. Their sensitivity to the feelings of others makes them good collaborators who thrive in team environments. They're well-suited for the helping professions, such as nurses, therapists, teachers, and so on. A good example of the amiable working style is that of Katie Couric.

Weaknesses of the amiable style

Amiables often have trouble asserting themselves and making decisions quickly. Generally, they don't like confronting disagreement with co-workers, and their reluctance to deal with conflict means that they don't always get what they really want. Their frustration about not resolving such issues can turn into resentment that is directed toward the same co-worker in later interactions.

Key amiable behaviors

People with the amiable working style tend to

- ✔ Have a friendly facial expression
- ✔ Make frequent eye contact
- ✔ Use nonaggressive, nondramatic gestures.
- ✔ Speak slowly and in soft tones with moderate inflection
- ✔ Use language that is supportive and encouraging
- ✔ Display plenty of family pictures in their offices

The expressive working style

The expressive working style, found in the bottom-right corner of the Figure 12-2 grid, has a high degree of assertiveness and a high degree of emotional expression. People with this style are outgoing and persuasive. They're enthusiastic, friendly, and prefer to work with other people. Expressives thrive in the spotlight. Words that describe this working style include:

- ✔ Outgoing
- ✔ Enthusiastic
- ✔ Persuasive
- ✔ Humorous
- ✔ Gregarious
- ✔ Lively

Sorting out your backup style

Although most people usually have one primary working style, many people have a backup style. This style is the one that you fall back on when you're under pressure. Your second highest questionnaire score usually indicates your backup style. For example, although your primary style may be expressive, when you're under pressure, you take on some driver style behaviors. When under stress, people with all four styles react one of two ways: They become either more active or more passive. Drivers and expressives (the more assertive of the four styles) become more active and aggressive under pressure. Amiables and analyticals (the less assertive of the four) become less active and less responsible under pressure. These general behaviors are associated with each style when under pressure:

✔ Drivers become more autocratic and demanding.

✔ Expressives show their emotions by verbally attacking others in conflict situations.

✔ Amiables give in and put their own feelings aside.

✔ Analyticals handle conflict by avoiding the situation.

Typically none of these responses resolves conflict. Therefore, being able to predict how you and others are likely to react under pressure and modifying those reactions can reduce conflict between you and your co-workers.

Strengths of the expressive style

Expressives have a lively nature, and because of that, they are able to motivate and generate excitement in others. They work at a fast pace and are good at building alliances and relationships to accomplish their goals. They are well-suited for high-profile positions that require them to make public presentations, such as trainers, actors, salespeople, and so on. Robin Williams is a famous example of someone with an expressive working style.

Weaknesses of the expressive style

When expressives are upset, they can often communicate their feelings with considerable intensity, and if criticized, they may lash out with a verbal attack. They may seem overwhelming to less assertive styles, because when they're enthusiastic about an idea, they press for a decision and may overlook important details.

Key expressive behaviors

People with the expressive working style tend to

✔ Use rapid hand and arm gestures

✔ Speak quickly with plenty of animation and inflection

  ✔ Have a wide range of facial expressions

  ✔ Use language that is persuasive

  ✔ Have a workspace cluttered with inspirational items

Getting in Step with Different Styles

Customers and co-workers with different working styles require different types of approaches. By understanding and adapting to the style of the person with whom you're dealing, you can create stronger rapport and deliver better service. This technique of *style stepping* is especially important in difficult situations in which the probability for misunderstanding or confusion is heightened.

Everybody uses aspects from all four working styles to some degree. Although the behaviors that you use the most reflect your particular working style, the others you use less frequently make up a smaller part of how you express yourself. Practicing style stepping gives you a chance to emphasize these little-used aspects of your working style.

The four scenarios in the sections that follow take place between a bookstore sales clerk and a customer. They show you how people with different work styles typically interact with one another. The first sketch in each scenario takes place before style stepping occurs, and although the sales clerk is polite and efficient, he or she misses the mark with the customer, because the conversation is on the service person's terms rather than the customer's terms. The second sketch in each scenario shows you how using style stepping enables the clerk to create more rapport and understanding by adapting to the customer's working style.

You first need to check out the scenario that features your own working style. Becoming more familiar with it can help you be more sensitive to how others view your style. Next find the scenario that contains the style of a customer or co-worker. Notice what you may have to change to get in step with their style.

Many people are concerned that style stepping means being artificial with people. If you're thinking, "Won't I seem phony if I am always being flexible to the other person's style?" take heart in knowing that style stepping doesn't replace your personality, but it does enhance your ability to get your ideas across to others.

Assessing a customer's style

Being able to quickly assess what working style your customer or co-worker has is a big part of becoming a good style stepper. Figuring out the styles of your co-workers is easy, because you're around them all the time. Customers, however, can be trickier, because you don't have a great deal of time to make an assessment of their styles. The more you use style stepping, though, the better you can become at recognizing each working style. When trying to evaluate a customer's style, we recommend that you keep it simple by asking yourself these two questions:

✔ Is this person asserting his or her needs, wants, and opinions a lot or a little?

✔ Is this person expressing his or her feelings and emotions a lot or a little?

The answers you come up with should point you in the right direction.

Amiable and driver

In this scenario, the clerk has the amiable working style, and the customer has the driver working style.

Clerk:	*(in a pleasant tone)* Good afternoon, how are you today?
Customer:	Fine. I'm looking for a book called *How to Get 25 Hours Out Of Your Day.* Do you have it?
Clerk:	I'm not sure; I'll have to look it up. Sounds like an interesting book. Where did you hear about it?
Customer:	*(impatiently looking at his watch)* A friend. The author is Stan Workmore. Do you have it?
Clerk:	*(looking at computer screen)* Let me see . . . Mr. Workmore has written several books. Have you read anything else by him?
Customer:	I'm really in a hurry; do you have it?
Clerk:	Yes, here it is. We have one copy left; it's in the back stockroom. Why don't you relax and look around while I go find it for you?
Customer:	I don't have the time. Could you get it for me now?
Clerk:	Sure, I'll be back in just a minute.

Getting in step with drivers

From this scenario, you find that drivers obviously are not big on small talk, and they like to get speedy results. Style-stepping behaviors for working with drivers include:

- Making direct eye contact
- Speaking at a fast pace
- Getting down to business quickly
- Arriving on time and not lingering
- Being clear, specific, and brief in your conversation
- Not over-explaining or rambling
- Being organized and well prepared
- Focusing on the results to be produced

Using style stepping

In this scenario, the clerk's natural style is amiable, but he style steps to bridge the gap between his style and the driver style of his customer.

Clerk:	*(with a pleasant voice)* Good afternoon, how are you today?
Customer:	Fine. I'm looking for a book called *How to Get 25 Hours Out Of Your Day.* Do you have it?
Clerk:	I can find out. What's the author's name?
Customer:	Stan Workmore.
Clerk:	We have one copy left. My co-worker, Nancy, can ring it up for you while I get the book from the stockroom.
Customer:	Thanks for taking care of this so quickly.
Clerk:	No problem.

The general rule when it comes to stepping into another style is this: A little goes a long way. In this revised scenario (and the ones to come later in the section), the clerk didn't go over the top when style stepping. Instead, the clerk shows just enough flexibility to make the customer feel comfortable and taken care of.

Analytical and amiable

In this scenario, the clerk has an analytical working style, and the customer has the amiable working style.

Clerk:	Can I help you with anything?
Customer:	*(pleasantly)* I'm looking for a book called *How to Get 25 Hours Out Of Your Day.* Do you have it?
Clerk:	*(matter-of-factly)* I've never heard of it, and I wouldn't want to guess. I can look it up in the books in print if you'd like.
Customer:	I'd really appreciate it if you would.
Clerk:	Can you tell me the exact spelling of the author's name, the publisher, and the year the book was published?
Customer:	The author's name is Stan Workmore. I'm really sorry, but I don't know who the publisher is. Can you still help me?
Clerk:	I'll do my best, but Mr. Workmore has written several books, and without more specific information, it will take me that much longer to locate it.
Customer:	That's okay. I'll be more than happy to wait while you look it up.
Clerk:	Okay, here it is. I've managed to find it. The publisher is Toilaway & Company. It was published in June of 1993. I have one copy left, and that should be located in our back stockroom. I'll go and get it. Will you wait here?
Customer:	I think I'll go have a cup of coffee in your cafe while I'm waiting.
Clerk:	Where exactly will you be sitting, so I can find you?

Getting in step with amiables

This scenario shows how the amiable customer couldn't care less about any of the details that are so important to the analytical sales clerk. Style-stepping behaviors for working with amiables include:

- Making eye contact but looking away once in a while
- Speaking at a moderate pace and with a softer voice
- Not using a harsh tone of voice or language
- Asking them for their opinions and ideas
- Not trying to counter their ideas with logic
- Encouraging them to express any doubts or concerns they may have
- Avoiding putting excessive pressure on them to make a decision
- Mutually agreeing on all goals, action plans, and completion dates

Using style stepping

In this scenario, the clerk's natural working style is analytical, but she style steps to bridge the gap between her style and the amiable customer.

Clerk:	Can I help you with anything?
Customer:	I'm looking for a book called *How to Get 25 Hours Out Of Your Day.* Do you have it?
Clerk:	*(with empathy)* I'm sorry, but I haven't heard of it. Would you like me to look it up for you?
Customer:	I would really appreciate it if you could.
Clerk:	Can you tell me the author's name and perhaps the publisher?
Customer:	The author's name is Stan Workmore. I'm really sorry, but I don't know who the publisher is. Can you still help me?
Clerk:	Of course; this will take me a few minutes to look up. Here it is. We have one copy left in the stockroom. Would you mind waiting here while I get it?
Customer:	No problem. Thanks for helping me out.
Clerk:	My pleasure.

Expressive and analytical

In this scenario, the clerk has the expressive working style, and the customer has the analytical working style.

Clerk:	Good morning. How can I help you?
Customer:	I'm looking for *How to Get 25 Hours Out Of Your Day;* it's by Stan Workmore and published by Toilaway & Company. Can you tell me where I can find it in the store?
Clerk:	*(enthusiastically)* Now that sounds like something we could all use. What did you say that author's name was again?
Customer:	Stan Workmore, W-O-R-K-M-O-R-E. Do you want to write it down?
Clerk:	No, I've got it. What a perfect name for the author of *that* book. Okay, here it is. You'll be pleased to know we have one copy left in the back. If you hold on just a second, I'll run and get it for you.

| **Customer:** | How long exactly will this take? I have an 11 o'clock meeting. |
| **Clerk:** | Just a second or two. |

Getting in step with analyticals

Remember that analyticals focus on facts, details, and logic. They are uncomfortable with expressing feelings and aren't very outgoing. When dealing with them, you need to emphasize the rational, objective aspects of what you're discussing. Style-stepping behaviors for working with analyticals include:

- ✔ Not speaking with a loud or fast-paced voice
- ✔ Being more formal in your speech and mannerisms
- ✔ Presenting the pros and cons of an idea, along with the options
- ✔ Not overstating the benefits of something
- ✔ Following up in writing
- ✔ Being on time and keeping it brief
- ✔ Showing how your approach has little risk

Using style stepping

In this scenario, the clerk's natural working style is expressive, but he style steps to bridge the gap between his style and his analytical customer.

Clerk:	Good morning. What a great day. How can I help you?
Customer:	I'm looking for *How to Get 25 Hours Out Of Your Day;* it's by Stan Workmore and published by Toilaway & Company. Can you tell me where I can find it in the store?
Clerk:	*(seriously)* I can locate that for you. Can you spell the author's last name for me please?
Customer:	Stan Workmore, W-O-R-K-M-O-R-E. Do you want to write it down?
Clerk:	Yes. I'll make a note of it. I have it. There's one copy left. It's in the stockroom; if you'll please wait, I'll go get it for you.
Customer:	How long exactly will that take? I have an 11 o'clock meeting.
Clerk:	No longer than five minutes.

Driver and expressive

In this scenario, the clerk has the driver working style, and the customer has the expressive working style.

Clerk:	Can I help you?
Customer:	*(enthusiastically)* Hi, how are you? I'm looking for *How to Get 25 Hours Out Of Your Day.* Isn't that a great title? All my friends have read it, and they just love it!
Clerk:	*(looking at his watch)* Who's the author?
Customer:	Oh, he's a wonderful man. I've met him. You won't believe his name; it's Stan Workmore. Isn't that the perfect name?
Clerk:	We have it. I need to go in the back to get it. Why don't you pay Nancy here while I go get the book?
Customer:	Sounds like a wonderful idea. I think I'll grab a cup of coffee in the cafe while you get the book.
Clerk:	No, don't do that — you won't have time. I'll be back in just a minute. Wait here. I will be right back with your book.
Customer:	Sure, I'll just talk with Nancy while I wait. Hello, Nancy. . . .

Getting in step with expressives

Expressives are the most outgoing and gregarious of all the work styles, and they're best approached by focusing on generalities rather than on details. Expressives usually respond well to playful people who focus on the big picture. Style-stepping behaviors for working with expressives include:

- Making direct eye contact
- Having energetic and fast-paced speech
- Allowing time in the meeting for socializing
- Talking about experiences, people, and opinions, in addition to the facts
- Asking about their intuitive sense of things
- Supporting your ideas with testimonials from people whom they know and like
- Paraphrasing any agreements made
- Maintaining a balance between fun and reaching objectives

Using style stepping

In this scenario, the clerk's natural working style is driver, but she style steps to bridge the gap between her style and her expressive customer.

Clerk:	Can I help you?
Customer:	*(enthusiastically)* Hi, how are you? I'm looking for *How to Get 25 Hours Out Of Your Day.* Isn't that a great title? All my friends have read it, and they just love it!
Clerk:	It sounds interesting. Can you tell me the author's name?
Customer:	Oh, he's a wonderful man; I've met him. You won't believe his name; it's Stan Workmore. Isn't that the perfect name?
Clerk:	It certainly is. Okay, you'll be happy to know that I found your book; it's in the back. Do you want to wait here while I go get it?
Customer:	I think I'll go grab a cup of coffee in your cafe.
Clerk:	Okay, I'll be back in just a minute. In the meantime, my co-worker, Nancy, can ring up the book for you, if you'd like.
Customer:	Thanks. I'll see you in a few minutes.

Style-Stepping Opportunities

Many situations at work provide good opportunities to use style stepping. They include:

- **Making a sales presentation:** We hear many success stories from clients who say redesigning their sales pitch to fit their customer's language has closed sales that previously were elusive.

- **Conflicts between you and a customer:** By stopping and listening to your customer's style, you can quickly redirect your approach to him or her so that you have a better chance of resolving disagreements.

- **Presenting your ideas to your manager:** Style stepping with your manager can make the difference between your ideas being acted upon or ignored. In our workshops, we often see good ideas lost, because the staff person wasn't able to present them in a way that made sense to the manager's way of thinking.

- **Developing teamwork:** Style stepping, in many ways, is the essence of good teamwork. Knowing and appreciating the different styles of the people on your team makes understanding their points-of-view and coming to a consensus decision easier.

Creating a Customer Profile

In some situations, taking the time to sit down and preplan an upcoming conversation can be useful for achieving a win-win resolution. The customer profile form shown in Figure 12-3 is best used when a challenging situation confronts you, and you have a specific objective that you want to achieve.

You can also use the customer profile form to plan conversations with co-workers and bosses, in addition to customers.

Create a customer profile by following these four steps:

1. **Determine the customer's primary working style.**

   Based on your observations, what is this customer's primary style? If you aren't sure, read the descriptions for each style found earlier in this chapter, and choose the one that fits the best.

2. **Set your objective.**

   One key to successful customer profiling is setting clear and achievable outcomes. Objectives that are too vague, such as, "I want to improve my relationship with Liza, my co-worker," make it difficult to assess what exactly needs to happen to achieve the goal. This assessment works better when you define your outcome more specifically, such as, "I want Liza and I to agree on how we are going to solve the overtime problem."

3. **Look at the big picture.**

   Step back for a moment, consider your working style and the working style of the customer, ask what potential trouble spots you may encounter, and decide what ideas you and the customer are likely to agree on or have in common. By thinking about trouble spots ahead of time, you can plan for a more successful interaction.

4. **Plan a rapport strategy.**

   After your analysis is complete, plan what actions you can take to create a rapport with your customer (or co-worker) and achieve the result you want. At this point, you may want to review the earlier section about "Getting in Step with Different Styles" and use that information as a basis for your strategy.

Be as specific as possible when you write down your strategy actions. For example:

- Be on time to my meeting with Bob.

- Prepare a chart with all the information on it.

- Ask Bob what his ideas are for solving the problem.

- Explain to Bob how I arrived at the solution, step by step.

- Give Bob a one-page overview of the proposed solution.

Customer Profile Form

Primary working style:

My objective is:

The big picture:

My strategy for building rapport is:

Figure 12-3:
The customer profile form.

Chapter 13

Turning Service Excellence into Sales Success: Five Timeless Techniques

In This Chapter

▶ Grabbing and holding your customer's attention

▶ Finding out what your customer really wants and needs

▶ Interrupting a customer when you have to get down to business

*I*n most companies, the sales and service departments are separate, but in reality, the services those departments provide are greatly interrelated. For example, if the sales department makes promises that can't be fulfilled (not that this ever happens), the firm's service reputation suffers. The same is true if the service department doesn't adequately support customers after the sale. Understanding the connections between sales and service becomes especially critical when your service staff is expected to cross-sell to existing customers or simply suggest alternatives that can lead to new sales.

In Chapter 2, we talk about the two aspects of your daily work: functions and essence. You can get so bogged down with the multitude of ceaseless tasks that the essence of your job, communicating and establishing relationships, is overlooked, and the customer ultimately suffers. The steps involved in successful selling also are functions, structured procedures that help deal with predictable customer responses and concerns. However, if these tools are used without a backdrop of appreciation and a commitment to relationship-building, they become nothing more than techniques that customers can easily construe as coercion.

Customers are far more likely to buy from you when they think you're listening to their needs and earnestly trying to serve them. By viewing sales as another great opportunity to serve your customer, you can use the five techniques we discuss in this chapter to aid you in creating better rapport and making your sales calls more efficient.

Technique 1: Getting the Customer's Attention

You may find it hard to believe, but your customers don't always pay a great deal of attention to what you're saying. Or, if they *are* paying attention, they may not be thrilled by what they hear. That's why beginning a sales conversation by saying something that grabs your customer's attention often is a good idea.

Foot-in-the-door, attention-grabbing methods are far from customer-focused. For example, most people hate getting a call from a telemarketer who sounds just a little too friendly and a tad too enthusiastic. Hearing an over-the-top, high-toned, "Hello, how are you today?" is one sure way of getting you to immediately hang up the phone. So, don't try and grab your customer's attention with false impressions or bogus offerings; it never works because they — like you — see through it every time.

In this section, we offer four approaches you can try to get your customer's attention in a positive and customer-friendly way.

Using a dramatic statement

Dramatic statements can be statistics or events that are surprising and/or thought-provoking. For example, we recently were stopped in our tracks when one of our vendors stated, "Sixty-eight percent of U.S. employees who use e-mail at work have sent or received e-mail that could place their company at risk." This statement grabbed our attention, because we thought it was a surprisingly high statistic — and it related to a subject for which we offer trainings.

Another example is a company that recently approached us regarding its facilities for printing our workbooks via the Web. One of its attention-grabbing statements was, "If you e-mail us your original by 7 p.m., it will be copied and overnight-shipped that same day." Wow! We were impressed and interested in learning more.

Making a third-party reference

Making a reference to a third party can turn a cold call into a warm call, because mentioning a mutual relationship adds a sort of instant credibility. For example, we recently contacted Gina, a potential client who had been recommended by Ted, a manager in another division of the same company, and a current client of ours. When we mentioned Ted's name at the beginning of the call, Gina immediately shifted gears, slowed down, and became more interested in what we were offering. Given her busy schedule, we doubt we would've grabbed Gina's attention without having a third-party reference.

When you're talking to a sales lead and referencing someone you know, or have worked with, be sure to mention how long you've known that person, the kind of projects you've undertaken, the results produced, and anything relevant about the relationship that adds more credibility and depth to the relationship.

Quoting an industry authority

Quoting an authority is similar to quoting a third-party reference, but the third party, in this case, is an industry leader rather than a business associate. This tool is especially powerful when your product or service addresses issues that have received recent media coverage. For example, a software company we work with encourages its sales team to quote recent reports and research that supports their products. To this end, it sends a monthly e-mail to its sales staff that provides Web links to all the latest, relevant industry findings.

Asking a key question

We know an investment advisor who often begins his sales pitch with the question, "Did you know that you can take the money you have sitting in your IRA account and invest it in real estate with all the same tax benefits?" He has found that asking a direct and compelling question usually gets a good conversation started.

Here are some ideas for topics for key questions accompanied by sample questions:

- ✔ **The benefits of using your product or service:** "Everybody knows how important it is to back up company data but can you imagine, with our automated product, never having to back up your data again?"

- ✔ **Recent findings related to your industry.** "Did you know that these types of engines are the most rapidly growing segment of the market?"

- ✔ **Compelling industry statistics.** "Are you prepared for the summer rush? We expect to see a 30-percent increase in tanning product sales this year."

- ✔ **Surprise questions.** "Would you like a free month of service so that you can really evaluate our product?"

Technique 2: Asking Questions

Asking a question is like opening a door. When you ask prospective customers questions, you're inviting them to talk, and if you're listening carefully, the customers will tell you what their needs or concerns are. That's how you can find out more about your customers. *Open-ended questions* are best for beginning a conversation and priming the pump for a productive interaction.

Sometimes, however, conversations can wander off into unrelated side waters that are unproductive and time-consuming. When that happens, you need to lasso the customer back on track by asking closed-ended questions.

Open-ended questions

Open-ended questions begin with the words how, what, where, why, and when. They cannot be answered with a simple yes or no answer. Here are some typical examples:

- How do you expect your business to change over the next year?
- What differences do you find between the larger and smaller models?
- Where would you foresee using our product?
- Why do you think that?
- When do you expect to make a decision?

Closed-ended questions

Closed-ended questions tend to evoke one-word answers. They are handy when you want to narrow the scope of the conversation and close the sale. Closed-ended questions usually begin with words like do, will, can, are, and so on. Here are some examples:

- Do you want me to invoice you?
- Will you send me the purchase order number?
- Can I send you a sample?
- Are you happy with your current vendor?

Technique 3: Making Benefit Statements

Benefits, as the word implies, let customers know what the product or service will do for them. Sometimes you find that when members of your service staff are selling, they get caught up in the features of their product but fail to go the extra step to extract the benefits of the features they're crooning about.

For instance, coauthor Keith Bailey and his wife went car shopping at a local dealership, and the showroom salesman began going over the many features of the model in which they were interested. As they listened to him go on and on about the number of valves, the intricacies of the strut bars, and the wonders of the four cams, they became more and more frustrated. They wanted to know how those features translated into something they could relate to — driving the car! Had the salesman been more benefit-oriented, he would've said things like, "It's a really quiet, smooth ride with easy steering and good road holding capabilities, even in bad weather."

Benefit statements can also be used to show a potential client your interest in him or her specifically. For example, "You've told me that your company is expanding rapidly, and that expansion creates a concern that communications in the organization will suffer. This software has the ability to produce real-time data that anyone can access at anytime, increasing the level of communications within your organization."

Table 13-1 provides a list of assorted features accompanied by the benefits they provide. At the end of the table, we provided a few blank lines for you to add the features of your product or service. After writing down your features in the left column, think about what benefits they provide for your customers, and write them down in the spaces in the right column.

Table 13-1	Comparing Features with Their Resulting Benefits
Features	**Benefits**
New formula paint with quick-drying ingredient	Saves time
We have a new fleet of vans to serve you	Faster, more frequent delivery and pickup
New online training offers an alternative to classroom study	Web classes save you money and are 8 easier to schedule
New sleek, ergonomic design	Attractive and comfortable

(continued)

Table 13-1 *(continued)*	
Your features	*Their benefits*

Have the members of your staff do the above exercise, and then have them develop a simple sales script that emphasizes the benefits of your product. Having some authorship interest in their scripts makes it easier for members of your staff to adopt the technique and sound even more authentic to your customers.

Technique 4: Backtracking

Backtracking is a technique that has two purposes: It tells customers that you've heard what they've said and gives you the opportunity to make sure that you understand the customer correctly. Sometimes called active listening, backtracking means that you paraphrase what you hear customers saying and then repeat it back to them.

For example, if a customer says, "I am very concerned about price. If I pay $250 per month now, can you guarantee that the amount won't fluctuate wildly in the months to come?" In response, the staff person backtracks by saying, "Mr. Smith I understand your concern about fluctuations in price and wanting some certainty about what you'll be paying month to month. . . ."

Paraphrasing is a simple and powerful technique that provides the customer with an important — yet often neglected — fundamental of excellent service: being heard and understood.

Speed isn't always as important as understanding, and solutions are more satisfying to everyone when they are presented with empathy and efficiency.

Technique 5: Bridging

Part of the challenge of selling services is balancing good listening skills with call efficiency. Customers can easily become derailed during a conversation or ramble on long after the point has been made. Waiting around for the conversation to get back on track can take a long time and therefore is obviously inefficient. *Bridging* is a three-part technique for politely steering the sales conversation in the direction you want it to go, while retaining good rapport. Read on for more info on each part of this valuable technique.

Step 1: Catching their breath

Bridging requires you to interrupt customers when they're talking. We know that sounds rude — but it doesn't have to be, if you simply wait for them to take a breath. If customers are excited or speaking quickly, you may have to listen intently as they suck up more air — but we guarantee they eventually will. And when they do, a short gap will occur in the conversation. That's when you seize the moment to interrupt. Because they're pausing momentarily, your cutting-in seems less abrupt.

Step 2: Showing empathy

Making an empathic statement further softens the abruptness of cutting into the conversation. For example, if you are cross-selling an enhanced insurance package to a customer, the conversation may go off track when the customer responds in the following way: "I want the policies mailed to my work address. The last time policies were mailed to my home, the dog got to them before I did, and they were shredded out of existence. She's a poodle, and they're not usually aggressive, but when she hears the mail man, she turns into a monster. I used to have a St. Bernard, and he could've taken the door off if he's wanted to. . . ."

Heard enough? Okay, wait for the breath and then show empathy by saying something like: "I can see how not receiving your policies would be a big inconvenience." Then move on to Step 3.

Step 3: Redirecting the conversation

Having interrupted with empathy, the last part of bridging is steering the conversation back in the direction you want it to go. Continuing the chewed-policy example, redirecting the conversation may sound like this: "I can see how not receiving your policies would be a big inconvenience. I'll make sure the policies are mailed to your business, but first I want to finish going over the new limits of the policy."

Bridging is useful in any situation in which you need to move forward and the other customer (or anyone else you're talking to) is hung up on a diversion. The good thing about bridging: It works both over the phone and in face-to-face situations.

Part IV

Road Blocks: When the Going Gets Rough

The 5th Wave   By Rich Tennant

COMPLAINTS

"First of all, I don't like sitting behind this window all day."

In this part . . .

*T*hink of a customer you dread dealing with. Imagine your phone ringing at work, and when you pick it up, it's him or her.

How do you feel? Are your palms starting to sweat? Is your throat getting tight? Are you reaching for the aspirin bottle? If so, read on. In this part, you find out how to reduce the effects of stress when dealing with conflict situations and how to calm angry and upset customers. You also discover how to turn a complaint into a valuable company asset.

To top it all off, this part of the book contains a process that we've taught to more than 50,000 people in companies and jobs like yours for turning difficult situations into win-win opportunities.

Chapter 14

Saying No: What to Do When You Can't Say Yes

*N*o! *Nein! Non! Nyet!* No matter which language you say it in, customers don't like to hear the word *no.* Regardless of where you are in the world, your customers want what they want, when they want it, and how they want it. If they don't get what they want, they're probably going to be disappointed, frustrated, or upset.

Imagine how you'd feel in any of the following situations:

- ✔ Your dentist tells you that he unexpectedly ran out of nitrous oxide, and you can't have the gas you requested for the root canal you scheduled.

- ✔ While out with some friends, you offer to pay for dinner. A few minutes after giving the waiter your credit card, he returns with an apologetic facial expression and tells you that your card was declined.

- ✔ You return from lunch and realize that you left your wallet or purse at the restaurant. You call the restaurant, and the hostess tells you that nobody has handed anything in.

- ✔ You arrive late at the airport and after running three miles to the gate, you discover that your flight has already departed. The service agent tells you that no other flight is leaving tonight.

Like it or not, you and every other service person from time to time must say no to your customers (whether you want to or not). Many companies tout the belief that service is giving customers what they want, and when you can, you should. The problem is that service providers often have this belief so etched in their minds that when they can't give customers what they want (in other words, they have to say no), they feel helpless and often fail to use other techniques that may bring about a satisfactory conclusion to a difficult situation.

In this chapter, we look at a few circumstances that make saying yes impossible, and then we show you how to say no (when you have to) and still make customers happy by making sure you're meeting their needs and giving them as much as you can.

Circumstances that Make It Impossible to Say Yes

No business in the world can say yes to every customer request and stay in business. Like it or not, circumstances exist that require you to say no to your customers. These situations include the following examples:

- ✔ **Federal regulations:** Certain rules and regulations may be imposed on your business (depending on the industry you're in) by an outside government agency. For example, if you work in a bank, you'd have to say no to a customer who wanted to open a business account that paid interest, because Federal Regulation Q prohibits banks from paying interest on business accounts.

- ✔ **The law:** Companies must comply with federal and state laws. For example, if you're a car rental agent and a customer can't produce his driver's license, you can't rent a car to him, even if you know him personally. A friend of ours is a vice president at a car rental company, and he was unable to rent a car to a friend when she visited from out of town, because she had an expired driver's license.

- ✔ **Company policies and procedures:** These restrictions are imposed not because of a legal requirement but rather as part of the company's rules regarding how it conducts its business. For example, if you work as a salesperson in a retail store, you may not be able to refund a return item that a customer brings in because she is unable to find the sales receipt.

- ✔ **Out of stock:** For whatever reason, the item the customer wants is temporarily unavailable. For example, you work in an ice cream parlor and a customer comes in salivating with excitement for a chocolate-fudge, double-malted shake with whipped cream — and you've just sold the very last scoop of chocolate-fudge ice cream.

- ✔ **Just not possible:** Sometimes a customer makes a request that just isn't possible to fulfill. For example: You're a hairdresser and one of your clients who has short hair asks for a style that would require her to grow another three inches of hair while sitting in the chair!

Saying no with style

In our book *Watercooler Wisdom: How Smart People Prosper in the Face of Conflict, Pressure and Change* (New Harbinger Publications), we talk about how to say no to your co-workers and customers. Knowing what your priorities are at work and having the energy and time to go after them requires learning to say no to some things. Here are some phrases that can help you gracefully get out of doing something you can't or don't want to do:

✔ I don't think I'm the right person for this job.

✔ I have a lot on my plate right now.

✔ I'm not comfortable with that.

✔ I can't do it right now.

✔ I don't want to; or, no thank you, I'm not interested.

✔ Doing this would require me to change priorities.

Saying Yes versus Making Customers Happy

The belief that saying yes and giving your customer what he wants will automatically make a happy customer is an easy trap to fall into. It doesn't always work that way. You can see on a visit to your local post office how this theory works. In general, the post office is well-stocked and rarely, if ever, runs out of stamps, money orders, and so on. Almost everyone who goes to the post office leaves having received exactly what he expected to get. If getting what you want were the only criteria, then the post office should be the greatest service provider on the planet. Yet, in our office, we toss a coin to see who has to go. One reason is the guaranteed long line; another is the somber attitude of the clerks and so on. The point is you get what you want (stamps, packages mailed, and so on), but you don't necessarily end up with that I-can't-wait-to-go-back-for-more great service feeling!

The opposite also is true. As a customer, you can end up not getting what you want and still feeling like you received good customer service. Imagine you're in the ice cream parlor again, asking for that chocolate-fudge, double-malted shake with whipped cream. The person at the counter apologizes and tells you that he unfortunately is out of chocolate-fudge ice cream. However, he doesn't leave it at that. Instead, he invites you to try a sample of a new flavor called Decadent Cocoa Overload. You try it and swoon! The counter person makes you a Decadent Cocoa Overload double-malted shake, and adds an extra-big blob of whipped cream. You leave in sugar shock — but happy.

In the ice cream parlor example, the service provider had to say no to the customer but knew that when he couldn't give the customer what she wanted, his job then was to fulfill as many of her other needs as possible:

- ✔ By apologizing, he showed empathy toward the customer's disappointment.

- ✔ When he offered the customer a taste of a second type of ice cream, he provided an alternative to the customer's first choice.

- ✔ By putting extra whipped cream on the shake, he provided the customer with a care token as part of bounce-back initiative. (Care tokens and bounce-back initiative are powerful service tools that are explained in Chapter 16.)

The key to scoring high marks with the customer, regardless of whether you say yes or no, is always asking yourself the question: "What does this customer need, and how can I provide it to the best of my ability?"

The Customer's Six Basic Needs — Are You Meeting Them?

By talking to thousands of customers and service providers during the past few years, we found that customers seem to carry around a sort of invisible report card in their heads. Without fully realizing it, every time they do business with you, customers are keeping score not only on how well you're giving them what they want but also on fulfilling six basic customer needs. In this section, we list those needs along with related scenarios as told to us by people attending our workshops.

A popular piece of customer-service folklore states that if you give customers what they ask for (just say yes), you end up with satisfied customers. This folklore is false. Customers do ask for what they want, but they usually don't ask for the six basic needs outlined in this section. When did you last go into a pizzeria and say, "I'd like one slice of pepperoni pizza, please," and then add, "Can you please be understanding, friendly, and fair?" Although customers don't ask for these other needs, they nonetheless expect such gestures and miss them when they aren't provided. So you need to move beyond the yes folklore and fulfill all your customers' needs to be able to provide top-quality customer service.

Friendliness

Friendliness is the most basic of all customer needs, and it's usually associated with being greeted politely and courteously.

Cliff, a San Francisco building contractor, always stops at the same coffee shop for breakfast, even though it's out of his way. He says the food is good, yet it's pretty much the same as he can get closer to home. He keeps going back because he loves the way the servers always are friendly and upbeat, calling him by name and usually having his coffee poured as he is walking in the door. By adding this extra value to Cliff's breakfast eating experience, the coffee shop separates itself from other cafes and competes on more than just the ham-and-eggs level.

Understanding and empathy

Customers need to feel that the person providing the service understands and appreciates their circumstances and feelings without criticism or judgment.

Gayle, vice president of a public relations firm, got an unexpected promotion and had to relocate within two weeks from Charlotte, North Carolina, to Atlanta, Georgia. To help her find a new home, she called Peachtree Realty (located, incidentally, in the Peachtree Shopping Center on the corner of Peachtree Road and Peachtree Avenue). Susan, the real estate agent at Peachtree Realty, understood the time pressure that Gayle was under, so she faxed Gayle a description of the various neighborhoods within 30 minutes of Gayle's new office (including houses for sale and prices). Doing so made Gayle feel that Susan was able to stand in her shoes and empathize with her situation.

Fairness

The need to be treated fairly is high on most customers' lists of needs.

Donna, a telephone receptionist, was waiting in line at a supermarket when a checker opened the next checkout lane. The person in line behind Donna pushed his cart past hers and made a mad dash to the checkout stand that had just opened. The checkout clerk, to his credit, politely asked the pushy customer to allow those who were in the front of the line to go first. By standing up for what was fair, the clerk impressed everyone (except, of course, the pushy customer) and fulfilled Donna's need for being treated fairly as a customer.

Control

Control represents the need of customers to feel as if they have an impact on the way things turn out.

Richard, a software engineer, planned to leave work early one day to meet the cable company representative at home for a repair. About an hour before he was supposed to leave work, the cable company called to let him know the representative was running about 30 minutes behind. This gesture by the cable company gave Richard control. He was able to reorganize his schedule so that he could stay and finish the project he was working on instead of waiting around at home and growing more angry and frustrated with each passing minute, wondering what was going on.

Options and alternatives

Customers need to feel that other avenues are available to accomplish what they want.

Rona, a lawyer with a Washington, D.C., law firm, was preparing an important case for a court appearance at the end of the week. As part of her research, she needed a recent report from a large U.S. car manufacturer. When she called to request the report, the car manufacturer informed her that it had not yet been published. She explained why she needed the report and the urgency of the situation. The car company came up with a solution by sending Rona, via an e-mail attachment, a draft copy of the report.

Information

Customers need to be educated and informed about the products, policies, and procedures they encounter when dealing with your company.

Milton, a human resources director, is a novice tennis player who went to a local pro shop to buy his first tennis racquet. Understanding that Milton needed to be educated about the fine points of buying a tennis racquet, the store manager took the time to explain the differences between the many types of strings and such and why prices varied from one racquet to the next.

By the time Milton left the shop, he not only had a tennis racquet that he felt good about buying, but he also had a better understanding of how a racquet can affect the game.

Different strokes for different folks

The needs of your customers not only vary according to their individual personalities, but they can also change depending on the nature of your business. A trip to Disneyland, for example, is remembered for the fun and safety of the park and rides. These two service qualities are part of what makes a day with the mouse so enjoyable and memorable. Compare this excursion with a visit to your accountants. In that situation, your needs are more in the realm of accuracy and certainty. You'd be mighty suspicious if your accountant was having fun — when you weren't — and started to laugh uncontrollably during a meeting.

Besides the six basic customer needs, dozens more exist that are specific to different businesses and occupations. See Table 14-1 for a list of some of the many customer needs we have discovered over the years.

Using the needs listed in Table 14-1, check off the six that you consider the most important to your customers. Ask your staff to do the same. Compare lists, and report the results to your staff. Then you can schedule a brainstorming session (see Chapter 6) with your staff to evaluate how well you think you're fulfilling those customer needs and how you can improve the ones that need more attention.

Table 14-1	Exploring Descriptions of Customer Needs		
What Customers Need Their Service Providers to Be			
Accessible	Dedicated	Honest	Reliable
Accurate	Dependable	Industry leaders	Respectful
After sales service	Discreet	Influential	Responsible
Alternatives	Easy to do business with	Innovative	Responsive
Attentive excellence	Easy to locate	Interesting	Reputation for
Attractive	Easy to use	Intimate	Safe
Authentic	Effective	Knowledgeable	Serious
Available	Efficient	Large in size	Sincere
Available inventory	Elegant	Leading-edge technology	Skilled
Careful	Empathic	Listens	Small in size
Caring	Entertaining	Low cost	Special
Cheerful	Exciting	Medium in size	Stimulating
Clean	Expensive	Moderate in cost	Technical support
Comfortable	Experienced	Modern	Timeliness
Committed	Experts	On time	Tranquil

(continued)

Table 14-1 *(continued)*

What Customers Need Their Service Providers to Be

Competitive	Extra amenities	Personal	Trustworthy
Concerned	Fair	Pleasant	Understanding
Consistent	Fast	Pleasurable	Unique
Convenient	Flexible	Private	Upscale
Cost effective	Friendly	Professional	Warm
Courteous	Healthy	Quick	Well-known
Creative	Helpful	Quiet	Well-planned environment
Customized	Homey	Relaxing	Well-stocked

What to Do When You Have to Say No

Given that saying no is a fact of life and that sooner or later you'll have to deliver bad news to the customer, your choice is not whether you say no but how you say it. You can say no the hard way, or you can say it the service way.

Avoiding the hard no

Nothing turns an uncomfortable no situation into a heated argument like a service person who thinks that her job is to be the brick wall that stands between the customer and what he wants. Saying no that way without empathy or any expression of desire to help is infuriating to the customer. The underlying attitude of the hard no is "no way, no how, never in a million years!"

You can always tell you're facing a hard no as a customer when you ask the service person whether any other easy solution is available to whatever situation you're dealing with, and she says, "No!" Then you ask for a recommendation about what to do next, and she says, "I don't know!" Finally, you come up with some possible options, and she systematically shoots them down, one by one. Get the picture? You're facing a hard no!

From observing customers and service providers during the last ten years, we're convinced that a hard-no approach takes more time and effort than the service-no approach.

How to drive a customer crazy

Nothing drives customers crazier than not getting what they want from a service provider who treats them like an adversary and isn't interested in looking for ways to help them resolve their situations. Some of the one-liners (said, of course, in a monotone voice) that clearly reflect this "I don't care," hard-no attitude are:

✔ That's not our policy.

✔ That's not my job.

✔ I'm not allowed to do that.

✔ I have no idea.

The body language that accompanies these responses can be:

✔ A blank stare

✔ Head held down

✔ Look-away eyes

✔ Distracted fidgeting

Opting for the service no

Although giving customers a hard no clearly doesn't work, we're not suggesting that you somehow try to make a no sound like a yes. No technique can accomplish that feat — except lying! We've seen many service providers who, not wanting to confront the situation honestly, tried to keep customers happy by bending the truth. Doing so gives customers the unrealistic expectation that they're going to get what they want, and sooner or later, when they discover that they've been misled, they're going to be even more upset! Manipulating customers into thinking you're saying yes when you're really saying no is not the answer and neither is hoping that a no will be received with joy and understanding.

Serving up a service-no sandwich

The solution is a technique that we teach our clients called the *service-no sandwich.* This technique requires no culinary training and helps ensure a successful outcome with a customer who can't get exactly what he or she wants.

We've used the sandwich technique for years when we have to say no, and it works with most customers — except the 1 percent who won't change their attitudes even if you levitate in front of them! It's called a sandwich technique because the slices of bread (so to speak) are represented by two phrases that are wrapped around a filling of recommended actions. The two phrases are:

✔ **What I can do is . . .**

This phrase tells customers that you want to help them and gives them specific actions you can take to get their problem(s) resolved. The alternative actions that you offer may not be exactly what the customer wants, but they usually can help create an acceptable resolution to the problem and reduce the customer's feeling of frustration.

✔ **What you can do is . . .**

This second phrase tells customers that they have some control over the outcome of the situation and that you consider them your partners in getting the problem resolved. Possible suggestions for customers may involve recommendations for a temporary fix to the problem or actions that the customer can take in the future to prevent the problem from occurring again.

Putting the sandwich technique into practice

Two common situations in which using the service-no sandwich technique turns a potentially hard-no situation into a service-no success are described in the two scenarios that follow.

Scenario 1: A customer calls the insurance office where you work, concerned and upset about a monthly bill he's just received that shows no record of last month's payment being made. In addition, the customer has been charged a late fee. Because the customer says he paid the bill on time, he wants you to waive the late charge immediately.

After sincerely apologizing for the inconvenience this problem has caused the customer, you whip out your ever-handy service-no sandwich technique and say, "What I can do is see whether we've received the check since your bill was sent. If we have, then I'll waive the late fee. If not, I can't remove the late fee today, but what you can do is fax me a copy of the canceled check, and as soon as I receive it, I can waive the late fee."

Scenario 2: A customer calls the store where you work to order a product that your company sells. You're temporarily out of stock and therefore must say no. After apologizing to the customer for the inconvenience and empathizing with her disappointment, you say, "What I can do is place the item on back order and ship it out to you by two-day mail when it arrives. What you can do is give me a credit-card number over the phone so that I can complete the paperwork now and ship the product out as soon as it arrives." You may still need to give the customer an explanation like the policy, but when you do, remember to put that phrase at the end of this technique, after you have given another option.

Chapter 15

Seeing Red: Dealing with Difficult Customers

* * *

In This Chapter

▶ Following a six-step plan for dealing with difficult customers

▶ Understanding the chemistry behind stress

▶ Overcoming personal stress and stressful situations

* * *

Service providers who don't know how to work well with difficult people lose their hair, their marbles, and their customers. The nature of your job as a service provider requires that you sometimes work with customers who drive you up a wall. Regardless of whether your customers are rude, frustrated, confused, or irate, most minor clashes don't have to turn into guerrilla warfare.

Six Steps to Beat the Heat of a Difficult Customer

Knowing when you're losing control when dealing with a difficult customer isn't always easy. However, certain red flags do pop up, such as:

✔ Tight neck and shoulders

✔ Cringing at the sound of the customer's voice

✔ Dreading the ringing of the telephone

✔ Headaches

✔ Anger

✔ Being short or curt

✔ Raising your voice unnecessarily

✔ Straining the tone of your voice

✔ Breaking out in hives

✔ Grinding your teeth

When you notice any of these symptoms, don't worry. Instead, use the basic six-step process that we outline in this section to help you get through the trying times with difficult customers. Practice makes perfect when dealing with the worst of the worst. The more you use these six steps, the better you become at winning over difficult customers and keeping yourself sane.

Step 1: Let the customer vent

When your customers are upset, they want two things: First, they want to express their feelings, and second they want their problem solved. The customers' need to let off steam can be so strong that they vent to the first person they get their hands on, even if it is just a receptionist. Some service providers view the customers' venting as a waste of time because they simply want to move on and solve the problem. However, trying to resolve the situation without first listening to the customers' feelings never seems to work. Only after your customers have vented can they begin to hear what you have to say.

Zip your lip

Nothing heats up already angry customers faster than being told to calm down while they're venting. If you try to stop customers from expressing their feelings, you can push them from annoyed to irate in a matter of seconds. The best plan is to stay quiet and not make matters worse by interrupting the customer. In particular, here's a list of phrases you want to avoid:

✔ You don't seem to understand . . .

✔ You must be confused . . .

✔ You have to . . .

✔ We won't . . . We never . . . We can't . . .

✔ You're wrong . . .

✔ It's not our policy . . .

Although you don't want to interrupt customers when they're venting, you do want to let the customers know that you're listening to them. You should do the following three things while they vent:

✔ Nod your head frequently.

✔ Say uh-huh from time to time.

✔ Maintain eye contact.

Don't take it personally

When customers vent, they may be expressing frustration, annoyance, disappointment, or anger. Of all of these emotions, anger is the one you're most likely to take personally because anger is such an in-your-face emotion. Raised voices, bulging blood vessels, rude comments about your mother, and wagging fists can make you want to run and hide or retaliate.

Anger is an emotion that's always looking for someone or something to blame. If you stub your toe on the couch, you get angry at the couch. If a mosquito bites you, you get angry at the mosquito. If you lock your keys in your car, you get angry at yourself and then give the tire a good kick to vent your frustration. Even though the customer's anger may appear to be directed at you, remember that you're simply the person she's venting to, so don't take it personally.

Step 2: Avoid getting trapped in a negative filter

The friction between you and a difficult customer is often worsened by how you interpret her behaviors. Take a moment and think of some of the names that you call your difficult customers — of course, not to their face, but privately, under your breath. You may even want to jot a few of your favorites down in disappearing ink.

Negative filter name-calling

Through our seminars, we hear many different names and descriptions for difficult customers. Some of the most popular are

- Jerk
- Bozo
- Rude
- Stupid
- Creep
- Liar
- Pushy
- Clueless
- Moron
- Turkey
- Loser
- X#%**&*!!

As soon as you pin one of these labels on a customer, it becomes a negative filter that dramatically changes how you see, speak, and listen to the other person.

How a negative filter is born

The following is an example of how a negative filter is created in a conversation between a bank teller and a customer:

> **Customer:** Good morning. I want to deposit this check.
>
> **Teller:** The back isn't signed!
>
> **Customer:** Sorry about that, do you have a pen?
>
> **Teller** *(sighing)*: Yes, here.
>
> **Customer:** By the way, I ran out of deposit slips and don't know my account number. Will you please look it up for me?

At this point in the conversation, the teller suddenly finds himself thinking: "This person is stupid!" The instant the teller has this thought, an invisible, negative filter comes down between him and the customer. From then on, the manner in which he relates to the customer is distorted by the negative filter. The teller's choice of words and his tone of voice reflects his silent opinion of the customer. The rest of the conversation would probably go something like this:

> **Teller:** Most people can remember their account number.
>
> **Customer** *(feeling scolded)*: I know and I'm sorry, but like I said, I don't have a deposit slip, and I didn't write down my account number.
>
> **Teller** *(annoyed and sighing again)*: You'll have to wait while I go look it up. Maybe you should write your number down and keep it in your wallet.

Negative filters are contagious

We were teaching customer service to the staff of a large hospital when we discovered that nurses on different shifts were unintentionally giving their negative filters to each other. The night nurses would write down a few comments about their patients' behaviors on the bottom of their charts. Sometimes the comments were positive, but sometimes they were negative. For example: "Mr. Smith has been in a very bad mood tonight." When the day nurse came on duty, she would pick up the chart and, boom, just like that, she had an instant negative filter about Mr. Smith. The day nurse, in turn, then noted her negative comments about Mr. Smith, reinforcing the night nurse's point of view, and so on. Within a day or two, word would get around that Mr. Smith in Room 206 was a pain in the elbow, and all the nurses on the floor, day or night, knew to be on guard when dealing with him. If left unchecked, negative filters can get out of control and spread like wildfire, creating a situation where positive communication with a customer becomes extremely difficult, if not impossible.

The service provider is speaking to the customer as if she is stupid. Being a professional, he knows better than to come right out and say, "Hey, lady, you're not too bright, are you?" Unfortunately, the negative filter still comes through, loud and clear.

Choosing to switch filters rather than fight

Inevitably, you have negative filters about some of your customers, some of the time. The idea is to avoid getting stuck in these negative filters. Understanding the harmful effects of a negative filter won't necessarily make them go away, but you do have a choice about whether you focus on them.

To get out of a negative filter, you need to switch to a service filter. You do so by asking yourself the following question: *"What does this customer need and how can I provide it?"* This question provides you with an alternative filter because as soon as you ask it, your focus changes. The negative filter instantly slides into the background, and the service filter slides into the foreground. The switching technique works in much the same way as a flashlight in a dark room: By changing where you aim your attention, you illuminate the issues that need to be addressed — instead of illuminating your personal feelings about the customer's behavior.

Step 3: Express empathy to the customer

If you give customers a chance to vent, they eventually run out of steam. When that happens, you can begin to participate more actively in the conversation. Giving a brief and sincere expression of *empathy* works wonders to calm a difficult customer. Empathy means appreciating and understanding someone else's feelings, even if you don't necessarily agree with them. By letting customers know that you understand why they're upset, you begin building a bridge of rapport.

Empathy is not *sympathy*. Sympathy is when you over-identify with the other person's situation. For example, say an angry customer comes up to you and says, "Your company really doesn't care about service!" A sympathetic response to that statement is, "You're right, we care more about the almighty dollar than anything else!"

Using empathic phrases

Empathic phrases are a simple and easy way of conveying that you understand your customer's situation. The types of phrases that best express empathy to a customer include the following:

> ✔ I can see why you feel that way.
>
> ✔ I see what you mean.
>
> ✔ That must be very upsetting.
>
> ✔ I understand how frustrating this must be.
>
> ✔ I'm sorry about this.

Always saying you're sorry

Some service providers feel uncomfortable apologizing to the customer because they see it as an admission of guilt. Saying I'm sorry to a customer doesn't imply that you or your company did anything wrong. Apologizing simply conveys that you're genuinely sorry that the customer has had a bad experience. See Chapter 17 for more details on apologizing to customers.

The tone of your voice goes a long way in helping you convey empathy. If you say all the right words but deliver them with an icy tone, the words may have an insincere ring to them. By using a genuinely warm and caring tone, you enhance the meaning and effectiveness of the empathic phrases.

Step 4: Begin active problem solving

Until now, you've been on the receiving end of the conversation with your customer. At this point, you can begin active problem solving by asking questions that help clarify the cause of the customer's problem.

As you ask the customer questions, be sure to listen to everything he says and don't jump to conclusions. Because you may have been through similar situations before, you may think that you already know the answer. However, this can cause you to miss details that are specific to this customer's situation.

Gathering additional information

Customers sometimes leave out critical information because they think it's unimportant or they just forget to tell you. When you need specific information from a customer, use the bridging technique. This technique, which is especially helpful when a customer's complaints have veered in an unproductive direction, builds a bridge between what the customer is saying and where you want the conversation to go. As you notice the conversation veering off track, wait for the customer to take a breath. (It may be a quick breath, but they all have to breathe eventually.) This is your cue to jump in with an empathic phrase followed by a question that steers the conversation back on course. For example, the customer may say

> *I never asked for a subscription to your publication. I don't even like your publication. How did you get my name? Did you buy it from a mailing list company? I get so much junk mail that I had to get a bigger mailbox . . . (breath).*

At this point, you quickly and politely say

> *Mrs. Jones, I understand your annoyance at receiving a subscription that you didn't want. May I have your address so that I can correct the situation for you?*

Chances are that the customer will immediately come back to the point and provide you with the information you need.

Double-checking all the facts

Upset customers rarely present the facts of their stories in neat little packages. You may have to do some detective work to make sure that you understand everything they're telling you. Use the mirroring technique to summarize your understanding of what the customer says, and then reflect it back to them. For example, imagine that your customer says

> *Last Tuesday I received a fax saying the order had been canceled, and then I got a phone call from your warehouse saying to ignore that fax. Today I still don't have the shipment, and nobody seems to know where it is!*

To make sure that you understand the situation, you can mirror it back by saying

> *What you're saying is that the order that should have been delivered last week still hasn't arrived, and you haven't been able to find anyone who can help you. Is that correct?*

The customer then has the chance to verify or correct your understanding of the situation.

Step 5: Mutually agree on the solution

After you gather all the facts, you need to work with your customer to come up with an acceptable solution to the problem. If you haven't already discovered what will make him happy, ask. You may, at this point, find it necessary to take a brief timeout from the customer so that you can do the behind-the-scenes work necessary to find out if you can actually solve the problem the way he wants you to. In this case, be sure that the customer knows exactly why you're asking him to wait and how long it'll take for you to get back to him. Finally, when you both agree on how to resolve the problem, explain the steps that you'll take to implement the solution.

Don't promise what you can't deliver. Be honest and realistic when telling the customer what you'll do. We always recommend that you under-promise and then over-deliver. Doing so sets an expectation (that you'll have a good chance of meeting and, hopefully, exceeding) in the customer's mind. For example, if you're sending a replacement product to the customer and you know that the shipping process usually takes three days, you can tell her to expect the package within a week. With this action, you build in a little time for unforeseen delays, and the customer is pleasantly surprised when the package arrives earlier than she expected.

Step 6: Follow up

You can score big points on the service scoreboard by following up with your customers — by phone, e-mail, or letter — to check that the solution worked. If you contact the customer and find out that he isn't satisfied with the solution, put out the "buck stops here" sign and continue looking for another, more workable solution.

Effective follow-up also includes fixing the procedures that are causing the problem to begin with. By spending time solving internal service delivery problems, you prevent them from occurring in the future. (For more information on how to do this, see Chapter 12.)

Understanding and Overcoming Stress

We read a *New York Times* article a while ago that highlighted the ten most stressful professions. Among the top ten listed were police officer, firefighter, air traffic controller, and customer service representative! Having a job that requires you to deal with angry, irate, or frustrated customers can make your blood boil (literally). Even if you aren't a customer service representative, some degree of stress is inevitable no matter what job you do (with the possible exception of sloth groomer at the zoo). Believing that you may find a stress-free job is wishful thinking. Imagine going into your place of work and hearing your manager say

> *As soon as you sense the customer getting angry, just put the phone down.*
>
> *You have all your work done — why don't you go home early and relax?*
>
> *I know it's Thursday and our deadline is Friday . . . but don't worry, I can always hire a few extra hands to help us get it done on time.*
>
> *I'm giving you a 20-percent raise because you're doing more than your job description calls for.*

Give it up. You won't ever hear your manager utter those phrases — not in this lifetime anyway. So, the answer isn't to wait for the circumstances of your job to change. Instead, you have to know how to manage the stress of dealing with difficult customers before the stress manages you.

Stress is your body's natural reaction to any demand (physical or psychological) that is put upon it. For example, imagine that you arrive at work a little late one morning and find a note on your desk from your boss. The note says that he wants to see you in his office. How would you feel? What thoughts would start running through your mind? Anxious to find out what he wants, you hurry to his office, but find that he's out until tomorrow. Now how do you feel? What are you thinking as you drive home that evening?

The next morning, you rush up to your boss's office and calmly ask him what he wanted to see you about. Beaming with pride, he says that he just heard back from an important client, and he was delighted with the work you put into his report. Well done!

When we run this scenario by people in our workshops, they usually start squirming as they visualize the amount of stress their negative thoughts would be producing. The anticipation and worry that the situation generated are all imagined, but the stress is very real and can ruin your whole day, not to mention keep you from getting a good night's rest.

Understanding how your mind works to create chemical stress in your body is an important part of both preventing stress before it occurs and curing stress once it hits.

Identifying the fight or flight mechanism

When physical or psychological demands become extreme, your brain alerts the hypothalamus gland (located at the base of your brain), which triggers a complex chain of events known as the *fight or flight mechanism.* This mechanism puts your body on red alert to gather the strength it needs to meet a challenging situation. Some of the ways your body prepares itself to meet a challenge are as follows:

- ✔ The heart pumps faster to get more blood to the muscles.
- ✔ Breathing speeds up to get more oxygen into the blood stream.
- ✔ Muscles tense up in preparation for action.
- ✔ Perspiration increases to reduce body temperature.

Recent research has revealed that the hypothalamus gland can trigger the fight or flight response in situations that are viewed as threatening even when, in actuality, they're not. The hypothalamus gland reacts to the signals your brain sends it without distinguishing between what is real and what is imagined. In other words, your negative thoughts are powerful enough to turn on the stress machinery in your body.

Different mammoth — same response

The fight or flight mechanism has been around for thousands of years. Our cave-dwelling ancestors had two basic responses when dealing with a hairy mammoth that was looking for a human snack: Stay and fight or run like the devil. This fight or flight response prepared the caveperson, within seconds, to have the extra strength needed to carry out either of these options.

The hairy mammoths of yesterday have been replaced by the difficult customers and deadlines of today, yet our hypothalamus gland continues to ignite our body's reactions in the same old way. Unlike our ancestors, however, we don't usually have the option of fighting or running away when confronted with an angry customer (although we're sure you've wanted to do both). The result is that your body gets all revved up with nowhere to go. The chemicals released into your system for extra strength don't dissipate and can keep you stressed out all day long.

The last time Keith was on vacation in Hawaii, he was lying on the beach looking up at the palm trees and heard, "No, Jack! They can't do that! They have a contract with us! That is unacceptable. We're in this deal to make money — not friends!" Aroused from his sun-drenched stupor, Keith looked around to see a man, in shorts and sunglasses, pacing up and down the beach yelling into a cellular phone. His head looked as if it were about to explode. He was oblivious to the golden beach, the blue water, and the red Hibiscus flowers that were in full bloom, and he was totally stressed out by his internal irritation. Keith suddenly realized that if this guy could create tension in the middle of such calm circumstances, then it stood to reason that Keith could also create calm in the midst of tense circumstances.

Changing from stress talk to smart talk

How you talk to yourself about your circumstances can either prevent or activate your cave dweller, stress-creating response. For example, imagine that you've just been on the phone with a difficult customer who insists that she get a refund on a product that she purchased from you six months ago. You sincerely apologize and explain why you can't offer a refund. The customer gets upset, interrupts you, and asks to be transferred to your supervisor. After talking with the customer, your supervisor comes up and tells you that he bent the rules and okayed a refund.

You now have to decide how you're going to talk to yourself about this situation.

Stress talk

If you put too much of a negative spin on the events, you may create stress talk and end up with your shoulders around your ears. Your stress talk in the above situation might go something like this:

> *I can't believe it! He always undermines my authority! He just doesn't have the guts to say "no" to difficult customers! He should support whatever decision I make. This always happens to me! I can't win with him! There's no point in talking to him about it because he never listens, and it wouldn't make any difference anyway . . .*

Some of the common themes found in stress talk include the following:

- **Exaggeration:** Using definitive words like always, never, and won't usually blows things out of proportion and exaggerates the incident. Things you say may feel true but probably aren't:

  He never listens . . .

- **Negative labels:** Taking a single action or behavior the person has done and putting a general negative label on it:

  He just doesn't have the guts to say "no" to difficult customers . . .

- **Negative outcomes:** Expecting the situation you're in to have a negative outcome and behaving as if the negative outcome is the only conclusion:

  There's no point in talking to him . . .

- **All or nothing attitude:** Looking at a situation as black or white or all or nothing:

  He should support any decision I make . . .

- **Eliminating the positive:** Ignoring all the positive aspects of the situation and focusing exclusively on the negative ones:

  It wouldn't make any difference . . .

Smart talk

Smart talk is constructive self-talk that helps you create less stress, live longer, and prosper. Your smart talk in the above situation may go something like this:

> *I'm really upset, but I know my manager was just trying to keep the customer happy. It must have been an awkward position for him to be in. It would've been difficult for me, too. I know that if I talk to him, we can work out a better way to handle this in the future. Since this doesn't happen all the time, there's no point in getting upset about it.*

Some of the common themes found in smart talk include the following:

- **Assuming good intentions:** Taking the point of view that whatever action the person took, whether it was good or bad, he did it with everyone's best intentions in mind:

  I know my manager was just trying to keep the customer happy . . .

- **Positive outcomes:** Expecting the situation you're in to have a positive outcome and behaving as if the positive outcome is the only conclusion:

  We can work out a better way to handle this in the future . . .

- **Focusing on the positive:** Seeing the positive aspects of the situation and including those in your self-talk:

  This doesn't happen all the time . . .

- **Seeing shades of gray:** Looking objectively at the situation from both points of view and seeing how each person is right in his or her own way:

  It must have been an awkward position for him to be in . . .

- **Empathizing:** Empathizing with the circumstances the other person is in, even if you don't agree with the outcome:

  It would've been difficult for me, too . . .

Chapter 16

Taking Initiative: Bouncing Back from Service Blunders

. . . .

In This Chapter

▶ Bouncing back from problems to keep your customers happy

▶ Spreading the goodwill to all from the get-go

. . . .

Service providers who show you unforgettable customer care are merely exercising the two kinds of initiatives that are needed to hang on to your old customers and gain new ones along the way.

We're talking in this chapter about the initiative needed to bounce back from those evil customer-service faux pas that plague many businesses and the simple act of goodwill, a commonsense service initiative that is top-of-the-line, the gold brand of service that goes beyond merely meeting your customers' expectations to exceeding them.

Taking the Bounce-Back Initiative

How you handle a problem situation with a customer can make the difference in whether she decides to use your company again. When you make a mistake with a customer, *bounce-back initiative* helps you (and your company) recover any respect, confidence, or faith that has been lost by your actions. Situations that require bouncing back often are the result of simple mistakes or oversights that hurt the customers' perception of your company. For example:

- ✔ The chef cooks your steak well-done instead of rare, the way you ordered it.

- ✔ Your car isn't ready by the time the auto shop said it would be.

- ✔ You're assessed a late charge on a bill that you paid on time.

- ✔ You have to wait for more than an hour at the doctor's office.

Satisfying the seemingly satisfied customer

Karen thinks most department stores do a pretty mediocre job of service these days. Having to hunt down the clerk, tie him up, and teach him how to use the cash register isn't unusual. So when she gets the kind of service she recently received, she is blown away!

While shopping at a local mall where the two main department stores are on either end of the building, Karen went to the first department store and immediately found what she was looking for: the perfect belt, in the perfect color, but wouldn't you know it, in the wrong size. Karen asked the salesperson whether the store had any more of the belts in stock in the back. She said "no" and added that the only belts like the one Karen was looking for already were on the sales floor. Disappointed, Karen turned to leave. "Wait a minute," the salesperson said. "Let me call some of our other stores to find out if they have that belt in stock." Karen thought that was nice of her. She came back a few minutes later

and said she had had no luck locating the belt. When Karen turned to leave again, the salesperson said, "Hold on, let me call the buying office and see whether they can get the belt from the manufacturer." Karen thought this offer was exceptional. Once again, she came back and said, "No luck." Finally, Karen turned to leave, satisfied that this woman had gone beyond the call of duty and done everything she could for her. "Don't leave yet," she said. "I think they carry this line of belts across the mall at the other department store. I'll go over on my lunch hour and see if I can find one for you. I'll call you later to let you know." What? Was Karen still on planet earth? She felt as if she were in the movie *Miracle on 34th Street* where Santa Claus sends the customers from Macy's to Gimble's.

Although extreme, this example of initiative proved to Karen that going out of your way for the customer creates a powerful and lasting impression.

When these types of incidents happen, the service provider needs to promptly bounce back by taking three specific steps and getting the customer back on his or her side.

Bouncing back in three easy steps

Imagine it's Monday, and a customer is on the phone screaming at you because the special order he was supposed to receive Friday still hasn't arrived. Simple enough to resolve this problem — you think. You'll just send his order by overnight delivery, and the disgruntled customer will have it by Tuesday morning.

Although this action may quickly fix or correct the problem, it doesn't necessarily convince the customer to stay on your side. He may receive the order on Tuesday, but what impression will he keep in the back of his mind about the way your company does business? A fair assumption is that the customer is relieved to get the package on Tuesday but may be a little wary about any delivery promises your company makes in the future. That's why only taking corrective action is insufficient and doesn't demonstrate initiative on its own.

You need to complete three key steps to help the disgruntled customer feel good about doing business with you in the future.

Step 1: Say you're sorry

Saying you're sorry is so simple, yet it's often overlooked. When standing in front of an upset customer, an apology can calm the fires of wrath. Apologize even if you're not the person who made the mistake, because a customer relates to you as representing the company that messed up.

Don't be stingy with apologies. Remember that an apology isn't an automatic admission of guilt. For example, if you're talking to a sick friend, you most likely say how sorry you are. Both of you know that the illness is not your fault, but you can still be sorry that your friend is having such an unpleasant experience. Apologizing is a way of letting the customer know that you care and want to right the wrong.

Some staff members resist the idea of apologizing to customers because they don't want to make the company look bad by admitting the mistake. This thinking is false logic, because customers already believe that you (or the company) blew it. Denials just agitate them more and make them even angrier.

Everyone knows that sometimes the customer is downright wrong. But, really, what difference does it make whether the customer is right or wrong? Your job as a service provider is to make customers feel valued and important and to solve their problems. Too many companies spend too much time trying to figure out who is at fault — who cares? The solution ultimately comes down to fixing the problem, not assigning blame.

Recovering from two bounce-back problems

Two distinct types of service problems require bounce-back initiative:

✔ **Predictable problems:** Some examples of predictable problems include running out of stock, misunderstanding a customer's request, and computer or technology breakdowns. These problems can happen as long as you're in business, but to a large degree, you can plan for them.

✔ **Surprise problems:** These problems are unique to the situation, the client, and your business. They aren't predictable and therefore you can't really plan for them. These instances are situations in which the service provider who uses initiative can save the day.

One way you can help to encourage members of your staff to take bounce-back initiative in your department is to meet with them to discuss predictable service breakdowns and come up with plans for how to deal with them.

Step 2: Fix the problem

This step requires you to listen to the customer's assessment of the problem. When she explains the situation from her perspective, your job is to fully absorb what she's saying about her unique set of circumstances. After you identify the customer's problem, the next step obviously is to fix it. Sometimes you can easily remedy the situation by changing an invoice, redoing an order, waiving or refunding charges, or replacing a defective product. At other times, fixing the problem is more complex because the damage or mistake cannot simply be repaired. In those instances, mutually acceptable compromises need to be reached. Whatever the problem, this step begins to remedy the situation and gives the customer what she needs to resolve the source of the conflict.

Don't waste time and effort by putting the cart before the horse and trying to fix the wrong problem. Jumping the gun and thinking that you know what the customer is about to say is an easy trap to fall into, because you think you've heard it all a hundred times before. Doing so, however, loses you ground on the recovery front and further annoys the customer. More often than not, what you think the problem is at first glance is different from what it becomes upon closer examination.

Step 3: Give the customer a care token

Many service providers miss the opportunity to score really big points after they've fixed the problem. They need to take one last, but critical step: giving the customer a care token. A *care token* is a specific action that you take as a way of letting customers know that you consider the mistake you made (whatever it is) unacceptable, that it won't happen again, and that you care about keeping their business. Care tokens say so much, and we're frankly surprised that companies seem so stingy with them. Here are a few examples of care tokens that responsible companies can offer:

- ✔ An airline gives you a $25 certificate off your next flight, because it didn't board enough meals and you were unable to eat (for some people this problem is a blessing in disguise).

- ✔ A restaurant buys you a glass of wine because you don't like the way your meal was prepared.

- ✔ The garage gives you a loaner car because your car isn't fixed on time.

- ✔ The one-hour photo shop gives you a free roll of film when it takes longer than an hour to process your holiday snapshots.

- ✔ The service provider who gives you her name and direct phone number.

What the care token costs is not important. It certainly doesn't have to be expensive, but it does have to show, in a tangible way, that you're sorry.

Bounce-back initiative is only effective when your basic services are in order and working. Customers find bounce-back initiative unacceptable when it replaces competent and expected services.

For example, a new copy shop recently opened near coauthor Keith Bailey's office. Modern and full of new, streamlined, state-of-the-art copiers, he just couldn't wait to use them. The first time he went over, he waited 45 minutes to be served because of a shortage of trained staff. They bounced back by apologizing, explaining the situation, and giving Keith a care-token coupon that was worth 100 free copies. Okay, he thought, fair enough, they're new and getting their act together, no big deal. A week later, Keith went back and waited 30 minutes for service. They apologized, explained the situation, and gave him a coupon for 100 free copies. This time Keith was a little less understanding. Two weeks later, he went back, and the same thing happened again. Keith didn't want another free coupon! The copy shop had bounced back once too often! Keith's opinion of its service was so soured that he began looking for another to have his copies made.

What have you done for me lately?

Taking initiative is most effective when it adds value to the customer experience by going above and beyond the core services your company provides. Some airlines, for example, think that they are giving you great service when they deliver you to your destination in one piece! This kind of service is only the ticket into the game. It isn't initiative because it's a fundamental expectation that all customers have about all airlines. Therefore, it's a basic core service.

Core services are not static, and they change with time. New innovations and ideas that your company adopts to show initiative today eventually are copied by your competitors and become so widespread that the customer begins to consider them normal core services

that no longer separate your business from the crowd. Some examples include:

- Hairdryers and TV remotes in hotel rooms
- Power windows in cars
- Frequent buyer or traveler programs
- 800 numbers for catalogs or other mail-order products
- ATM machines at supermarkets, gas stations, and so on

Companies that stay on the cutting edge of customer service always take a leadership role by looking for ways to improve their own services rather than playing catch-up with their competitors.

Understanding when to bounce back

Recovering from service blunders and breakdowns is not only about knowing how to bounce back but also when. Although we can't tell you every potential situation in which you may need to bounce back, at least five basic service breakdowns for which bounce-back initiative is critical occur when:

- A deadline is missed.
- An order is incorrectly filled.
- The customer is treated rudely or unprofessionally.
- The customer is given incorrect information.
- The customer is unhappy with the product or service.

Recovering from a missed deadline

When you fail to deliver your goods or services by the expected time, the result is more than likely going to be an upset customer. Situations include:

- Being late for appointments with your customer (and not calling)
- Giving a specific date or window of time for a service to be delivered and not meeting it
- Promising delivery of a product by a certain date and not meeting the deadline
- Telling your customer he will be on hold for only a few minutes and returning to the phone 30 minutes later
- Telling the customer you will call her back tomorrow and not calling back until the day after tomorrow, if ever

The closer to the agreed upon deadline that you cancel, the more upset your customer will be. The reverse is also true: The farther away from the deadline time you cancel, the less upset your customer will be.

For example, if you call at noon to let your customer know that you will be late for your 4 p.m. appointment, he will react differently than if you call at 3:59 p.m. to tell him you'll be an hour late.

Fixing an incorrectly filled order

When a customer places an order (for a meal in a restaurant, goods from a mail-order catalog, and so on) she has a natural and understandable expectation to receive exactly what she ordered. If, upon delivery, the customer's expectations aren't met, she may be upset because she is

✔ Disappointed about not receiving what she expected.

✔ Inconvenienced by having to return the wrong item.

✔ Forced to waste more time waiting for the correct order to be redelivered.

Changing rude or unprofessional treatment of a customer

The roots of rude or unprofessional treatment of a customer are poor communication and the customer's negative perception of the way he is treated by one or more service providers. Some typical situations include:

✔ Being put on hold abruptly and without any choice in the matter

✔ Arguing with a customer

✔ Not returning phone calls

✔ Accusing a customer of doing something wrong or lying

✔ Ignoring a customer

Correcting incorrect customer information

Your customers rely on you for accurate information. Even little mistakes can cause the customer big problems. Imagine the following scenario: You receive a letter from the IRS stating that your tax return is inaccurate and inconsistent with its records. The IRS is demanding an explanation with accompanying paperwork. You call your accountant who says he must look into the matter. He calls you back and explains that he made a mistake and accidentally omitted an important document from your return. Without bounce-back initiative, your faith in your accountant may diminish to the point of desertion. As customers, we have very little tolerance for inaccuracies from professionals whose sole job it is to eliminate them. The same is also true of internal customers; co-workers expect a consistent level of professionalism and competency from us. If they don't receive it, a weak link is created in the customer chain. Other examples that often require bounce-back initiative are

✔ Wrong or poor directions on how to reach your place of business

✔ Mistaken invoicing, billing, and so on

✔ Incorrect dates or times for specific events

✔ Incorrect information about company policy or procedure

Soothing the unhappy customer

Perception is everything. If, in the customer's mind, she has been wronged by your company, it's up to you to do what you can to fix it. Situations in which a customer feels wronged may not be fair, but life is tough, and the reality of your customer service exists only in your customers' perception of it. If a customer is unhappy with your product or service, bouncing back works much better than excuses, reasons, and hard-luck stories.

Bounce-back classics

The following list shows some key ways that you can go the extra mile with your customer when taking bounce-back initiative.

- **Giveaways:** Giveaways usually involve, you guessed it, giving away items, goods, or services that were incorrect or messed up to start with.

- **Discounting:** Because of a service failure, the company gives a customer a coupon authorizing a discount (usually anywhere from 10 to 25 percent) on his or her next purchase. This policy helps ensure that the company will have a repeat customer.

- **Absorption of extra costs:** When mistakes result in inconvenience to the customer, any extra cost involved in putting things right as soon as possible need to be absorbed by your company.

  For example, the refund check that the customer was promised by Tuesday did not arrive, so you offer to send it by overnight courier at no cost to the customer.

- **Personal touch:** In this situation, calling works much better than writing because it's more immediate and enables you to follow up faster. Calling a customer after a service breakdown has occurred helps ensure that the problem has been completely resolved to the customer's satisfaction and that no other action is required. This personal touch helps reestablish your company's credibility while confirming your sincere concern about the problem being resolved.

Defining Service Heroism: Goodwill

Every once in a while, if you're lucky, you may have the good fortune of being on the receiving end of something we call service heroism — the goodwill initiative. Although the term may evoke images of an overnight delivery courier pushing through waist-deep snow to deliver a package by 10:30 a.m., in reality service heroism is often one person going out of his or her way to make the customer's life easier.

Service heroism has a *wow quality* to it. When customers experience it, they say, "Wow!"

On one of Keith's many visits to the San Francisco airport, he checked in at the airline club desk. Without realizing it, he left some important documents on the countertop. Later that evening, he was ripping his luggage open looking for the documents. Of course, they were nowhere to be found. So he did what he usually does when he's being resourceful; he called his wife. She calmly informed him that the airline-club counter agent who had checked him in had noticed the documents, seen his name on them, looked up his records in the membership files, and called his home number to let somebody know that the documents were safe. The agent also confirmed that she had Keith's correct address and mailed the documents to him so that he received them the next day. Wow!

The power of goodwill

At one time or another, you've had a service person take initiative and show such exceptional customer care that you couldn't wait to tell your friends and family about it. As customers, you remember the companies that go the extra mile on your behalf or take the extra step to ensure that you are delighted with the service you receive.

The difference between good service (which, in our opinion, is not so easy to find) and "I-can't-believe-I'm-still-on-this-planet" excellent service is the amount of goodwill initiative you take. It's the service person's willingness and ability to provide customers with something they can appreciate and don't expect.

Goodwill initiative is only as good as the goodwill with which it is given. Going into your local bank and being thrown a free ball point pen by a grouchy, impolite, and impatient teller just doesn't cut the mustard, especially when the message on the barrel of the pen reads: "The bank that cares." About what? That's what we want to know.

We were consulting with a company that had conducted a survey of its customers and had received a good rating for the quality of service it provided. A short while later, the company lost about a third of its customer base to a new competitor. Confused and concerned about why it had lost so many customers, the company conducted another survey, but this time lost customers were queried, and the response the company received was pretty much unanimous:

> Your service is good, but your competitor's is excellent.

The lesson the company learned was that good customer service is not necessarily enough in a tough market. Goodwill initiative helped the newly arrived competitor elevate its service beyond good to excellent.

Develop a goodwill mind-set

Consider these simple acts of goodwill initiative:

- ✓ The cab driver who gets out of the taxi and goes around to open the door for you

- ✓ The store clerk who offers to let you use the store's phone instead of the pay phone

- ✓ The local computer consultant who calls back a week after he sets up your computer system to make sure that everything is working okay

- ✓ The salesman at the car dealership who calls you one month after you purchase your new car to see whether you need anything

- ✓ The hair salon that sends you a greeting card each year on your birthday

- ✓ The restaurant that provides free valet parking

- ✓ The gas station attendant who washes your windows, even though you're in the self-serve lane

- ✓ The dry cleaner who puts a little tag on your shirt or blouse informing you that she has replaced a button or two as part of the store's complimentary service

All of these examples have one quality in common: They reflect initiative that is taken out of pure goodwill toward the customer.

The service provider or company isn't required to take the action. Instead, it is extra, unasked for, and has a pleasing impact on the customer. Unfortunately, this type of goodwill is usually reserved for the holidays when you expect to get free calendars and other giveaways that show a company's appreciation of your patronage. Although these efforts are praiseworthy, goodwill initiative has less of an impact at that time of the year, because they are more common and therefore more predictable. Goodwill initiative has the most impact when it is unexpected.

Chapter 17

The Gift of the Gaffe: Dealing with Customer Complaints

In This Chapter

▶ Understanding how customer complaints can improve your service

▶ Exploring ways to calm angry customers

*O*ne of the things that can drive customers to the brink of hysteria (or more importantly, into a competitor's arms) is the feeling that they have no outlet for communicating their frustrations to a company that has, in their minds, done them wrong.

One study conducted by the Technical Assistance Research Program, Inc., (TARP) found that:

- Customers who have a problem with a product or service voice their objection to the company directly 50 percent of the time. Nine out of ten of these customers usually take their future business elsewhere.

- Customers who do voice a complaint to the company aren't thoroughly satisfied with the company's effort to resolve the situation 50 percent of the time. These dissatisfied customers tell, on average, between seven to nine other people about their unsatisfactory experience with the company.

With statistics like these, which show the relationship between the customers' unhappiness with service and their taking their business elsewhere, you can't afford to take the issue of customer complaints lightly. Knowing how to deal with customer complaints is an essential part of offering excellent customer service.

The eight principles and practices in this chapter help you craft an approach to dealing with complaints that encourages your customers to communicate with you and assures them that you'll take quick and reasonable actions to resolve their problems and concerns.

Viewing Complaints as Gifts

Even though customer complaints can, at times, be stressful and challenging, they're really a gift. If you're willing to open your mind and listen, complaints can prove to be a great source of information, innovation, and inspiration. They can help you do the following:

- ✔ Gain valuable ideas for new products or services.
- ✔ Recover a customer who may otherwise have decided to go elsewhere.
- ✔ Fix problems that could be frustrating to other customers and could cause them to leave.
- ✔ Gain a lifelong customer, if you resolve the complaint quickly and efficiently.
- ✔ Discover problems that you didn't know existed.

Don't think of a complaint as just another problem taking up your time and energy. Think beyond that and teach yourself, and the rest of your company, to view customer complaints as valuable opportunities to learn from your customers and to improve your business.

Make It Easy for Your Customers to Complain

The TARP study, which is mentioned earlier, concludes that the three primary reasons customers fail to register their complaints are

- ✔ They believe it isn't worth their time.
- ✔ They don't know who to complain to.
- ✔ They feel that complaining produces no results.

You can minimize the frustration your customers may experience by creating (and introducing to your customers) a specific company complaint policy that, in detail, spells out

- ✔ How customers can contact you when they have a complaint or problem.
- ✔ Where in your organization a customer can make specific complaints.
- ✔ Who's responsible for dealing with different types of complaints.

Remember that the goal is to make communicating with you easy — even if your customers are only communicating to tell you about problems. Don't frustrate, confuse, and annoy your customers by making them chase person after person, from department to department, to get their complaints resolved.

Complaints come in all forms

Most complaints your company receives come in one of four packages: letters, e-mail, face-to-face contact, and phone calls. An effective complaint policy takes all complaints seriously and responds according to the gravity of the complaint instead of by the method it was received.

✔ **Letters:** Complaint letters are considered by customers to be an official record of their grievance. If for no other reason than making it easy for your customers to send you a complaint letter, your address should always be listed clearly on your Web site. The upside of complaint letters is that they give you, as the company, the time and opportunity to reflect on the problem, take steps to resolve it, and get back to the customer with a response and, hopefully, a resolution.

✔ **E-mail:** E-mail has become one of the most commonly used methods for customer complaints. However, because it still remains a more informal communication medium, customers usually use e-mail to voice their displeasure regarding smaller, less significant problems. The downside of e-mail complaints is that the customer expects that your company will respond quickly, usually within 24 to 48 hours. Your company e-mail policy and procedures should include quick response times to all e-mail inquires and complaints received via your Web site.

✔ **Face-to-face contact:** In brick and mortar businesses such as retail shops, restaurants, hotels, and so on, face-to-face communication is the most common form for customer complaints. These interactions are often the most challenging for front line staff since the customer's emotion is front and center, not to mention in the service provider's face. Off-handed comments, such as "I always have problems with your company" or "Could you guys make this any harder" or "Come on, I don't have all day" are general in nature and may not reflect a particular circumstance, but instead a general dissatisfaction. By teaching your employees to not only apologize when they hear these types of comments but also to probe for more details and pass on what they're hearing to management, current problems can be corrected and future problems prevented.

✔ **Phone calls:** Similar to the face-to-face complaint, phone calls are an immediate expression of dissatisfaction on the customer's part. Usually complaints made by phone are less serious than those that require a letter, but they nonetheless impact the customer's experience of doing business with your company. Many customers prefer speaking to a real, live person about their problem, rather than sending an e-mail or letter. For this reason, it's critical to list a company phone number on your Web site. Don't compound an existing problem by making it difficult for your customers to locate your phone number. The downside to phone call complaints is that you must either solve the problem on the spot, which isn't always possible, or call the customer back, which delays the resolution of the problem.

Identifying the Elements of the Complaint

In order to resolve a customer's complaint, you need to make sure you understand exactly what's contributing to the dissatisfaction. Even though this isn't the complete list (you'll find hundreds, if not thousands, of ways that customers' expectations aren't met), the following are the most common elements found in customer complaints:

- Billing mistakes
- Complicated or confusing product or service instructions
- Delays in delivery of goods or services
- Failure to fulfill product or service warranties
- Failure to provide refunds and adjustments as promised
- Incompetent or discourteous employees
- Incorrect or misleading information
- Misleading advertising
- Misleading statements by sales staff
- Order filled incorrectly
- Poor quality repair work
- Product or service not performing as promised
- Products are back-ordered or unavailable
- Unfriendly user interface

Don't waste your effort (and your customers' time) trying to fix the wrong problem. Assuming that you know what a customer's problem is within the first few sentences of the dialogue is easy — you've probably heard it all a hundred times before. Often, however, the problem changes or becomes unique upon closer examination.

Thanking Your Customers for Complaining

Most complaining customers don't expect to be greeted with sincere and heartfelt appreciation. Yet, a simple thank-you is one way to let your customers know that you appreciate the time and effort they've taken to inform you about a problem with your company's service or product.

In addition to simply expressing thanks for the complaint, let your customers know why or in what way their complaints have contributed to your business. For example, you may want to say

Thanks for your suggestion. It'll help us improve this process in the future.

Thank you for giving us a chance to resolve the problem and keep you as a customer.

I appreciate your bringing this to my attention so that we can correct the problem.

I appreciate your telling me this because it helps me do my job better.

Sincerely Apologizing for All Problems

Nothing extinguishes the fires of wrath like a well-timed, sincere apology. Simple enough, right? Yet, many workers resist the idea of apologizing to customers because they don't want to make the company or themselves look bad by admitting a mistake. The problem with this logic is that upset customers already believe that you (or the company) have made a mistake! Strongly professed denials or refusals to apologize just cause more aggravation.

A few guidelines for apologizing to customers include the following:

- **Don't be stingy with apologies.** An apology isn't an automatic admission of guilt. Instead, it's a way of letting the customer know that you care and want to right any wrong that has been done.

- **Apologize even if you're not the person who made the mistake.** Remember that your customer thinks of you as a representative of the company. She takes your apology as a corporate mea culpa, not a personal one.

- **Apologize even if the customer is wrong.** Say something like, "I'm sorry you're having a problem." What difference does it really make if the customer is right or wrong? Don't waste time trying to figure out who's at fault in a situation. You need to fix the problem, not assign blame.

- **Time your apology carefully.** Don't use your apology as a preemptive strike by making it the first thing you say to an upset customer. Instead, give customers time to provide the necessary details so that you can make your apology more personal and specific to their circumstances.

Fixing the Problem

Fixing your customer's problem requires an understanding of the elements of the complaint and of your customer's unique perspective on the situation.

After you accurately identify the factual part of a problem and your customer's point of view, the next step, obviously, is to fix it. Often, you can quickly remedy the situation by changing an invoice, redoing an order, waiving or refunding charges, or replacing a defective product.

Other times, however, fixing the problem is more complex. The damage or mistake can't simply be undone. In these instances, you have to reach mutually acceptable compromises. Any solution you come up with should take into account any of the following issues that apply:

- ✔ Contractual commitments you've made or warranties that may be in place

- ✔ Your customer's expectations and any promises you've made to the customer

- ✔ The possible cost of all the potential solutions

- ✔ The value of this customer to your business and the probability of losing the customer's future business

- ✔ What a fair and reasonable action to resolve the problem would be

- ✔ The chances that the problem will get larger if not fixed immediately

- ✔ Your ability to deliver on the chosen solution

You won't always be able to resolve an issue immediately. In such cases, offering a realistic time frame for resolution is important. You should explain why the delay is necessary and what steps you're taking toward resolution.

Practicing Prevention

The information you gather from customer complaints can provide your company with a valuable source of process-improvement opportunities. In order to capture this information and make sure that you're using it to prevent future problems from occurring, create a formal procedure for recording all incoming customer complaints. The information you record should include

- ✔ The date of the complaint

- ✔ The name of the person who made the complaint

- ✔ The nature of the complaint

- ✔ Specific details relating to the complaint

- ✔ The actions taken to resolve the complaint

- ✔ The follow-up contacts made

Over time, management or an employee task team can analyze complaint logs to determine patterns, trends, and root causes of recurring problems. In addition, complaint logs allow managers to check the system by making sure that complaints are being handled quickly, fairly, and to the customer's satisfaction.

Following Up

After you've resolved a customer's complaint, call or e-mail the customer to bring closure to the situation. This follow-up contact ensures that the problem has been completely resolved to the customer's satisfaction and confirms that no further action is required. This personal touch also helps reestablish your company's credibility while reinforcing your sincere hope that the problem has been resolved.

Part V

Working in a Wired World: Customer Service on the Web

The 5th Wave   By Rich Tennant

"I like getting complaint letters by e-mail. It's easier to delete than to shred."

In this part . . .

1 t seems like only yesterday that e-mail, e-commerce, and Web sites were new ideas that really didn't affect everyday relationships with our customers. Today, even those of you in the deepest technological denial realize that the online world is a vital part of offering responsive service.

In this part of the book, we explore the nitty-gritty of how you can use e-mail and the Internet to better serve your customers and improve communication with your co-workers and staff. We provide you with specific techniques and tools for making your e-mails effective and elegant and for designing your Web site so that it's Web-wise and customer-friendly.

Chapter 18

Clicking with Your Customers: Online Content and Commerce

In This Chapter

▶ Attracting visitors to your Web site

▶ Encouraging visitors to make purchases at your site

▶ Creating an online community via your company's Web site

*I*ndustry pundits, Web marketers, and Internet gurus alike agree that after you develop a strategy for pointing customers to your Web site (see Chapter 21 for the various ways of optimizing the "findability" of your site or pick up a copy of *Search Engine Optimization For Dummies,* by Peter Kent [Wiley]), getting them to come back more frequently and to stay longer when they do are keys to success on the Internet. This goal of increasing the overall amount of time and attention that visitors give to your site often is referred to as making your site *stickier* (think of flies stuck on flypaper). Of course, the longer and more often your customers spend time on your site, the better the chances are that they'll buy something. We agree with most experts that the key to making your site stickier is focusing on the quantity and quality of information you provide and the ease with which you enable visitors to make purchases on your site.

Content: Giving People a Reason to Visit Your Site

Given the vast amount of Web sites out there, what can you do to inspire a Web surfer to spend time (in a sense, develop a relationship) with your site? One answer is to make sure that you have free, useful, and relevant content. Remember that the Internet originally was a vehicle for scientists and academics to freely share ideas, theories, and findings with each other. And although e-commerce is a growing part of the Web, the culture of the Internet still values the sharing of information and emphasizes the "for free" aspect of this sharing. You can add value to your site by featuring many of the useful forms of content that we discuss in this section.

White papers

Although *white papers* traditionally refers to reports produced by governments, today it's a generic term used to define a five- to ten-page document that expounds on an industry issue such as: "Making your call center more profitable" or "The five fallacies of modern management." By writing a not-too-detailed essay that provides compelling information you add a valuable reason for visiting your site. Sites that offer white papers usually headline a descriptive paragraph and then require registration for accessing the complete document. White papers target a specific demographic — those interested in your subject — so while registration is usually free, capturing your visitors' names and contact information is invaluable for future marketing follow up.

How-to articles

You can empower your customers by presenting how-to articles that identify common tasks and offer concrete methods to accomplish them. Including how-to articles on your Web site does the following:

- ✔ Provides value to your customers by giving them relevant and valuable information in small, bite-sized chunks
- ✔ Establishes your company as an expert in its field and, as such, increases your customers' comfort level when buying from you

The more up-to-date the content on your site, the better. When you regularly add to or update the content on your site, your customers come to know you as a source of consistently current and helpful information. They keep coming back to see what's new and improved.

Relevant links and resources

Links on your Web site to other companies or sources of information that complement your business add value and convenience to your site, and your customer will recognize that. You can extend the boundaries of your service by anticipating what additional products or services your customers are likely to need and then providing online links to companies that offer those goods or services. If you're running a photography Web site, for example, you may want to include links to photo retailers, photography associations, photography book links with an online bookseller, and so on.

Make sure that the links you provide direct your customers to sites you know and trust. Customers commonly view links as endorsements.

Online tools

The content on your site isn't limited to passive print; you can also provide your visitors with an online tool as part of the content offering. Examples include

- Questionnaires
- Surveys
- Tests
- Industry-specific calculators (for example, a Web tool that calculates mortgage payments)
- Real-time stock quotes
- Syndicated news

You can check out an online tool by logging on to our Web site at www.scg training.com. Just click on "Quality Service Audit" and take an interactive audit that evaluates how customer-focused your organization is and then, based on your score, provides recommended actions.

Advice

If your company has a particular area of expertise or specific information you want to share with your customers, try adding an advice section to your site. Having advice on your site can be as simple as offering a FAQ (Frequently Asked Questions) section, where you post and answer typical questions a visitor may have. FAQ pages can be frustrating if the visitor doesn't find the answer they're looking for, so by necessity the section must also offer an email address for posting such questions, along with a specific time frame by when the question will be answered.

E-mail newsletter

One of the best ways to provide valuable information to your customers and, at the same time, promote the commerce side of your business is to create an e-mail newsletter. Among other things, the newsletter can include

✔ Feature stories about your customers and how they use your products and services

✔ How-to articles written by your company's employees and designed to empower newsletter recipients

✔ Articles by guest writers on topics relevant to your business, its products, and your customers' interests. (You can create an arrangement in which writers contribute to your newsletter in exchange for your listing their Web addresses.)

Make sure that you archive all your past newsletters on your site; someone's bound to want to read them. Set up a system by which visitors can search previous newsletters using keywords to find what they're looking for.

Live interview or Web-cast event

A great way to attract people to your site and provide them with interesting and useful information is to offer a *live interview,* which is the equivalent of a text-based Q&A session presented in real time. Your Web site plays host to the interview, which is set for a specific date and time and features a guest who is of interest to your audience. A moderator facilitates questions from the online audience.

Alternatively, you can offer a *Web-cast event,* which is more like a live lecture. Web casts are set up much like a live interview, but they have the added features of audio and/or video and often are accompanied by synchronized PowerPoint slide presentations. Interviews and Web casts can be presented either live or prerecorded and made available on demand.

Commerce: Making It Easy for Your Customers to Buy

The obvious first step toward e-commerce glory is getting your product ready to sell and your technology up and running so that you enable customers to buy from you. Although numerous issues are related to conducting commerce on your Web site, we've discovered that the nine items presented in this section form a good foundation for providing your customers with the confidence needed to make purchases from your company. Just follow our advice in this section, and you'll be far ahead of many e-commerce sites.

Make it safe

Even simple e-commerce transactions require buyers to provide a great deal of personal information, including their name, address, phone number, and billing data. Naturally, many consumers are a bit leery about giving this information over the Internet. You can go a long way toward making your customers feel safe in purchasing from you by:

- ✔ Using credit-card data encryption
- ✔ Maintaining all customer-provided data as confidential (in other words, not selling it!)
- ✔ Giving customers the choice of keeping their credit-card data on file at your site — or not

Make it convenient

If your purchasing processes aren't quick and easy, you run the risk of not only losing the sale, but potentially losing the customer.

Make your purchase processes as easy as possible by:

- ✔ Asking your customers to provide you with only the data that's needed to fill their order
- ✔ Not making customers enter the same information into the system more than once
- ✔ Allowing your customers a means of easily updating their information on your system, a feature that can save customers significant hassle on subsequent visits to your site

After you collect your customer's information, make sure you remember who each one is the next time any of them visit your site. A couple of good examples of this technology are `my.yahoo.com` and `Amazon.com`.

Confirm order status

When customers place orders over the Internet, they expect an immediate confirmation, either at the end of the order process itself or by e-mail immediately afterward. To avoid confusion, mistakes, and problems down the line, order confirmations need to include

- ✔ A list of the items that were ordered
- ✔ The total cost of the order, including shipping and handling
- ✔ The address to which the order will be delivered
- ✔ The date the order will be shipped (if backordered, the expected date of shipment)
- ✔ Tracking information (usually via a link to the shipper's Web site)

If a customer orders a product that has a long lead time or is backordered, e-mailing her weekly updates to keep her apprised of the situation is a good idea. Alternatively, you can provide your customers with a Web link to check the status of their own orders.

Make suggestions

Internet customers have come to expect Web sites to suggest products and services that may be of interest to them based upon their specific buying patterns. For example, Amazon.com offers its customers a section under each book listing called "Customers who bought this book also bought." It lists other, related books the customer may want to purchase. This type of suggestive selling is ideally suited for the Web because it gives customers information about what's available, yet allows them to choose whether to click through.

Offer financial incentives

Consider the success of warehouse and outlet stores in general. Everyone loves a bargain! One strategy for encouraging customers to buy from you online is to offer a variety of financial incentives that are available through purchase only via your Web site. You'll need to experiment to find out which ones work best for your type of business. Some of the incentives to try include

- ✔ **Lowering online prices.** Offer your online customers a lower price than they'd get when purchasing through one of your other distribution channels (phone order, mail-order, or retail). You may want to explain to customers that when they order online, your costs are reduced, and you're able to pass those savings along to the customer in the form of lower prices.

- ✔ **Limiting the offer time.** Send an e-mail notification to your customer list alerting customers to a special, limited-time offer. Advertise it on your home page, too. The offer can be a "special of the week," a coupon good for a certain amount off of the customer's next purchase, a gift with purchase, or free shipping and handling. The key to this incentive is to be absolutely clear that the offer is valid for a limited time only.

✔ **Establishing a bonus program.** A bonus program is based on the idea that every time a customer makes a purchase from you, she racks up points toward a future discount, free merchandise, or a bonus gift. To encourage participation, offer free bonus points just for signing up. After your customers establish an account, they're more likely to come to your site and buy your products.

List recent projects

You can help your customers determine whether your business has what they need and want by posting a "Recent Projects" section on your Web site. The aim of this section is to demonstrate your company's capabilities to potential clients. This section needs to list three to six of your past projects in chronological order. Make each project description no more than a paragraph and include the following elements:

✔ Client name or type of company

✔ Dates of the project

✔ General project description

✔ Results of project

A sample paragraph may look like this:

> *April, 2006: We worked with a large national bank to design and implement a customer-relations training program for all 40,000 of its staff and managers. The program focused on teaching day-to-day customer-relations skills that the employees could use with customers face to face, over e-mail, and on the phone. Topics included: Dealing with difficult customers, creating rapport via e-mail, team-oriented problem solving, etc. The coordinating management program helped managers understand how to create a day-to-day environment for service excellence with a focus on creating a specific plan for improving service within their work areas. Evaluations of the program averaged 4.5 on a 5.0 scale.*

Get permission to use your client's name in association with a particular project before posting it as part of a Recent Projects or other online reference tool. If doing so proves too difficult, you can substitute a general reference to your client's type of business, size, or industry category for the actual company name.

Post testimonials

Nothing is more powerful than a well-placed quote from a satisfied client. Give visitors to your site the option of clicking onto a page or two of testimonials from current and past clients. Knowing what other customers say about you helps to influence a potential buyer's decision to purchase from you. Testimonials need to be short and sweet — no more than three to four sentences — and must be attributed to the name, company, and title of the person giving the quote. As always, get permission before posting the quote on your Web site.

Provide customer lists

Although you don't need to include a complete list of every customer you have ever had, a customer list can inspire confidence in potential buyers whenever they see that others in their industry or well-known companies have made purchases from you. You can arrange your customer lists alphabetically or by industry, depending on what best suits your type of business. You may actually want to give visitors to your Web site some sorting options (alphabetically, by industry, by size, and so on), so they can check you out according to their preferences.

Always make sure that you have permission from your customers before adding them to your online customer list.

Show samples of your work

If possible, showcase a sample of your work on your Web site. By all means, toot your own horn! For example:

- ✔ If you're a photographer, try posting a stunning example of your work.
- ✔ If you're a public speaker, use streaming video and audio of you delivering a speech.
- ✔ If you're a creative writer, provide a sample of your writing.
- ✔ If you're a building contractor, display photos of completed projects (maybe before and after shots).
- ✔ If you're a Web developer, post a link to a Web site you've designed.
- ✔ If you're a landscape architect, show a rendering of a landscape plan you've designed.

If your business has recently won an award or been the subject of positive publicity, post that information on your Web site. Anything that makes your company appear more competent, trustworthy, and knowledgeable in a customer's eyes is worth putting on your Web site.

Encouraging People to Share Ideas about Your Company

Think of the last trip you made to a mall near your home on a sunny day. You probably were browsing for the perfect gift for a friend, communing with your fellow citizens, and sipping a Starbucks coffee — ahhhh . . . all was right with the world.

Okay, perhaps we've gone a bit too far. But the point is that today's mall is more than just a collection of stores selling everything from shoes to stereo systems. The shopping mall has become an icon of interactivity, a place for us to meet and greet others in our community. In the online world, your Web site has the potential of becoming an electronic community, a gathering place your customers will want to visit again and again.

Consider the success of America Online, which started out as a service provider of value-added information and only brought online shopping into the picture later, after it had a strong community of users already in place. The bottom line is that the greater the sense of community you can create on your site and the more you can tailor your offerings to a specific topic, lifestyle, age, or social group, the stronger the customer relationships you will be able to establish with your visitors.

Although you may find the idea of adding community features to your site overwhelming, in reality all it takes is utilizing just a few relatively simple tools.

Message boards

Also called *forums* or *bulletin boards, message boards* enable your visitors to post and reply to messages on various topics. Thus large numbers of your visitors can have conversations that take place over a period of time (days, weeks, months, or longer). One of the advantages of this type of community activity is that people don't have to be online at the same time to interact with one another.

Putting a message board on your Web site also presents you with an opportunity to understand how your customers perceive your company. By reviewing the content of these discussions, which remain posted on the board, you can find out a great deal about your visitors' interests and concerns. This information helps you identify significant issues and pass useful knowledge on to your customer base.

Blogs

A *blog* (short for Weblog) is a personal journal that expresses the opinions and ideas of the author or *blogger*. Usually a blog hosted on a Web site supports and reflects the purpose of the Web site. There are blogs on every subject you can imagine, from pets to politics, and the blogging pages of a Web site are created with a user-friendly interface so that typing in new entries is easy and requires no technical expertise. The interactive aspect of blogging invites site visitors to add their comments and opinions so that in-depth discussions can go on for days or weeks, with the blogs being updated daily. Blogs add a dynamic element to a Web site because they foster a virtual community of people who are interested in similar issues.

Broadcast e-mail lists

The simplest of all community-building methods, *e-mail lists* (formerly called *LISTSERVES*) are similar to traditional mailing lists in that your correspondences are sent simultaneously to everyone on your list — but they require no postage or printing. You can encourage users who have subscribed to your e-mail list to visit your Web site by sending regular information about what your company is doing, special offers, or any other information your customers may find valuable. Unlike *open e-mail lists* where anyone can post a message, *broadcast e-mail lists* are one way, and only the host company publishes and sends the e-mails.

Chapter 19

Making Your Web Site Shine with Site Design

*T*he nature of your customers' online interactions with your company plays an important role in the overall success of your site, the reputation of your company, and the strength of your online brand. If your online customer finds herself confused and frustrated, you've undercut all your other efforts. Underneath the jazzy graphics, clever *URL* (that's your Web site address that usually begins with www), and marketing hype lies the crux of the matter: You're not just creating a Web site, you're creating a customer experience.

If you're anything like us, you may have good ideas about what your site should look and feel like, but you have no idea how to actually produce it. What you need is a *Web developer*. Web developers are those brave souls who spend each day in the depths of digital design and who produce Web sites that are (we hope) user-friendly from aesthetic and technical points of view. In short, your Web developer can make your online presence magical. However, if you're not careful when choosing a Web developer, he can make your presence much less than desirable.

In this chapter we walk you through three key steps to finding the right Web developer for your company — someone who fits with your company culture, can provide the expertise you need, and is able to work within your budget. We also provide you with tips for how to outshine your competitors' Web sites. Finally, after all that hard work, you want to make sure that people actually find your site, so we give you some pointers for doing just that.

Determining Your Web Site Goals

Before you log on to the Internet, begin thumbing through the yellow pages or call your local graphic design firm to look for potential Web developers. Also, spend some time thinking about what you specifically want to achieve with your site. Some questions you may want to ask yourself include the following:

- ✔ What is the purpose of this Web site?
- ✔ Who is the target audience for this site?
- ✔ What are the long-term goals for this site?
- ✔ What are the short-term goals for this site?
- ✔ What is the scope of this particular project?

The more specific the information is that you provide a Web developer, the more accurate an estimate the developer can give you of the time and cost involved in achieving your site goals. Beyond determining what your main objective is, you should be prepared to answer these questions before you speak with a Web developer:

- ✔ Do you already have a domain name or do you need to register one?
- ✔ What specific products or services will be sold on the site?
- ✔ Who do you have in mind to host the site?
- ✔ How do you plan to maintain and update the site?
- ✔ Do you have company literature that can be used on the site?
- ✔ How sophisticated a design do you want for the site? (For example, do you want text, animation, audio, or video, or a combination of them all?)
- ✔ Are you planning to include interactive features, such as feedback and response forms?
- ✔ What special technologies will you need to meet your goals? (For example, shopping carts, databases, or animation?)
- ✔ What is your budget for site creation, maintenance, and marketing?
- ✔ Are you planning to accept payments over the site?

To stay within your budget and avoid any financial surprises we strongly recommend sketching out a site map. By planning ahead and estimating the overall number of pages your site needs, you'll create a flowchart that represents the structure of your site by showing the main content categories and subcategories you plan to include. Planning the details and having a grasp on how the pages relate to one another will save frustration, time, and money.

Exploring Ways to Reach Your Goals

Now that you know what your site goals are, before sitting down to interview potential Web developers, you need to decide how you want to divide up the work of the project. For example:

✔ What aspects do you want to hire a Web developer to handle? For example they can secure your Web site name; manage the overall site development; perform regular updates of Web content, and so on.

✔ What parts of the project will go to other vendors such as graphic artists who might design your logo; develop the overall look and feel of each page; copywriters who take your ideas and create compelling copy, or simply spruce up your written material or they may edit contributions that you gather from other sources such as other publications, professional organizations and so on.

✔ What role do you want your existing staff to play? For example you might ask your staff to collect customer testimonials that you publish on your site, or contribute how-to articles or submit a list of the FAQs (Frequently Asked Questions) that they receive from customers.

Using specialists for each part of your Web design will rack up the costs of development. If you don't want to overtax your budget, consider limiting the number of pages and finding a Web developer that shows skill in both technical and design abilities.

A Web developer can contribute to your site development project by doing the following:

✔ Setting up all the technology necessary to achieve your site goals.

✔ Designing, implementing, and maintaining all aspects of your site.

✔ Advising you on ways to implement plans you've already begun to draft.

✔ Converting materials, such as brochures, product descriptions, and testimonials, to *HTML* (or, for those who really want to know, Hypertext Markup Language, which is the programming language used on the Web).

✔ Creating an overall graphic style that represents your business. Or, a developer can transfer your established graphic image to your new Web environment.

Print designers who have limited experience with Web development often make the mistake of thinking that anything they produce in print will easily translate to the Web. They don't realize the limitations of the HTML environment.

For this reason, it's a good idea to hire a graphic designer for general direction, but then supplement that person with a Web designer. Working together, the graphic designer and the Web designer should

- ✔ Develop graphics that are bandwidth friendly.
- ✔ Create interfaces that are user friendly.
- ✔ Design layouts that recognize HTML limitations.

Engaging the Right Web Developer

You know your objectives, you have a budget in place, and you have the thumbs up from management. It's finally time to take the big leap and hire a Web site developer. What now? The questions race through your frenzied brain, which was stimulated by that triple espresso you downed at lunch. Where do I find a Web site developer? How much will it cost to develop my site? How can I make sure they'll do a good job? The questions go on and on.

Unfortunately, many companies don't put the same care, concern, and attention to detail into choosing a Web developer that they would into hiring a graphic designer to create their annual report or an accountant to handle their books. To make matters even more complex, the job description of a Web developer is constantly evolving. This uncertainty makes determining who they should hire to develop their site even more difficult for the average businessperson.

The job of putting together a Web site is complex and involves a variety of skills. For this reason, Web developers often have a group of other experts available to work for them either as employees or on a subcontract basis. To avoid having to find and hire a separate contributors, look for a Web development firm that has working relationships with graphic designers, HTML programmers, database programmers, and others who can work together to form a Web development team that can get your job done with the quality you expect.

If you're looking to develop a site that is relatively simple and small, you can probably find all the capabilities you need in a *solo practitioner,* which is a person who can develop your site without a large support team and has a decent skill level in the full spectrum of technical and artistic requirements. If your site is going to be mid-sized and offer more bells and whistles, a small *Web shop* (a company whose business is creating Web sites) can, more than likely, take care of your needs. In general, the advantage of a hiring a solo practitioner or a small Web shop is that your site gets developed by the people you spoke with when you were making the decision of who to hire. Solo practitioners, after all, can't really delegate the job to someone else!

If you're looking to develop a large and highly complex site that uses leading-edge technology, you may need to hire a major Web development firm. The advantage of hiring a large firm is that it employs large numbers of highly-specialized staff members who are available to work on your site.

Regardless of which way you decide to go, certain criteria exist that you can use to evaluate potential Web developers, whether they are solo practitioners, small Web shops, or large Web development firms. The following sections pave your way to finding the perfect Web developer for your company.

Technical competence

Ask the developers to describe specific projects they've worked on that incorporate the type of technology you expect to use in your site. For example, if your site is going to be animation heavy, take a look at Web sites that the developers have already created to make sure that they've had prior experience incorporating animation that has the quality you expect. Other technological issues to look for on sites that the developers have created include the following:

- ✔ Clear site navigation
- ✔ Innovative storytelling
- ✔ Appropriate mix of media (audio, video, text, and so on)

In today's rapidly-changing business environment, technical competence requires constant updating. Be sure to ask the Web developers what kinds of continuing education they participate in. They should have some method to stay on top of the latest technological bells and whistles in Web site development.

Creative style

In general, you should feel that the sites the developer has created previously are attractive and are to your taste, in terms of overall look and graphics. Ask the developer to provide you with a few sites it has created so that you can review them for overall design quality. If you don't see design concepts that you like, chances are you have incompatible design tastes. Move on and find another developer.

Ongoing maintenance capabilities

One of the biggest complaints clients have about working with Web developers is that, after the site is up and running, getting the developer to promptly make changes is difficult. One reason for this difficulty is that some developers are strictly in the business of creating the initial site and aren't interested in or capable of offering ongoing maintenance. Although hiring one company to do the site development and another to do the maintenance is a perfectly acceptable and common alternative, you want to know beforehand where you stand, in terms of maintenance, with the particular Web developer. Communicating in advance insures that expectations are clear and prevents future problems and frustrations.

Communication skills

Because they've focused most of their attention on honing their technical expertise, many people who develop sites are a whiz at programming — but are weak in their interpersonal communication skills. Since the Web developer needs to work hand in hand with you and others, pay attention to how the person communicates in the interview stage. In addition, you may want to call the developer's references and inquire about the following:

✔ Was the person's general manner helpful and customer-focused?

✔ Was the person cooperative in working with others?

✔ Did he provide periodic updates on the project's progress?

✔ Did he communicate when a problem occurred?

✔ Did he let you know if he was going to miss a deadline?

Professional conduct

Because a Web developer is often made privy to the most intimate aspects of your business, including client lists, pricing structure, marketing strategies, and so on, you need to feel confident that the developer does the following:

✔ Keeps the details of your business confidential.

✔ Avoids putting herself in a position where a conflict of interest between you and any of her other clients exists.

Many firms ask the Web developer to sign a nondisclosure agreement. Speaking with the Web developer and specifically asking her to tell you if she's currently working with, or has immediate plans to work with, any client where a conflict of interests may exist with your business is a good idea. Dealing with these issues upfront is an important step in establishing a professional relationship with the Web developer. It also helps prevent misunderstandings and problems farther down the line.

For the protection of all the parties involved, always get a contract — in writing — prior to the beginning of work. It doesn't matter how great the rapport is between you and your developer. Having a contract protects the developer and ensures that you get what you pay for. Among other items, the contract should spell out the project scope, technologies to be used, deadlines, fee arrangements, and payment schedules. You can find generic or boilerplate contracts that will probably fit your needs in *Business Contracts Kit For Dummies,* by Richard D. Harroch (Wiley).

References and credentials

One of the great things about the Internet is that it's given birth to an array of new jobs, including the Web developer. The downside of this boom is that virtually anyone, regardless of their background or qualifications, can hang a sign outside his door to declare himself a Web designer. For example, a graphic artist who may be great at designing print brochures, but who may have no technical knowledge on implementing an e-commerce site, can still declare himself a Web developer! Likewise, a technical-type person with outstanding programming skills may decide to go into the Web development business even though he has no sense of how color and design should be used.

Checking the credentials and references of any potential Web developer is critically important to ensure that the person you hire has the skills necessary to complete the job to your satisfaction. Some issues to consider when considering a developer include the following:

- ✔ **Has the developer done this type of Web site before?** Is this person qualified, given the goals of your project and the various services you need (including graphics, writing, and technology)? Ask the Web developer to provide you with examples of Web sites (and the addresses) she has designed that are similar to the type of site you're looking to create.

- ✔ **Does this person have any industry or software certifications?** Even though being certified doesn't guarantee that the Web developer is able to get the job done, certification is a good place to start in evaluating the person's knowledge base. However, keep in mind that many top-of-the-line Web developers have no certification, but still deliver a high-quality job based on their practical experience and the knowledge gained from self-education.

- ✔ **How long has the developer been in the business?** The more experience a developer has, the more professional, effective, and unique your Web site will be. Look for someone who has a minimum of three to five years of Web development experience. Remember that the fewer years of experience a developer has, the more likely she will be to use templates from an off-the-shelf program. Even though a novice developer may only cost you a few hundred dollars, she could leave you with a mediocre site that could cost you thousands of dollars in lost business.

✔ **What do the developer's references have to say about her?** As old fashioned as it may seem, one of the best ways to determine the credibility of a Web developer is to call a few of her clients and ask how their project went. Getting the information straight from the horse's mouth can be invaluable. Don't limit your questions to the person's technical capabilities. To get the big picture, focus your questions on the creative and interpersonal aspects of the reference-giver's relationship with the developer. Consider asking the following questions:

- How easy was it to do business with the developer?

- Did she take a collaborative approach or was she very opinionated and difficult to deal with?

- How well did she follow through on what she promised?

- Did she get work done on time?

A good source of information on Web developers is the International Webmasters Association (`www.iwanet.org`). Among other services, it offers referrals to resources in your area, certification programs, and up-to-date information and developments in the field of Web development.

Polishing Your Web Site to Outshine Your Competitors

Your Web developer (or you, if you are technically inclined) should know how to polish your site so that it outshines the competitors. The following sections show the many ways to ensure that your site is pleasing to your potential (and current) customers.

Make site navigation easy

To search any Web site effectively, a customer needs to use a *navigation system,* a clearly labeled set of buttons that directs them to different parts of the particular Web site they're exploring. The navigation system you and your Web developer establish for your company's Web site is what enables your customers to find the information they're looking for. On the other hand, a poor navigation system may only frustrate the customers in their attempts to find that information.

Because you want your site to be as customer-friendly as possible, you need to make exploring the various pages on your Web site as easy as possible. Creative and original design, although aesthetically valuable, is less important than organizing your site in a way that enables visitors to find their way around quickly and easily.

When designing a navigation system for your site, make sure that the site architecture answers more questions than it raises. If you and your Web developer don't create clear and easy-to-use site navigation, most visitors will become frustrated and leave. Here are some factors to consider when evaluating your existing site design or deciding on the method that customers will use when navigating a new site:

- ✔ **Provide visual feedback so users know where they are.** If you highlight and reinforce your site's section names so that users who come to your site know exactly what section of the site they're currently exploring, you greatly improve your site's accessibility.

- ✔ **Make the site's section names easy to understand.** Because the goal is to make navigating through your site a no-brainer, logical names are more important than cleverness.

- ✔ **Keep navigation buttons consistent from page to page.** Presenting the same navigation system on every page increases your customers' comfort. Consistency and repetition in the navigation elements prevents your customers from having to search for the buttons on each page.

- ✔ **Make site navigation self-explanatory.** The best navigation systems require no thought. For example, the "Products" button takes you to a page that describes the company's products, and the "Company Information" button takes you to information about the company. Ask yourself whether a typical 10-year-old could easily navigate the site. If not, the navigation system is probably too complicated.

- ✔ **Use a variety of navigation elements.** Simple links, graphic icons, navigation buttons, fancy graphics, photos, and plain old text can all be used in navigating a site. Use a combination of these elements so that your customers can go to any section of the site they're interested in and easily find their way back to the home page.

- ✔ **Group together the navigation buttons that lead to the main parts of your site.** Site navigation buttons that send the customer to the main parts of your page should be grouped together. Don't spread them all over the page. They can be placed either at the top, bottom, or side of the page, as long as they're together. In general, finding these buttons is easiest if they're placed vertically on the left side of the page.

- ✔ **Give customers a textual description of what the links on your site provide.** Placing a short sentence underneath each link makes finding what they want easy for the customers because they understand what pages the links connect to.

Answer their questions before they even ask

After so many years in business, you know the questions that your customers or potential customers are most likely to ask. Create a *Frequently Asked Questions* (FAQ) section on your Web site that clearly states, then answers, these questions.

If you include a FAQ section, it's a good idea to have an e-mail link on the same page for those people who can't find an answer to their question. The link opens up an e-mail page that allows the customer to write to you with his problem and get an answer back. The e-mail link reduces some of the frustration customers feel when they can't find what they want.

Hit a home run with your home page

Have you ever visited a Web site and, after a few minutes of looking around, realized that you had no idea what the heck the site was about? The number of sites, especially those of small- and medium-sized businesses, that leave visitors scratching their heads and wondering, "What do these people do?" is amazing — even though a mystifying site is a clear violation of all the rules you learned in Business 101. Make sure that your home page clearly states the business you're in and the types of products and services you offer. Within a few seconds, your visitor should know exactly what your site is about and should have received the main message that you're trying to get across.

Offer something for free

"Free" is one of the words that has defined the culture of the Internet from the beginning. Even though the Internet is a hotbed of commercial activity, the attraction of going to a site and finding something for free is still deeply ingrained in the online culture and a big part of what brings visitors to your site.

One of the best and most popular giveaways you can offer is relevant, clear, and useful information in the form of white papers, articles, and company newsletters. Your strategy for service on the Internet should include offering enough information and services for free that you become a bookmark destination for your current and potential customers.

Make your downloads fast

Look around at the hurried pace of today's business world and you'll see that your customers have neither the time nor the patience to wait for anything — not in line at the bank, on hold on the phone, or for the Web pages on your site to download. Consider these facts:

- ✔ The majority of Web pages take anywhere from 3 to 11 seconds to download.
- ✔ The average viewer will click off a site if a page takes more than eight seconds to download.
- ✔ These click-offs (bailouts when users get tired of waiting and click away from a slow Web page) cost e-businesses an estimated $4.35 billion annually in lost revenue.

Speed does make a difference. You can reduce your customer bailout rate from 30 percent to 8 percent just by reducing your download time by one second per page! Remember that if your site is slow, your customers will go.

To decrease the download time of your pages, avoid over-designing the site with too many fancy graphics. In general, photos and graphics with large file sizes take a long time to download.

Begin with high-quality, professional photos, and instead of simply scanning them, try using a photo-editing software program, such as Adobe Photoshop, to compress the image so that the file size is small enough to load quickly. Be aware that compression may reduce the quality of the image somewhat. We suggest using a professional Web page designer who can help you strike the delicate balance between speed and quality.

Offer contact options

Many of the business owners and executives who attend our seminars have told us that customers often see something on their company's Web site that they're interested in, and then want to contact the company to ask a question or to place an order. The philosophy, "Do business with your customers the way they want to do business with you," is one of the principles behind excellent service. In other words, you need to make sure that your Web site has an easy to find "Contact Us" link on the home page. Because some customers won't be accessing your site through the front door, you may want to post your contact information on all the pages within your site.

Many companies provide too little detailed contact information, limit the contact information to only an e-mail address, or provide no contact information at all. Your contact section should provide all the possible options for contacting your company, including phone number, street address, fax, and e-mail.

Don't limit your customers to one method of contacting you, such as e-mail. Instead of only one method, give customers all the options and let them choose how they want to contact you. Providing a variety of contact options makes you look more like an established business and less like a fly-by-night company. Providing multiple contact options makes it look like you actually *want* customers to contact you and reflects your company's dedication to excellent customer service

Use multiple media

Imagine receiving a brochure from two different companies on the same day. One is all text, and the other is a combination of words and images. Which would seem more interesting to you? Create a more dynamic and interactive online experience for your customers by using animation, video, and audio files to enhance the text on your Web site.

As the saying goes, "A picture paints a thousand words." In the online world, pictures can give your customers a feel for who you are and the kind of business you're in. Think about what types of pictures you could put on your site that would help your customers get a better understanding of your business. You could include a picture of yourself, your entire team, or your products.

Video and audio clips are two effective ways to introduce yourself and your company to your customers. These clips give customers a taste of what you're offering and add value to your site. However, be careful that these video and audio files don't take too long to load. You could also include an interactive media tool, such as a self-scoring questionnaire, to provide value to your customers by helping them evaluate some aspect of their business or to identify a business need (that your business could fulfill) in some relevant way. For example, a flooring manufacturer might win customers by providing questions that ask them where they plan to use the flooring, the amount of traffic it will get, and so on and then use the answers they enter to direct them to the floor covering it carries that is most suitable for their needs.

Update your site often

After their Web sites are up and running, business owners too often sit down, put their feet up on their desks, wipe their brows, and exclaim with relief,

"Whew, I'm glad that's done!" Unfortunately, getting your Web site up and running is just the beginning of the process of maintaining quality online service. If you want your customers to consider your site a valuable destination, you have to make constant updates.

Visitors are always looking for fresh and new information. In addition to the basics, such as updating your contact information if it changes, removing time-sensitive material, and updating current specials, you can create a "What's New" section and update it daily, weekly, or monthly, as appropriate.

Keep your site design simple and clean

Hundreds of books, magazine articles, and Web sites have addressed the serious business of Web site design. Unfortunately, many businesses don't seem to be paying attention to this important concept. In their attempts to be unique and to use cutting-edge technology, they've created Web site design disasters by jamming their sites full of:

- Busy backgrounds
- Hard-to-read fonts
- Too many buttons
- Jumping, twirling, and spinning animations

Resist the temptation to clutter up your Web site. If you opt for a simple and clean layout, you'll have a Web site that's well designed, interesting, and customer focused. Here are a few tips to keep in mind:

- Although one well-placed *banner* (those little commercial billboards you see on so many Web sites) isn't hard on the eyes, imagine a Web page that has three banners, four Amazon buttons, and a variety of links all competing for attention. You risk making your site look busy, confusing, and unprofessional when you include too many of these banners.

- A nice, clean background on your site makes text easier to read, looks more professional, and is less distracting than a busy background with some wild pattern that reminds browsers of the bathroom wallpaper they grew up looking at. When choosing your site background, stick with a basic color that's consistent with the image you want your company to portray.

- Graphics make a site visually appealing but, if overused, can leave a poor impression. Remember that your customers (and potential customers) don't like to wait for graphics to download. Make sure that any graphics are compressed enough to download quickly.

Practice e-mail excellence

Most of the e-mails you send to customers will probably be responses to their queries. Don't underestimate the impact your e-mail responses have on your customers' perception of the service they receive.

Try these four simple, yet effective, ways to ensure that your e-mail creates goodwill and a positive service experience for your customers:

- **Be timely.** The sooner you get back to your customer, the better. However, a general rule is to return all e-mail inquiries within 24 hours. If you don't have the information the customer needs within this time, you may want to consider using an automated response system. These systems respond to incoming e-mails with a note saying that the e-mail was received and is being dealt with. This note acts to fill the gap until you can get back to your customer with the necessary information.

- **Personalize your response.** One of the best ways to add a human touch to your e-mail responses is to use the customer's name in the greeting. Too often, e-mails to customers are impersonal and cold. Although it may seem like a small thing, consider how differently you would feel if you received an e-mail response that began with "Dear Ms. Smith" (assuming that you're a Ms. Smith) than one that started "To Whom It May Concern" or that had no greeting at all.

- **Refer to the original e-mail.** Keep in mind that not only do you receive hundreds of e-mails a day from your customers, but that your customers also send countless e-mails each day. When you respond, make it easy for your customers to remember their question by including or referring specifically to their original question, comment, or problem. If appropriate, you may want to include the text from their original e-mail. This extra effort on your part saves your customers time and shows that you're really paying attention.

Allowing Customers to Find Your Site

The repeated message in the movie *Field of Dreams* is "if you build it, they will come." Although this message may be true of a baseball field, the same is decidedly untrue of a Web site. The reality is that even if you build the Eiffel Tower of Web sites — a shining example of design and interactivity — you won't get the online traffic you're hoping for if people aren't aware that your site exists or don't know how to find it.

In order to maximize your Web site, you must create an overall plan for promoting your site that compels current and potential customers to visit you online. First, determine who you're trying to attract by asking yourself the following questions:

✔ What audience are we trying to reach?

✔ Who would benefit most from visiting our site?

✔ Who do we have the best chance of selling our services and products to?

After you know who your target audience is, the next step is to determine how you're going to reach them. Following are three of the best ways to reach your audience:

✔ Getting listed with search engines

✔ Establishing beneficial links with other Web sites

✔ Creating a public relations campaign that showcases your Web site

In the following sections, we show you what you need to know to list your site with search engines, to maximize the number of hits your site receives, and to establish link exchanges to increase traffic at your site.

Getting listed with search engines

Visitors access your Web site one of three ways: They can type in your Web address on a browser, open your Web site via a bookmark, or find your site on a *search engine,* which is a site, such as Google, where customers enter a word or two that describes what they are searching for and then presents them with a list of relevant sites. Search engines are only one method of attracting visitors to your site, but they're critically important. A few of the myriad of benefits of getting listed with a search engine are as follows:

✔ Most search engines list your site for free.

✔ Search engines make it easier for your current customers to find you.

✔ Search engines bring new customers to your site.

Submit the following information to each individual search engine that you want to list your site:

✔ Company name

✔ Nature of your business

✔ Web site address

✔ Some key words describing your business

Following are the four main ways to do so.

Manual submission

You can manually submit your Web site address, as well as specific information for each separate Web page you have, to the individual search engines of your choice. You can find out from the search engine companies exactly what they need. It usually includes the following:

- Web page titles
- Web site title
- Key words regarding XXX
- A 10-word description of your business
- A 25-word description of your business
- A 50-word description of your business
- Your company's name, address, e-mail, phone, and fax numbers

A search engine is likely to refuse to list your site if you don't provide all the information it requests in exactly the format that it wants. It also may not list your site if your site isn't active enough or, in some cases, if the search engine doesn't like the way your site looks.

Paid submission services

If you have more money than time and you don't want to go through the submission process yourself, you can pay someone else to do it. One advantage of paid submission services is that they allow you to focus on the content of your Web site, while the submission service takes care of the promotional work of listing your site with search engines.

Search engine consultants

One result of the Internet is the creation of never-before-heard-of job titles, such as *search engine consultant*. Unlike most submission services, these consultants offer a personal service by analyzing your site and using their expertise to get your site listed and, for a fee, they can help you:

- Evaluate your site.
- Design an overall search engine campaign.
- Design key words and content to attract visitors to your site.
- Suggest ways to get high rankings.
- Maximize every file in search engine submission forms.
- Submit your site to a targeted list of search engines.
- Make multiple submissions for individual pages of your site.

If you use a paid consultant, you have access to a professional who can look over your key words and titles and recommend ways to achieve a higher placement within the search engines. The common goal is to get your site listed on the first page of search results because most people never click past it. The ultimate goal is to have your listing be the first result presented — or at least within the top five — which allows you to attract to your site the greatest number of visitors possible. However, if your budget doesn't stretch to paying experts there are other, less expensive options.

Submission software

An alternative to the other submission methods is to purchase one of the software packages available on the market today that help you with search engine submissions. Some of these products are better than others, so you need to do some research to find the best one. Basically, the software works like a submission service – without the fee. Using submissions software can save you time, but be aware that most of them don't allow you to customize your submissions to gain higher rankings.

Achieving the highest possible ranking and position in search engine results

The average person accessing a search engine only looks at about 15 listings before she chooses one or move on. Getting your Web site listed with a search engine is only half the battle. The other half is getting it ranked as highly as possible in the search engine results. If you're not in the top 50 results that a user sees after she types in a search, the chances of new customers finding your site are slim to none. You should aim to be in the top 20.

We can't make any guarantees because the rules for ranking seem to change daily, but usually you can improve your placement by doing the following.

Selecting your words for maximum hits

A simple four-step strategy exists for choosing the best words to describe your site on the search engine submission forms. The strategy involves a bit of research, but the benefit of increased traffic on your site is well worth your time. You don't want to lose Web traffic because you didn't do your homework!

1. **Jot down a list of words and phrases you think your customers and potential customers are most likely to use when trying to find services and products that relate to the type of business you're in.**

2. **Enter these words into the top search engines to see what the top 10 to 20 sites are.**

3. **Go to each one of these sites and count the number of times that the words and phrases from the list you generated in Step 1 appear on the first page of that site.**

   In addition, view the source code of the page to see what title, key words, and descriptions have been used to achieve the high ranking.

4. **After you've seen which key words, when used repeatedly, are giving your competitors an upper hand in the rankings, check your own use of these words in your search engine submission forms and adjust your language as needed.**

In general, the more often a key word appears on your page, the higher any search engine is likely to rank your site. Be sure to repeat the key words and phrases that you have determined are the most valuable at least three or four times within the first 100 words of your page.

Monitoring the status of your position

Many individuals and companies simply submit their site to a search engine, do what they can to get a high ranking, and, with fingers crossed, hope for the best. But this mediocre strategy isn't good enough if you want to capture as much business as possible with your Web site. After you've gone to all the trouble of submitting your site — properly using all the techniques available to get you a high ranking — don't waste your hard work. Regularly check the status of your positions and work to improve them. This way, if your position starts to fall, you'll be able to catch it and fix it right away. You can and should stay on top of things by checking your ranking once every few months on each of the top search engines.

Even though you may have obtained a high ranking with a search engine when you first submitted your site, your position can slip over time because the Web is dynamic, and competitors, having the same goals as you, can displace you and push you further down the list. You'll occasionally be completely dropped from a search engine's database for no apparent reason. Since your position in the rankings determines how many people find your site, staying on top is as important as getting placed.

Maximizing your hits with link exchanges

Link exchanges are a good way to promote your site. A link exchange is a reciprocal agreement in which you and another site list each other on your respective Web pages. The beauty of a link exchange program is that you can select other companies with whom exchanging links would be a natural fit, mutually beneficial, and inexpensive to boot. Here we discuss the four steps involved with creating a link exchange program.

Step 1: Define your audience

In order to know which sites you could most beneficially link to, you need to identify your *target audience* — the people you want to attract to your site. Generate a list of what types of customers you want to reach, what types of Web sites they're likely to visit, and what related products and services they're likely to buy.

Step 2: Create a target list

After you know what types of sites your potential customers may visit, surf the Web to see what sites you may want to exchange links with. Come up with a target list of companies you plan to approach.

Let's say you own a company that sells baskets. You've just come out with a spiffy new kid-friendly bicycle basket made of titanium and available in hot pink, black, and the ever-popular chartreuse. Some, but certainly not all, of your natural link exchange partners include the following:

- ✔ A site belonging to the manufacturer of children's bicycles
- ✔ An online magazine for children's sports
- ✔ An online magazine for bicycle enthusiasts
- ✔ A site focusing on parenting
- ✔ A site dedicated to baskets

Step 3: Customize your contact

After narrowing your list of possible link exchange partners, send a customized e-mail message proposing the link. In order to avoid creating the impression that your message is *spam,* a message sent indiscriminately to a multitude of recipients, send your e-mail directly to the decision maker and make it easy for him to welcome your proposal by including the following information in your message:

- ✔ Your name and position
- ✔ Your company's name and the type of business you're in
- ✔ The types of customers you have
- ✔ The reason you think a link would be mutually beneficial (this information is the key!)
- ✔ Your contact information, including phone number and address
- ✔ A request that the person get back to you within a specific time range

Step 4: Decide where to place links

After you've agreed to exchange links, you need to negotiate the specific placement of your link on your partner's site and your partner's link on your site. Base your decision for determining link placement on traffic. Think of your Web site as real estate. Since your home page represents the most valuable real estate on your site, reserve that space for those links from which you receive the most traffic.

Pick your partners carefully

Any link exchange you establish reflects your company. The way your partner company does business can affect your customer's perception of you. Remember that visitors to a Web site assume that a link is an endorsement. Therefore, regardless of potential benefits, never link to a site that can hurt your reputation or credibility. Make sure that any partner company you link up with:

✔ Is reputable

✔ Has an interesting and well-designed site

✔ Provides useful and valuable information on its site

✔ Updates its site regularly

✔ Shares the business values that your company has

Because determining how much traffic a link will generate at the beginning of a partnership is almost impossible, we suggest that you establish a probation period with any new link exchange partner in order to test the benefits of the link and to determine future placement. If a link exchange isn't working out, a probation period allows you to get out gracefully.

If a company you exchange links with puts you on its home page, you do not need to place its link on your home page. Even if you decide that a link is worthy of occupying the prime real estate of your home page, it should be placed on the bottom of your page so that customers see your information first.

Since the goal is to have your customer stay at your site as long as possible, avoid putting too many links on your site, since doing so increases the chances that your customer will jump from your site to another, and may or may not come back.

Chapter 20

E-Mail Etiquette and Writing: Making the Most of the Medium

*T*ake your typical day at work. You arrive at the office by 9 a.m., turn on your computer, and pull up your "to do" list for the day. Some of the many things that you must accomplish during your typical workday include:

✔ Confirming the details of an upcoming business trip to China

✔ Informing a colleague about a schedule change that affects him or her

✔ Congratulating one of your teammates on closing a sale

✔ Running a few ideas by your staff members for their input regarding a service problem

In the business world of ten years ago, you probably would've dealt with at least some of these items with a phone call, a memo, or a face-to-face meeting. Today, however, chances are you'd probably handle most, if not all of these, by *electronic mail* (e-mail).

A recent survey of more than 850 companies by the ePolicy Institute found that more than 50 percent of employees surveyed reported that they spend between one and two hours each day on e-mail. Another 10 percent surveyed stated that they spend three to four hours a day.

Weighing E-Mail Pros and Cons

Although we aren't advocates of using e-mail to the point where it eclipses all other methods of communication, we do believe that in the hectic pace of today's business world, e-mail can be an invaluable tool for receiving and disseminating information quickly and easily. As with any communication technology though, the use of e-mail brings with it both pros and cons.

The pros of e-mail

Face it: Who hasn't been grateful at one time or another to be able to send an e-mail rather than pick up the phone or, worse still, get on a plane? Using e-mail provides customers with round-the-clock convenience and service while reducing costs and increasing productivity at work. For example, artificially intelligent, automated e-mail software enables businesses to process up to 1,000 e-mail queries a day from customers for as little as 25 cents per e-mail. Compare that amount with an estimated $2.75 per e-mail when answered manually by an individual service provider. Other advantages of e-mail include:

- It enables you to communicate with many people simultaneously, by using multiple addresses.
- It leaves a trail, so that the history of a conversation can be traced.
- It provides an easy reference to past communications.
- It doesn't require that your customers be available when you send them a message (a great benefit when working across time zones — you can accomplish things even while you sleep).
- It saves you time when you need to communicate with someone, but don't have time for small talk.
- It enables you to attach pertinent files that recipients can easily open (usually) without the delay involved with other mail delivery systems.

The cons of e-mail

Although e-mail has big upside potential, its use doesn't always mean that customers get better service or that communication is improved. E-mail communication, although convenient, doesn't always obey the rules of conversation. Electronic messages cannot convey your facial expressions, body language, tone of voice, or other clues to the real meaning of your words.

Consequently, e-mail communications are far more likely to be misinterpreted than if you were to have those same communications face-to-face. Some of the other perils to using e-mail as a main medium of communication in business are that it:

- ✔ Isn't the best medium for communicating certain emotional or highly charged issues

- ✔ Often is overused as a substitute for phone and in-person communications

- ✔ Isn't as secure, private, and confidential as people think

- ✔ Can be used in a court of law as evidence and increases company liability and risk

- ✔ Can be problematic when dealing with time-sensitive issues that require immediate responses

Recognizing real-world limitations of e-mail

Although e-mail provides a fast and convenient means of communication, it doesn't work well for all messages. Using e-mail most often is inappropriate:

✔ **When sending messages of a confidential nature.** Because e-mails are not private — in other words, they can be forwarded to the moon and back — don't use them for anything that is of a private nature. Have a face-to-face meeting or use the telephone for topics that are emotional or related to coaching or counseling an employee.

✔ **When sharing big news, such as a takeover by another company.** We once conducted an employee survey for a large company. The overriding feedback was that a lack of communication existed from top echelons down.

Executives defended themselves by stating that during the recent takeover by another company, they had sent monthly e-mails to staff members to keep everyone informed. The point these executives missed was that most employees want to hear important (potentially life-changing) news from a live person with whom they can interact and ask questions.

✔ **When dealing with time-sensitive issues.** Consider that most people don't check their e-mail as often as their voice mail when they're on the road and away from their desks. Urgent matters, especially when a customer needs a speedy response, need to be pursued via the telephone, although you can certainly send an e-mail as well.

✔ **When distressed customers need immediate problem resolution, or at least a sympathetic ear.** Sending an e-mail isn't as personal as engaging in a conversation. When dealing with matters that require empathy, understanding, and a resolution, you need to have a dialogue.

Testing Your E-Mail Etiquette

E-mail is ubiquitous and as such requires an established etiquette that helps ensure that good manners are the rule rather than the exception in cyberspace. The age-old idea behind etiquette, electronic or otherwise, is to show consideration for other people. The simplest way of doing just that is to ask yourself, "How would I feel if I received this message?" After you peruse the e-mail message that follows and answer this basic question, read through the ten most common e-mail mistakes that the sender makes and the "E-Mail Etiquette Solutions" section. Finally, think about whether you unwittingly commit any digital *faux pas* in your e-mail communications.

The following is an actual e-mail (with a little creative license taken by the authors) from an employee of a software firm to the company's accounting department regarding an expense report. Test your e-mail etiquette by seeing whether you can find the ten most common mistakes made in this posting.

```
To: actng.mny@lpa.com

From: peterrut@lpa.com

re: screw up

CC:  Jackie.colr@lpa.com

     Steve.bldr@lpa.com

     Molly.daut@lpa.com

     Aron.sn@lpa.com
```

I submitted my expense report last week and I stil don't have a check back : - (

I always have prolbems recieving my checks on time! I know that you have cutoff times and I usually make them, so I don't know what is happening?

I sthere any way that you could notify people when you do'nt process thier reports on time? CAN YOU CLARIFY EXACTLY HOW YOUR PROCESS WORKS? - as well as review the policy that you have regarding cutting checks after the standard cut off times? I'd like to get my check Fedexed to me by tomorrow. I realize that TNSTAAFL but there might be a better way to handle this!!!!!!! How do you process chekcs for direct depositi? Do you have the same cut off times? Can you process last week's expense report and get it into my Wells Fargo Account as soon as possible? I really don't want to have to wait an extra week on this if at all posssible. Please advise. Please don't just give me the typical RTFM accounting response.

ANECDOTE

Better etiquette = happier people

We were consulting with a well-known high-tech company, when the subject of e-mail arose. Much to our surprise, the group turned ugly at the mere mention of the topic. It turns out that poorly written e-mails had contributed to a hostile working environment between individuals and, in some cases, entire departments. We'd assumed that being high tech the company naturally would make its e-mails high touch. We were wrong. As is true with developing phone tone and writing winning letters, crafting effective e-mails is a learned skill. Even in an environment where folks should've known better, the rules of online excellence weren't clear and certainly not universally used.

We hope it's obvious that the author of the preceding e-mail didn't take the time to think about how his or her message was coming across to the reader. What impression did you have of the person who wrote this? If you received this message, would you want to go out of your way to help this person? Probably not. Although it's obvious that the general tone of the message is unfriendly, the sender has made ten common mistakes that are guaranteed to create a lukewarm response and possibly a quick tap of the reader's Delete key.

- ✔ **Mistake 1: Unclear subject line.** The subject line in this e-mail is simply titled "screw up." Not only does this title create a negative tone, but it also provides the reader with no idea of what the e-mail is about until the document is opened.

- ✔ **Mistake 2: A poor greeting or no greeting.** The writer makes no attempt to create rapport by greeting the reader. Instead he/she simply starts with a description of the problem. Not only is this unfriendly, but it also may put the reader on the defensive. A greeting is one of the few ways to convey "tone" through e-mail.

- ✔ **Mistake 3: Using abbreviations not commonly used or understood.** The writer has included two abbreviations that are not in common use by business people today. Using such hard-to-understand language is roughly the equivalent of sending an e-mail in English to someone who speaks only French! The possibilities for misunderstanding and misinterpretations abound. By the way, to see what the abbreviations mean, check out solutions section in the next section of the chapter.

- ✔ **Mistake 4: Unnecessary CC (carbon copy) of the posting.** The four people to whom the author has CCed the message more than likely have no real impact on solving the problem, and the copies are just a way for the author to cybergossip and vent his or her frustrations.

✔ **Mistake 5: Sloppy grammar, spelling, and punctuation.** By not taking the time to spell- or grammar-check his e-mail, the composer runs the risk of creating a negative online impression. Sloppy e-mails, especially those with flagrant misspellings, lower your credibility with the receiver.

✔ **Mistake 6: Uses all capital letters to make a point.** By using all caps in one of the sentences, the author basically is throwing an online hissy fit. In the digital community, putting all or part of your e-mail in capital letters is equivalent to shouting and yelling.

✔ **Mistake 7: No closing or sign-off.** In the same way that the sender uses no introductory salutation or greeting to set a friendly tone upfront, he or she also omitted a closing or sign-off to end the posting on a positive note.

✔ **Mistake 8: Difficult to read.** The run-on sentences, repeated points, and absence of paragraph formatting make it obvious that the author isn't concerned with making his e-mail user-friendly. Instead, the message rambles on, reflecting no respect for the reader's time or ease of understanding.

✔ **Mistake 9: Unfriendly tone.** The tone of this e-mail is accusing and hostile. Because the reader immediately is put on the defensive, the likelihood of a helpful response is about the same as Larry Ellison and Bill Gates going on vacation together.

✔ **Mistake 10: Lack of a clear request.** What does the author of this e-mail really want from the accounting department? Because this message is full of so many questions and requests, the person reading it will be hard-pressed to figure out which actions need to be taken to best satisfy the sender. E-mails are either requests for actions or FYIs. Let your reader know upfront which one it is.

E-Mail Etiquette Solutions

The ten mistakes described in the preceding section can all be corrected and avoided by following basic rules of e-mail etiquette. In this section, we discuss each of these rules and how to carry them out.

Providing a context

Picture this question being asked over the phone or during a meeting: "When can I get the fourth-quarter report? I know it was scheduled to be out yesterday."

Myriad different vocal tones, facial expressions, and hand gestures help convey the context and meaning behind the question.

Now imagine checking your e-mail inbox and seeing this same sentence pop up on your computer screen. Without body language and tone of voice, vital signals are removed from the message, increasing the potential for misunderstanding, miscommunication, and hurt feelings. Keeping that in mind, here are some ways of providing a context for your e-mails that help your reader accurately interpret the meaning of your message.

When in doubt, ask. If the context of a specific message isn't clear to you, send it back and ask for clarification. This solution is by far better than proceeding on what can be a mistaken assumption that creates more problems.

Setting a tone

How would you interpret the importance and significance of each of the following?

- ✔ A co-worker writes you a sticky note and posts it on your desk while you're out to lunch.
- ✔ A memo is distributed to your department from company headquarters.
- ✔ A formal letter is sent to you from the president's office.

Chances are that the form in which these messages arrived gave you a clue as to the importance of the communication. E-mail messages, on the other hand, all look alike! You can't tell by the format the intended level of significance or importance. By going beyond the straight presentation of the facts and adding tone to the message, you can help your reader distinguish whether your communication is a formal request, a casual inquiry, or a firm instruction.

If letterhead and precise formatting are important parts of conveying your message, consider creating the document in your word processing program and then adding it as an attachment to your e-mail cover introduction.

Using a specific subject line

One easy way to establish the context of your message is to write a subject line with a few well-chosen words that provide the reader with a clue to what you're writing about. Avoid writing generic subject lines such as:

- ✔ Re: Problem
- ✔ Re: Report
- ✔ Re: Request

You can help the reader understand the bigger picture of your message by referencing any related e-mail to which you're responding or taking a few lines upfront to explain the reason for your message.

Saying it with electronic emotion

One disadvantage of e-mail is that feelings you're normally able to get across in person or by phone are more difficult to express in the colder medium of electronic mail. Because emotions add flavor to your conversations at work, finding a way to integrate them into your e-mails is essential.

Emoticons

One quick-and-easy way to add feeling or tone to your e-mails is to use what are popularly referred to as emoticons or smileys. *Emoticons* (a hip word if ever we heard one) are just that — icons that express emotions. Some are useful, some are bizarre, and a few convince you that some people just have too much time on their hands.

Because this book is rated PG, we won't go into the racier emoticons that we've seen, but here are some of the more commonly used ones:

: -) The smile is the most popular symbol used in e-mail today. It represents humor or pleasure and is made by a colon symbol, followed by a dash, followed by a right parenthesis. As in:

```
What I especially liked about this morning's meeting
was the muffins :-)
```

: - (The frown is the second most popular of emoticons and is used to conveys sadness or disappointment. It is made by a colon symbol, followed by a dash, followed by a left parenthesis. As in:

```
I wish Alexis had been able to make the meeting today
:-(
```

Too many emoticons spoil the soup. Avoid the tendency to be overly cute in your e-mail messages by peppering them with an overabundance of emoticons — especially in more formal business communications, where misused or overused emoticons trivialize the power of your message and make you look unprofessional.

Bracketed expressions

Another useful way to express emotion in your electronic communication is through the use of bracketed expressions. These are feelings put in angle brackets at the end of a sentence; they generally leave less room for misunderstanding than emoticons because the actual feeling is being specified rather than represented in picture form. For example:

```
I think we should proceed slowly on this agreement
<apprehension>.
```

Minimizing abbreviations

Because e-mail culture leans toward brevity rather than length, abbreviations are popular in this medium. Messages that rely too much on acronyms to get their ideas across can confuse and annoy your reader. Use acronyms sparingly and try to stick to the ones that already are commonly used — like the ones in Table 22-1.

Table 22-1	Commonly Used E-mail Acronym Abbreviations
Abbreviation	*What It Means*
FAQ	Frequently asked question
FYI	For your information
BTW	By the way
IMO	In my opinion
WYSIWYG	What you see is what you get
AKA	Also known as
CYA	Cover your assets

Respecting the reader's time

Survey after survey shows that people in the workplace have more work to do and less time to do it than ever before. Remember that when you send an e-mail, you are, in a sense, contributing to this work overload by requiring your co-workers or customers to take the time to read and answer your message. By following the guidelines provided here, you can compose better e-mails and show more respect for your reader's time.

Exploring the true meaning of TNSTAAFL

You're probably saying to yourself, what the heck does that mean? That's what we wanted to know, so we went searching the Internet until we found it. Here goes . . . . There's no such thing as a free lunch. Hundreds of abbreviations are out there on the Net, and some of them are understood only by members of the ISDN (International Society of Dweebs and Nerds). Here are a few:

Abbreviation	What It Means
ROTFL	Rolling on the floor laughing
IMHO	In my humble opinion
IMNSHO	In my not so humble opinion
RTFM	Read the blankety-blank manual
YMMV	Your mileage may vary
LOL	Laughing out loud
ITRW	In the real world
HNN	Hey nonny nonny
OTT	Over the top

Keeping messages clear and concise

An award-winning writer once said that the key to great writing is editing. That adage is as true with e-mail messages as it is with a Pulitzer Prize–winning novel. Good e-mails are to the point but not so short that they create the impression of being rudely curt. Most people, however, lean toward being one or the other of overcommunicators or undercommunicators.

Overcommunicators

Some people think of e-mail as the perfect place to hone their skills as budding novelists. They fill the screen with tons of text and agonizing detail that not only is unnecessary but detracts from the power of their messages. The motive for this overcommunication often is often a CYA mentality. If you fall into this category, use the following questions to keep your e-mails short and sweet:

- ✔ Have I included so many points that my main point is lost?

- ✔ Is there a way that I can say this in fewer words?

- ✔ Have I unnecessarily repeated information that has been confirmed by a prior e-mail?

- ✔ Is my message longer than 25 lines? If so, is there a document I need to attach instead?

Undercommunicators

Equally as ineffective are people who believe less is more. These writers don't put enough information in their messages and shorten them to the point where they run the risk of being seen as rude and offensive. If you think your e-mails can use a little fattening up, ask yourself the following questions:

- ✔ Have I provided enough information for the reader to understand what I am saying or requesting?
- ✔ Are there any previous e-mails to which I need to refer so that I enhance the context of this message?
- ✔ Do I need to add any detail to this message, or is it understandable as it is?
- ✔ Would an attached document be helpful?

Avoiding multiple media

A few eager beavers out there (you know who you are) insist on sending the same message to a co-worker in every communication medium possible. For example, they send an e-mail, leave a voice mail (telling the recipient that they sent an e-mail), and just for good measure, they fax the information contained within the e-mail to the e-mail recipient. Let us be blunt: Don't! Just plain don't do this! Overkill is annoying and wastes time. If an e-mail is the best format for your communication, stick to it and have some faith that your message will get through.

Whenever you're concerned about receiving verification that an important message was received by a colleague, use the *return receipt* feature available on some e-mail systems. If this feature isn't an option for you, wait at least two days before sending a second e-mail to inquire about the status of the first one. Of course, if your e-mail is urgent, don't hesitate to ask the reader to reply within a given time frame so that you can confirm receipt of your message.

Don't OD on the CC

For our readers who aren't old enough to remember where CC came from, it stands for *carbon copy,* which in ancient times way back in the 20th century was the only practical way to duplicate letters. The best thing about carbon copies was that they were limited; you could make only three good copies from any one document. E-mail, however, enables you to make virtually unlimited copies to be shot off effortlessly and instantaneously with a quick click on the CC box. Of all the e-mail complaints we hear about in our training sessions, sending out too many CCed copies is at the top of the list. Before you CC anyone, ask yourself the following questions:

✔ Is this information critical/important for the recipient to know?

✔ Is this information that the recipient would want to know?

✔ Does this information require some action on the part of the recipient?

✔ Am I just CCing this person to cover my electronic behind?

If you answer yes to any of the first three questions, then CC away. If the answer to the fourth question is yes, resist the temptation, live dangerously, and don't pass on information that clogs up the exit on your co-worker's electronic highway.

 Always make sure that your CC box is empty when replying to an e-mail. Depending on how your e-mail preferences are set, hitting the reply button for a message to which a whole string of people were CCed with the original message may automatically attach the e-mail addresses of those same people to your reply. Repeating, make sure that your CC box is the way that you want it before sending your reply.

Reviewing your e-mail before you send it

The number of people who merely type a quick e-mail message on their keyboard and then shoot it off without reading it through is astounding. Falling into the trap of thinking, "It's e-mail; I can be casual about this," is so easy. But don't be fooled by the apparent informality of the medium . . . you're still representing yourself, and you're still sending out a communication that can be seen by an untold number of people. Customers are slow to forgive bad manners and probably won't take the attitude, "Oh well, it's only e-mail." Review your document carefully, because after you press the send button, you can't take it back!

 Nothing is harder to read than a solid block of text with run-on sentences and paragraphs that meld into each other. Create an easier-to-read document by using no more than 75 words per sentence, starting new ideas with a distinctly separate paragraph, and remembering that italicized and bolded text doesn't often translate.

Starting and finishing on the right foot

Start all e-mails with the standard salutation of "Dear So-and-So." A couple of guidelines to keep in mind are:

✔ If you're contacting the person for the first time and want to maintain an air of formality, use his or her respective courtesy title (Ms., Mr., Mrs., or Dr., for example) and last name.

✔ If you're responding to a message, use the same level of formality the sender uses with you. If the writer uses your first name, use the writer's first name; if the writer uses your last name, address the writer in the same manner.

Follow the salutation with an introductory sentence or two such as:

✔ It was a pleasure meeting you yesterday.

✔ It was a pleasure speaking with you.

✔ Thank you for responding to my earlier e-mail.

✔ Thanks for your quick response.

✔ In response to your e-mail . . .

✔ I am contacting you on the recommendation of . . .

A perfectly good e-mail can be ruined by an abrupt ending. At the end of your message, be sure to sign off the same way you would with any letter or fax. Most e-mail programs have a feature that enables you to automatically add a personalized footer. Use this signature to include your full name and contact information for the reader's convenience.

Conduct a training session with members of your staff to go over the basics of e-mail etiquette, use, and ethics. By getting everyone within your group onboard, you make e-mail an effective tool within your office. If you need some help, check out our online training program titled "Essential E-mail" at www.scgtraining.com.

Applying the rules of grammar and spelling

Two camps have formed regarding the necessity of proper grammar and spelling in electronic messages:

✔ The first camp (usually the ones who don't spell well) thinks that worrying about spelling and grammar defeats the spontaneity and convenience of e-mail.

✔ The second camp (the kids who got *A*'s in English) thinks that e-mail is a written communication and therefore should be subject to the same rules and regulations that apply to its cousins the letter, the memo, and the fax.

We're definitely huddles around the bonfire at the second camp, although Karen (coauthor Karen Leland, that is) would be in deep trouble without her spell-checker. The bottom line is that bad grammar and poor spelling create a negative impression and take away from the message you mean to get across. Any business communication on which you place your name needs to represent the competent professional that you are.

Don't get into the habit of overusing question marks and exclamation points. What would you think if a simple sentence was followed by a dozen question marks???????????? Overpunctuation is definitely OTT (over the top) for business communication!!!!!!!!!!!!

Making your message visually appealing and easy to read

Few things are harder or more annoying to read than an e-mail that has no paragraphs. Be sure to create a new paragraph for each different idea and topic. Remember that in many cases, formatting — such as bullet points, bold, and italics — is lost in translation and may not show up on your reader's pages in the same way that it does on yours. The best approach is to keep it simple so that anyone who receives your e-mail can read it with ease.

Writing E-Mails that Produce Results

Obviously, no guarantees exist that an e-mail you send will produce the result that you want. However, you can improve the odds that you'll get the response that you're looking for if you carefully craft the language you use in your messages.

In this section, we introduce a few techniques that can help make your e-mails more effective, and we include a few exercises to help you practice the techniques.

Prioritizing your paragraphs

Many of our clients receive more e-mails than they can possibly read — unless they give up weekends and family life. To be able to deal with the bulging mailbox problem, many of them read only the first paragraph of all but the most important of messages. So if your e-mail doesn't qualify as an A1, most important, top-of-the-line priority in the reader's eyes, it may never get a full read. Thus getting your message across in the first sentence or two is crucial, because anything that follows may not be read and therefore is of questionable worth.

We found out the hard way when we were using e-mail to set up dinner arrangements with a busy executive. Rather than sending an e-mail for the specific purpose of arranging dinner, we simply added the invitation to the end of a business-related message we needed to send to the executive. He always sent very courteous and speedy replies to our other questions, but he never responded to our dinner invitation. Eventually, we figured it out. He wasn't reading beyond the first paragraph. Like it or not, we realized that this was his way of dealing with an overburdened mailbox. As soon as we sent a short e-mail, specifically asking for possible dinner dates, he responded immediately.

We're not suggesting that you always write one-paragraph e-mails, but it does make sense to make sure that the first paragraph in each of your messages contains the most important information. We call this technique *top-down writing*.

Top-down writing exercise

Practice your top-down writing skills by looking at the following e-mail. We scrambled the order of the paragraphs. Find out whether you can rearrange them in order of importance. A space is provided at the end of each paragraph for you to write in the number that represents what you think each paragraph's priority is. You can check your answer in the next section.

```
To: all@company.com

From: J.Jones@company.com

Re: upcoming meeting

Hello everyone,
```

I know how hard most of you have worked on preparing your reports. I appreciate all the effort and work put into each of them. Your findings are extremely important to the future of company.com. *(Priority # _____)*

Each report needs to be completed, copied, and bound for presentation. Please do not have any loose handouts, because they will cause confusion. However, for your convenience, the overhead projector will be available. *(Priority # _____)*

Because we have a limited amount of time, I have to ask you to limit your presentation to 2 minutes. We have a lot of material to cover, and by having a short presentation coupled with a copy of each report, we can at least begin the necessary discussions. *(Priority # _____)*

This Thursday's meeting is of utmost importance. For us to complete our agenda, I need everyone to be prepared to present their findings within 2 minutes. Please have enough copies of your reports for all 25 participants. *(Priority # _____)*

Two weeks after Thursday's meeting we will all meet again, I expect everyone to have read all five reports by that time so we can have a meaningful discussion regarding the direction company.com needs to take. *(Priority # _____)*

Answers to top-down writing exercise

Priority #1: This Thursday's meeting is of utmost importance. For us to complete our agenda, I need everyone to be prepared to present their findings within 2 minutes. Please have enough copies of your reports for all 25 participants.

Priority #2: Each report needs to be completed, copied, and bound for presentation. Please do not have any loose handouts, because they will cause confusion. However, for your convenience, the overhead projector will be available.

Priority #3: Because we have a limited amount of time, I have to ask you to limit your presentation to 2 minutes. We have a lot of material to cover, and by having a short presentation coupled with a copy of each report, we can at least begin the necessary discussions.

Priority #4: Two weeks after Thursday's meeting we will all meet again. I expect everyone to have read all five reports by that time so we can have a meaningful discussion regarding the direction company.com needs to take.

Priority #5: I know how hard most of you have worked on preparing your reports. I appreciate all the effort and work put into each of them. Your findings are extremely important to the future of company.com.

Use concise and meaningful subject lines. Some people judge an e-mail by the subject line alone and delete messages before ever reading the contents.

Putting your request upfront

In the prioritizing exercise, you saw the importance of making the first paragraph count. It follows, therefore, that if your e-mail is asking the recipient to take some kind of action, your request needs to be included within that first paragraph of the message.

After you realize that you must place your request where it's likely to be read, you must do whatever you can to ensure that it produces the results that you want. Obviously, you can't guarantee that other people will do what you say or ask (unless you're a hypnotist), but writing a clear request can definitely improve your chances. The sections that follow discuss four factors to think about when you send a request.

Specify the action you're requesting

Make sure the recipient understands exactly what is expected of him or her. For example, you may write something like, "To investigate your claim, I will need a letter stating the circumstances."

But you can be even more specific, because the recipient of such an e-mail can easily respond with a letter that's not detailed enough or with a small phonebook of information.

A better request would be, "To investigate your claim, I need a one- or two-page letter that states the general circumstances."

Set a time frame

When you send a message that requires some action, be sure to state specific time requirements so that no misunderstanding (or missed deadlines) can arise. For example, saying something like, "I need the report as soon as you can get it to me" can be interpreted by the recipient as, "Just send it as soon as you've dealt with all your other, more pressing priorities."

A better request would be, "I would like the report by 2 p.m. Wednesday."

Establish mutual understanding

Much confusion can arise whenever people on the sending and receiving ends of an e-mail don't completely understand the contents of the message. You may not get the response you're hoping for if the person to whom you're sending an e-mail doesn't understand all the underlying circumstances. For example, sending an e-mail to your Chicago office (when you're working in San Francisco) requesting a conference call at 4 p.m. may not produce the result you'd like — when it's 4 p.m. in Chicago, it's 2 p.m. in San Francisco, and when it's 4 p.m. in San Francisco, it's 6 p.m. in Chicago.

Evaluate the competence of your recipient

Make sure you send your request to someone who is capable of responding satisfactorily. No matter how well formed your e-mail request, if the person to whom you send it is not competent to fulfill it, then your request won't be answered. For example, sending an e-mail to a newly hired front-line employee asking her to put together an intranet staff directory would be inappropriate. This new person wouldn't have sufficient knowledge to complete the job quickly or competently.

Trimming the fat

Using unnecessary words is a major obstacle to e-mail efficiency. Many people write the same way they talk. The problem with that is the spoken word is much less tightly woven than the written word; when you write, you ought to be more succinct than when you talk. A customer reading an e-mail has far less tolerance for repetition and unclear phrasing than a customer with whom you're having a conversation.

The spoken word also is accompanied by many visual and auditory cues that generate interest and understanding. When you read, you're focused on the words — nothing more. The words alone need to be sufficient to convey your point concisely yet courteously. We include the exercise that follows to give you practice adjusting language to make it tighter and clearer.

Trim the fat exercise

Go through the following e-mail and remove the words that you believe dilute the message. Feel free to add a new word or two if they help make the message more concise.

```
To: all@company.com

From: K.Smith@company.com

Re: Last Thursday's Meeting

Hello to all,

I just wanted to take a moment to give you my perspective
of the very heated discussion that occurred during the
first part of last Thursday's lively meeting.

First and foremost, I felt it was not supportive of our
teambuilding efforts for all of us to be so defensive
about our reports. Let's face it, I believe we all tend to
take on a personal attachment to those things that we pro-
duce, but rarely are we willing to have the necessary
degree of objectivity to be able to discuss it in a posi-
tive and open way.

As a result, I feel that some of us felt, to some degree,
betrayed by the rather negative comments made by others.
Likewise, I personally felt attacked and otherwise not
supported for both my content as well as my efforts.
```

If we are to move forward as a team, then we need to support each other as a team. At this point in time, I welcome any and all discussions regarding my thoughts here as long as they are in constructive form. Furthermore, if any of you wish to meet to clear the air, I would most definitely welcome that as well.

Answers to trim the fat exercise

To: all@company.com

From: K.Smith@company.com

Re: Last Thursday's Meeting

Hello to all,

I ~~just~~ wanted to take a moment to give you my perspective of ~~the very heated~~ ~~discussion that occurred during the first part of~~ last Thursday's lively meeting.

~~First and foremost,~~ I felt it was not supportive ~~of our teambuilding efforts for all of us~~ to be so defensive about our reports. ~~Let's face it, I believe we all tend to take on a personal attachment to those things that we produce, but rarely are we willing to have the necessary degree of objectivity to be able to discuss it in a positive and open way.~~

~~As a result, I feel that some of us felt, to some degree, betrayed by the rather negative comments made by others. Likewise, I personally felt attacked and otherwise not supported for both my content as well as my efforts.~~

If we are to move forward as a team, then we need to support each other as a team. At this point in time, I welcome any and all discussions regarding my thoughts here as long as they are in constructive form. Furthermore, I welcome the idea of discussing this with you further. If any of you want to meet to clear the air, I would ~~most definitely~~ welcome that as well.

E-Mail Ethics

The explosion of e-mail has led to new spins on age-old issues, such as privacy rights, intellectual property, copyright, freedom of speech, and political correctness. Few areas in recent history can compare with the challenges that the legal system now faces as it's stretched to the limits by the popularity of e-mail and the Internet in general. In this section, we cover issues that we think are the most critical for you to be aware of in today's working world.

ANECDOTE

Careful, big brother may be watching you

We were having lunch one day with a client, and inquired into how one of the staff members was doing. To our surprise, we were told that the individual no longer was employed by the company. It seems he had developed a habit of surfing the Web for personal reasons on company time.

A company investigation showed that this employee was spending an average of three to four hours during the workday, accessing sites for personal use. Upon discovering of the employee's wayward ways, he was given the choice of resigning or being fired.

Whose e-mail is it anyway?

If you're like most people, you probably assume that the contents of the e-mail messages you send are private and belong to you. Well, think again.

The Electronic Communications Privacy Act ruled that internal e-mails are the property of the company that pays for the e-mail system, thereby giving companies the right to search your mailbox. According to a study by the American Management Association, 20 percent (and growing) of all companies are regularly and randomly taking a peek at their employees' e-mails.

The next time you write an e-mail, consider how the following factors impact the privacy of the message you're about to send:

- ✔ Because most messages are sent in ASCII text, anyone can read them. Only encrypted text cannot be read without first being decoded by a computer.

- ✔ In any large corporation, a systems administrator has access to all messages sent to, from, and within the company.

- ✔ E-mails frequently are sent by accident to someone or a group of some-ones who are not the intended recipients.

- ✔ People often forward e-mails sent to them by someone else without the sender's knowledge or permission.

- ✔ E-mail can automatically be forwarded to another employee when one of the employee's co-workers is out of town.

- ✔ Some companies have policies that include regular screening of employee e-mail.

- ✔ Firms specializing in recovering e-mail, even deleted ones, can and do use e-mail for evidence in civil and criminal court cases.

No place to hide

Robert Anderson and Norman Shapiro wrote a study titled "Toward an Ethics and Etiquette for Electronic Mail." In the study, Anderson highlights that e-mail's greatest "phenomenon is its propensity to lead to misinterpretation and . . . the strange permanence yet volatility of electronic messages." The funny thing: Mr. Anderson wrote this passage in 1985, when less than 1 million Americans were regularly using the medium. His advice then still holds true: "Never say anything (on e-mail) you wouldn't want appearing, and attributed to you, in tomorrow morning's front-page headline in *The New York Times*."

Here today, not gone tomorrow

Despite the seemingly fleeting nature of your e-mail messages, they are nonetheless a permanent record of your communication, and that's a good thing to keep in mind when considering what you should and should not send into cyberspace. Careful consideration will avoid your having said something electronically that you may regret and possibly have to defend, weeks, months, or even years later.

The bottom line is that e-mail has become a form of evidence as acceptable in legal disputes as any written document. As a recent article in *Wired* magazine states, "Old e-mail never dies." In fact, a whole new industry known as computer forensics has come into existence in the past few years. Companies in this field specialize solely in locating e-mails (usually for litigation purposes) that people believe are deleted and long gone.

Flames, spam, and harassment

A difference exists between an e-mail that is poorly written or has an unfriendly tone and one that has crossed over into the realm of e-buse. Question: What is the online equivalent of

- A co-worker leaving you a nasty note on your desk with a few choice words that can't be said on a prime-time television show?
- A telemarketer calling you at home, during dinner, to sell you swamp land in Florida?
- Your boss making uninvited advances toward you?

Answer: A flame, spam, and harassment. No, that isn't the name of a new rock group but rather three of the worst and most common breeches of etiquette/ ethics possible in business cyberspace.

Support a flame-free environment

In short, a *flame* is a verbal attack in electronic form that oftentimes can set into motion an equally heated response. You may someday send what you consider to be a harmless message and find that you get back a not-so-harmless response. Or you may just be on the receiving end of a customer or co-worker's anger and frustration. In any case, if you are flamed, the number one rule is: *Do not engage.* Despite all temptations to enter a flame war by shooting back an equally bad, nasty response, don't. Stop flaming in its tracks either by ignoring the offending comments, calling the person and telling him how you felt, or sending a response back that politely asks the person to clean up her e-mail.

Never send an e-mail that you've written when you're angry, exhausted, or on the verge of tearing your hair out from frustration. Always compose yourself before composing your e-mail.

Zero tolerance for spams

Spamming has unfortunately become all too commonplace in the e-mail environment. According to industry experts, an estimated 10 billion pieces of spam shoot through the Internet each year. The most common type of *spam* is when a company, hoping to find a few fish to bite on its line, sends out a single advertising message to huge numbers of e-mail users. These messages arrive in your mailbox as unsolicited e-mail — the electronic equivalent of all the junk mail you get everyday courtesy of the post office. The big difference is that the letters that come in the mail can be thrown away unopened, while junk e-mail often requires taking the time to open and then delete. This problem is fast becoming a big one for businesses as advertisers find ways to reach online mailboxes in the workplace.

You can avoid becoming part of the problem by never, under any circumstances, sending non-business related, unsolicited e-mail of a sales, marketing, advertising, or inappropriate personal nature to your business associates or colleagues. That means don't

- ✔ Forward your electronic newsletter — unasked for
- ✔ Advertise that your 1967 Chevy Camaro is for sale
- ✔ Send a chain letter threatening the recipients with a hideous future if they don't forward it to ten others
- ✔ Complain about what a yahoo your boss's wife is

Remember, people's e-mail boxes do not function as a company bulletin board for posting your personal agenda.

Banning spam

In a recent California court case, a former Fortune 500 Company employee who had been fired retaliated by sending bulk e-mail to 29,000 of the company's employees, criticizing the company and his firing — your basic slam spam. As a result, the company had to spend time and money trying to block the e-mails and addressing employees' concerns about the mailings. The ex-employee claimed he was just exercising his right to free speech. The state court decided he was trespassing on company property by sending the mass mailings and granted a permanent injunction barring him from doing it again.

If you legitimately were referred to someone by a third party, state that fact upfront in your message line and greeting. Similarly, don't give any of your colleagues' e-mail addresses to any mailing lists without their permission.

Online harassment

Using cyberspace for harassment, sexual or otherwise, goes beyond bad manners. It is a deep violation of the receiver, and it's against the law. Many cases in which advances and/or threats were made via e-mail using company computers have been documented. We heard of one case in which a male manager was sending one of his female employees e-mails regarding routine business items and peppering them with occasional outrageous sexual suggestions as if it were an acceptable part of their business relationship. The employee simply filed the e-mails electronically, made hard copies, and went to the human resources department. Her manager, needless to say, was fired.

Under no circumstances is it permissible to harass anyone using the medium of e-mail. Even if you think the other person is receptive to your personal attentions, using the Internet in this way is an open invitation for problems and even legal action.

A more innocuous form of harassment is the person who likes to send out dirty jokes to his customers and colleagues. We recommend that you ask before you send to avoid offending those you work with.

Creating Online Rapport

Rapport is defined in *Webster's New World College Dictionary* as "a close or sympathetic relationship." Good customer service requires that you establish rapport with your customers. Having good rapport makes your customers feel like they're more than just a source of income. They'll be much more likely to give you valuable feedback or stick with your company through a few service blunders if rapport has been established. As a business professional, you probably know how to quickly build rapport — look your customers in the eye, make chit-chat, get to know them.

But how do you establish rapport over e-mail? You don't have those long business lunches to bond over. You don't have body language to read, as in even brief face-to-face contacts. You can't even listen carefully to the tone of a customer's voice, as you can over the phone. In this chapter, we give you a few great techniques for establishing what we call *e-rapport*.

We all speak the same language. Or do we? In our workshops, we often get participants to think about language by asking them what comes to mind when we say "orange." Responses include the fruit, the color, the county in southern California, and offbeat ones like "the sweater I wore yesterday." The point is that, although we all use similar words, we each use them in our own unique way. Creating e-rapport requires honing in on the language choices that the other person is making and then responding with similar language. In other words, figuring out the other person's wavelength, and then putting yourself on it.

E-rapport is the skill of using e-mail to get closer to your customers by getting on their wavelength, so that you don't have to fly blind simply because you don't receive visual or auditory cues. Two powerful techniques that help ensure harmonious relations online are using sensory language and backtracking key words. Read on for more about these techniques.

Using sensory language

When they speak or write, most people use words that relate to the senses of seeing, hearing, and feeling. Without realizing it, individuals often use one sense more than another, and so that person's e-mail messages contain words relating specifically to that sense. Here are three sentences that say the same thing using different sensory words:

- ✔ I *see* your *perspective* (visual).
- ✔ I *hear* what you're *saying* (auditory).
- ✔ I *feel* that you have a *point* (tactile).

By using sensory words that are consistent with your customers' main style, you add a rapport-building quality to the messages you send. The following sentence is written in neutral language (language that has no sensory relationship):

I am interested in knowing more about your products and services.

Now, here is the same sentence translated into language that uses the three primary senses:

- I *look* forward to *seeing* the information about your products and services.

- I'd like to *hear* more about the service and products you offer.

- I'd be happy if you'd get in *touch* with me about the products and services you offer.

All four sentences contain the same basic message, yet the change in sensory language gives each one a different flavor.

Before responding to an e-mail, quickly scan the words in the original message to find out which sense dominates the language the sender uses. After you know the writer's sensory preference, reply to the e-mail using a preponderance of those sensory-specific words. The chances are that the recipient will feel a sense of rapport with you — usually without ever knowing the specific relationship-enhancing steps that you've taken.

Crafting visual messages

Writers with a visual preference use words to paint pictures and create images of what they want to communicate. Some words that you can use when communicating with a person who leans toward visual language include

- Clarify

- Focus

- Look

- See

- Vision

- Perspective

- Clear

- Observe

The following phrases are visual:

- I see what you mean.

- That looks good.

- I'm a little hazy about that.

- Let's try and shed some light on . . .

- I have a different view of the situation.

- I get the picture.
- I appreciate your insight.
- I look forward to seeing you.

Incorporating auditory language

Writers with an auditory preference use words and phrases that give tone to what they're saying. Some words that you can use to give an e-mail an auditory style include

- Sound
- Hear
- Say
- Tell
- Volume
- Loud
- Listen
- Tone

The following phrases are auditory:

- I'm glad to hear it.
- Let me explain.
- We're in tune.
- Tell me what you hear.
- Everything just clicked.
- That sounds good to me.
- On that note, we should end the discussion.
- That rings a bell.

Using tactile language

Writers with a tactile style use words and phrases that refer to physical sensations when writing a message. Some words that you can use when you want to create a tactile style include

- Touch
- Feel
- Firm
- Pressure

- Relaxed
- Rough
- Solid

The following are tactile phrases:

- It feels right.
- Stay in touch.
- Warm regards.
- It leaves me cold.
- Get a grip.
- Hold on.

Responding to upset customers using e-mail

When sending e-mails to customers or colleagues whom you know are upset or angry, use the following tips to help maintain rapport.

- **Delay sending emotional messages.** If you must send an e-mail about a highly emotional topic (face-to-face or phone conversations usually work much better), compose the note but don't address it or send it. Read it again a few hours later and then revise it, if necessary, before sending it. Make sure that you've responded appropriately and haven't reacted inappropriately.

- **Soften e-mail messages.** If an e-mail message you're sending sounds too curt or abrupt, add an opening line, such as, "Thank you for the e-mail" or "It was a pleasure hearing from you."

- **Reread your e-mails.** Before sending an e-mail, reread it from beginning to end and ask yourself whether any parts of it can be misconstrued by the reader. In certain instances where there has been a lot of e-mailing back and forth, it's a good idea to revisit the original message just to make sure that you are still on track and haven't lost the point of the original message.

- **Get a second opinion.** Before sending a sensitive or emotional message, have someone you trust read the e-mail and give you suggestions for making it more customer-friendly.

The following is an example of a neutral e-mail received from a customer. Note that the message creates a feeling of distance rather than of closeness because of the absence of any sensory words.

Dear Mr. Smith:

Thank you for your acknowledgment regarding the instrument that my institution returned to your company. I am not convinced that this matter has been fully taken care of at your end and request that you forward me the details of the credit return we are expecting.

Sincerely, Ms. Jones

Recognizing the effect of neutral language

Neutral language seems formal and business-like compared to sensory language. Although neutral language can seem cold and impersonal, it's useful when you want to send a formal response to an official or legal document or when your customer has demonstrated a preference for neutral terms. Some examples of neutral words include

- ✔ Think
- ✔ Seems
- ✔ Know
- ✔ Involve
- ✔ Denote
- ✔ Recall
- ✔ Matter

Backtracking key words

When writing e-mails, people choose specific words and phrases that they think are great ways to describe the situation or that they have a predilection for using. The e-rapport skill of *backtracking key words* requires you to pick up on the key words that the other person uses. Then you repeat back some of the key words or phrases. What do you think are the most important words and phrases in the following e-mail?

```
Dear Esther:

I strongly suspect that our customers are mystified by the
pricing information on our Web site. I would like to meet
at your earliest convenience to remedy the situation.

Regards, Sarah
```

The key words are:

- ✔ Strongly
- ✔ Suspect
- ✔ Mystified
- ✔ Remedy

Now use some or all of these key words in composing your response. For example:

```
Dear Sarah:

I think you are right in suspecting that customers are
mystified by the Web pricing. Can you meet me tomorrow
morning at 10:30 to work on a remedy?

Regards, Esther
```

By using a sprinkling of the senders' words in your response, you mirror back to them something familiar. The more they recognize their style in your response (consciously or subconsciously), the more they feel a sense of rapport and trust.

Chapter 21

CRM: Automating the Personal Touch

*F*ast, inexpensive, and easy-to-access technology has hatched a new world of customer tracking possibilities. Any size company can now maintain a database and effortlessly track all the comings and goings of its customers. In this chapter, we look at the latest online customer service technology, *customer relationship management* (CRM), and give you ideas for using its principles in your business, big or small, so that it serves you, rather than vice versa.

Defining Customer Relationship Management

Customer relationship management, when used in conjunction with a customer-centric business strategy, enables your company to track every aspect of the customer relationship. You can determine who bought what and when they bought it. When you have a profile on each customer, you can transform each business interaction into a dialogue. In effect, you can talk to the customer as if you know him or her. By using CRM technology to understand the customer's relationship with your company, you create a one-to-one relationship with hundreds or thousands of customers at a time.

Too often, the relentless pursuit of higher profits is the sole driver for many CRM initiatives. A corresponding commitment to customer care is sadly lacking. Customers become frustrated and disheartened by companies that mistakenly believe that every human interaction can be replaced by technological applications. Customers love technology when it resolves a problem quickly; they're not so crazy about it when it hinders progress and creates an even bigger problem. After all, most of us have lost brain cells through the stress of trying to navigate a poorly designed voice-mail system.

The fundamentals of online customer service are the same on this side of the digital divide as they were on the analog side. Quality customer service still consists of listening to customers, doing everything you can to fulfill their needs, and knowing what to do when you can't.

Customers who feel they're in a dialogue with your organization — who feel as if they're listened to — become lifelong customers. As the relationship matures, they spend more and more of their money with your company while requiring little or no incentive to continue purchasing. The more you understand about CRM, the more the line blurs between sales and service (read more about turning service into sales in Chapter 13).

Developing Trust and Loyalty Online

When implemented effectively, CRM can add tremendous value to your company by helping you create and retain loyal customers. This loyalty is developed through the types of experiences customers have with your company. If you can consistently provide competent and immediate service, you increase the likelihood that your customers will stay with you.

In a perfect world, CRM is

- ✔ **Immediate** — allowing your customers instant gratification, whether the interaction involves processing a request or solving a problem
- ✔ **Personalized** — enabling you to tailor each interaction to your customers' unique needs and preferences

So, regardless of whether you're selling dog collars or offering cleaning services, CRM can help you make every customer encounter positive and rewarding. And that's good for business!

In the following scenario, we demonstrate how CRM technology, when implemented well, can have a positive impact on cyberservice by creating satisfied, loyal customers. The interaction is a practical balance between providing a set of personalized help options to the customer and maintaining an efficient, low-overhead support process for the company. Here goes:

> Imagine that you receive your monthly bank statement in the mail and discover that your balance is less than you expected. You're close to being overdrawn. You look through your register and discover that a deposit you made two weeks ago isn't recorded. You do some of your banking via the Web, so you access your checking account online by entering your account number and password.
>
> *Customer profiling* has provided the bank with a detailed understanding of how you use its Web site and what information you're usually seeking. The bank has customized its presentation of your information by providing you with easy access to the functions that you use the most. Running across the top of the screen are special introductory offers for investment opportunities to help with future education and schooling costs. By crunching its stored customer data, the bank uses data mining to analyze customer information and then look for spending patterns and common demographic trends. This has shown the bank that given your age, income, family situation (two young children), and zip code, you're very likely to be looking for investments that help cover your children's educational needs a few years down the road.
>
> As you scan your online statement, you discover that the deposit isn't recorded there either. The Web site provides a Please Call Me button that initiates an immediate telephone call back from the bank. You click the button, enter your phone number and a few other details, and wait.
>
> The request is automatically sent to a customer-service agent at the bank's call center who specializes in bank statement inquiries from the specific customer segment to which you belong. The computer screen that alerts the agent to call you also supplies him with your personal information, your history with the bank, the reason for your call, and what Web page you were looking at when you initiated your request for a call back.
>
> With the press of a button, the agent returns your call. You speak with an agent, who, having all the relevant information in front of him, has an immediate understanding of the situation.
>
> The agent scans your other accounts and discovers the money was mistakenly deposited into your money-market account. He then corrects the mistake and apologizes for the inconvenience it has caused.
>
> The agent explains that, if you sign up via the Web, the first month's fee for the service is waived. You agree, he directs you to the site and asks if you'd be willing to fill in a brief customer survey regarding your satisfaction with the service you've received. You go to the survey page, fill in a brief questionnaire, and then sign up for overdraft protection. The Web

pages explain the details about the service, how it works, and what it costs. You fill in the application form and press the Submit button.

The following morning, to your surprise, you receive an e-mail from the agent. He apologizes again for the mistake and assures you that everything has been taken care of as promised. You're impressed with the service and, when you arrive at work, talk enthusiastically about your bank and what a good job it does. You forget completely that it misplaced your money.

This scenario shows how you can effectively use the information you gain through CRM to provide better service. The result? Satisfied customers.

You can gain a deeper understanding of how the balance between customer needs and company benefits is achieved by taking a look at the scenario from both sides of the equation — the bank and the customer.

Meeting customer needs

Assume that you're the manager of the bank. You need to decide whether your investment in CRM is paying off. Thinking about the earlier example, you see that the integration of CRM technology and your commitment to delivering excellent service have fulfilled a number of customer needs, including:

- ✔ **Personalization:** With the information you gather through CRM, you can tailor your customers' experiences according to what they routinely request. CRM helps you to predict what new products they're likely to buy or what concerns they're likely to have. The bank has designed its Web site to change its appearance according to the individual customer's unique usage patterns.

- ✔ **Convenience:** Everyone is busy these days, including your customers. Always being accessible to your customers ensures that you'll never miss a business opportunity. In the bank scenario above, both the Web site and a call center response are available 24 hours a day, seven days a week.

- ✔ **Responsiveness:** Whenever a problem occurs, most of us want to be able to take action to resolve it. At the beginning of the scenario, the customer is understandably concerned about the missing money. Through a self-service Web interaction, he's able to verify the most up-to-date information and easily contact — by using the convenient **Please Call Me** button — a service agent.

- ✔ **Understanding:** We all need somebody to lean on. The service agent, through viewing pertinent data on his screen, is able to immediately ascertain why the call has been made. As a result, the customer thinks his situation is immediately understood.

✔ **Expertise:** When you have a specific question, you need a specific answer. In the scenario, the call is routed to an agent who specializes in the area of the customer's query.

✔ **Speed:** Whether you're purchasing a new sweater or solving a troublesome problem, in this fast-paced world, when you want something, you usually want it *now!* Because the agent in the scenario is familiar with the customer's circumstances, he doesn't have to ask the customer questions to get up to speed with the customer's issue.

✔ **Resolution:** Knowing that something is taken care of is always satisfying. If customers feel like they're in good hands, they're much more likely to stick with you as a customer. In the scenario, the agent resolves the issue by seamlessly transferring the money to the correct account without having to ask the customer for account numbers.

Reaping company benefits

One of the biggest benefits that CRM provides for a company is that it creates happy, loyal customers. Yet other benefits to your company exist too, such as:

✔ **Feedback:** Whenever you can gain insight into your customers' experiences with your company, you have an opportunity to improve your service. The customer in the scenario is delighted with the efficiency with which the bank resolves the problem and willingly fills in a short survey.

✔ **Up-selling:** Offering an existing customer new services is more effective on inbound calls. The agent uses the interaction in the earlier example to better service the customer and to generate a new revenue stream for the bank.

✔ **Marketing** No company can ever have too much exposure. During the banking interaction above, targeted banner ads are displayed by the bank and its third party vendors or partners.

✔ **Referral:** Hardly any better advertising exists than a satisfied customer. The customer in the banking scenario was pleased with the overall experience and considers the bank to be very customer centered. He becomes a walking referral.

Learning from CRM

No off-the-shelf, generic CRM template perfectly fits every company's needs. However, regardless of your organization's size and future plans for CRM, every savvy business person needs to understand the principles that are part of its successful implementation. The following three areas are common denominators among companies where online service is flourishing:

- ✔ Segmentation of the customer base
- ✔ Consistency across communication channels
- ✔ Developing a multichannel strategy

Although not every company is big enough to implement CRM, these three elements can help any business offer better online customer service by making products and services more customized and accessible.

Segmenting your customer base

Because of the newly developed ability to industrialize the trust- and loyalty-building processes with customers, business people are required, as never before, to analyze which customers they need to spend resources on and which ones they shouldn't. It makes sense to invest heavily only in the ones who have a high probability of being lifelong and profitable customers. This prioritization is the heart of customer segmentation.

A segmentation strategy is a three-step process that sorts customers who meet the criteria you set for gaining a return on your investment. The criteria may be based upon how much a client spends with your business in a year, the average dollar amount the client spends per purchase, or the potential growth rate of the client (which, in a business-to-business situation, signals increased sales for your company). Segmentation then categorizes these potential spending habits in a way that makes creating distinct customer populations easy.

Each distinct customer population can be offered specific products and services that may be too expensive to offer to your entire customer base. A simple example is a company that offers free delivery to customers who purchase goods of more than a certain amount. Another is the credit-card company that offers you a lower-than-advertised rate because of your repayment history (and, no doubt, the strong possibility that you'll use the card extensively). Twenty percent of the CRM investments that companies make go toward the loyalty-building aspects of profiling customers and segmenting markets.

The *80/20 rule,* which states that 20 percent of your customers are responsible for 80 percent of your revenues, is accurate for almost every business. If you take this analysis one step further, the *1/10 rule* reveals that about 1 percent of your customers account for about 10 percent of your profits. These numbers are a good place to start when segmenting your customer base according to profitability.

Step 1: Sort your customer base into profitability segments

Select the customers from whom you're making the most money. Say you have a customer base of 5,000. Using the 1/10 rule, select the 50 customers who contribute the most to your profitability. They are your premium customers, and you'll probably discover that you're garnering most of their business already. However, the true value of CRM is that it not only is about getting more business from your customers, it's also about finding ways to better serve them and to deepen their loyalty to your company.

Here are some of the key traits of customers in this primary segment (other than their contribution to your bottom line):

✔ They have the potential to become customers that you make an even higher profit from.

✔ They are market-savvy and are interested in establishing strategic partnerships with their suppliers.

✔ They are profitable and financially sound.

✔ They are industry leaders.

Next, sort out the 40 percent of your customers from whom you don't make tons of money but who can become lucrative accounts with diligence and cultivation. Creating a dialogue with these customers will more than likely give you rich information regarding why they give some of their business to your competitors. By discovering what they need in the way of service and products and supplying what they need, you help move them toward the most-profitable bracket. For a company with 5,000 customers, approximately 2,000 customers are included in this secondary segment. Along with the key traits for high-profit customers (see the previous list), medium-profit customers also have these characteristics:

✔ They are innovative and flexible.

✔ The possibility for cross-selling is high.

✔ Your product or service is significant to their businesses.

✔ They show a trend toward increased revenues.

Next you deal with the customers that are marginally profitable. In the sample customer base of 5,000, about 3,000 customers are in this category. We believe that giving every customer the highest possible level of service is important, and we think that good business sense requires you to carefully consider who your premium customers are and, when appropriate, offer them premium services that may be too costly for you to offer to smaller or less-frequent buyers. In other words, the highest possible level of service that you can give to an occasional customer who tends to pay you late and is rumored to be going out of business probably isn't real high. But for the big accounts, the highest possible level of service means pulling all the stops.

After you know which customers you're going to invest in, the next job is finding out what they need from your organization — not only now but also in the future. You discover this information as you implement the second part of your segmentation strategy.

Step 2: Segment the markets and functions of your customers

The more refined your customer segmentation, the better able you are to determine your customers' specific needs and tailor your services to them. In this second step, you initially need to segment the vertical markets of the companies that you serve into categories such as:

- Financial
- Engineering
- Manufacturing
- Healthcare

Next, segment the specific customers from each of these markets into functional responsibilities, such as:

- Executive
- Management
- Marketing
- Sales
- Clerical
- Accounting

Sort this list of individuals by their areas of responsibility, such as:

- Corporate
- Division
- Department
- Individual

By segmenting your customers vertically, you're better able to hit the mark when it comes to product design, marketing, and sales. For example, a training company that has identified a large customer segment of corporate-engineer managers, for example, may design and market a seminar that deals with the specific concerns and issues that it knows are of interest to that group.

Step 3: Segment the habits of your customer base

Your customer database obviously is the central tool for CRM. New database technologies such as *data warehousing*, which enables you to store information in a single place, and *data mining*, which enables you to retrieve specific information about your customers, have brought about a new sophistication in forecasting what your customers want from you. Keep reading this section for more about data warehousing and data mining. The purchasing habits of your customers can partially be predicted by customer information such as:

- Previously purchased products
- Frequency and volume of purchases
- Zip code
- Gender

Online service presents a means for more comprehensive customer profiling and data collection. Many companies now collect customer information that helps provide a deeper knowledge of customers so that interactions are smoother. These areas of familiarity may include

- How many times the customer has encountered a problem with a product or service
- How many times a customer has called in or e-mailed a product-related question
- How much working experience the customer has had with the product
- How many company-offered product-familiarity courses the customer has attended
- The customer's personality over the phone (chatty, curt, bitter-and-twisted, and so on)

Although building your customer database is the beginning of the segmentation process, it is *only* the beginning. The average organization has about ten separate databases, and these disparate systems need to be brought together into one place — a *data warehouse.*

A *data warehouse* is a database that is used to store information that originates from the many different corporate databases and external market data sources. Because of the way information technology has evolved, most companies have different databases, in different formats, using different languages. The process of bringing all this information together is data warehousing.

Given the need to have all departments (reception, sales, marketing, credit, manufacturing, and so on) access and update the same customer information, the data must be manipulated and cleansed so that it is consistent and compatible with the format developed for the warehouse. After this consolidation has taken place, special software programs can be used to sort through the data, which otherwise is known as data mining. *Data mining* enables users to sift through large amounts of data, using specialized software tools, to uncover data content relationships and build models to predict customer behavior. Predictive modeling can segment and profile customers, and that information, if appropriate, can be integrated with other marketing-oriented applications.

Maintaining consistency across channels

The second element in assuring effective CRM is maintaining consistency across communication channels. A *channel* is any avenue that enables you and your customers to communicate with each other, including:

- ✔ The Web
- ✔ E-mail
- ✔ Fax
- ✔ Telephone
- ✔ Face-to-face meetings

CRM brings one of the most distinctive aspects of online service into sharp focus — the multiplicity of channels. These channels are used for many different aspects of operating your business, including:

- ✔ **Distributing information,** such as the specifics on your product or service. This information may include models, colors, characteristics, availability, the warranty, pricing, and service agreements.

- ✔ **Communicating** by answering customer inquiries about products and services, for example.

- ✔ **Making transactions,** such as sending invoices and payments.

- ✔ **Distributing** products in innovative ways. Many software companies, for example, allow you to download software directly from a Web site after you've paid.

- ✔ **Providing service** through the many channels, which makes it easier for your customers to connect with you.

Your organization's reputation for being customer centered hinges largely on your ability to create a consistent service level regardless of what channel your customer chooses. If you're not convinced that you need to be strong across all channels, consider this: Forty percent of online shoppers in a recent survey say they'd use more than one route to obtain customer service. It isn't just phone calls anymore.

Many bricks-and-mortar companies that have moved into Web sales are having a hard time serving customers across all channels. They aren't in the habit of keeping up with the details of customer interactions. One scenario in which a customer gets bad service: A customer calls a catalog company about a recent store or Web purchase only to be greeted by a service rep who has no record of any previous purchases via other channels.

Although realizing that customers value consistency across all channels is extremely important, the most successful online service providers also know that different customer segments have different channel preferences. These preferences can change depending on circumstances. For example, customers who normally use the Web to ask questions will make a telephone call if they need an answer quickly.

Developing a multichannel strategy

Although many different methods exist for developing a multichannel strategy that suits your organization, it is wise to consult your different customer segments to discover their needs and their *loyalty drivers* — those things that keep them coming back for more. A survey will help you capture valuable information that can become the basis of your strategy. Three key steps are involved:

Step 1: Design a customer survey

Conduct a brainstorming session with key staff members to come up with a list of interview questions. You may want to create a slightly different set of questions for different customer segments. The following list can get you started thinking about potentially useful questions:

- Do customers have access to the Web, or at least to e-mail?
- What is the customers' preferred channel for receiving new product information?
- What is the customers' preferred channel for obtaining answers to questions regarding products or services not yet purchased?
- What are the customers' invoicing and payment preferences?
- Do customers have concerns or feedback regarding privacy and security?
- What are customers' preferred channels for technical support and problem resolution?
- How satisfied are your customers and what impacts their loyalty?
- What products or services do your customers not know about?
- What are the customers' future spending plans and via which channel?
- What services would you need to supply to get a greater share of your customers' spending?

Keep your survey brief. Regardless of whether they're responding to a live person or filling in a form online, customers soon grow weary of answering questions.

Step 2: Conduct customer interviews

After you develop the questionnaire, decide how the surveys will be delivered to your customers. The fastest and least expensive method undoubtedly is by e-mail; however, because e-mail questions are so cut and dry, no opportunity is created for the in-depth dialogue that can, potentially, spin off from a live conversation. For some of your clients, the expense and time of a live interaction with an in-house person who has knowledge of the client's history may be worthwhile.

We recommend that interviews generally be conducted:

- ✔ **Face to face** for big accounts and accounts with great potential
- ✔ **By telephone** for medium-size accounts
- ✔ **In writing** for small accounts that probably will stay small
- ✔ **By e-mail or the Web,** an increasingly popular method that can be used, if appropriate, with small- and medium-size accounts

Step 3: Use collected data as a basis for your strategy

The next step is to analyze the information that you collect from your surveys and begin building a channel strategy. Your strategy will be unique to your products and services and to your customers' needs. Some things to keep in mind include

- ✔ Some customers use the Web far more than others. Because Web interactions require dramatically lower overhead than voice interactions, many companies offer incentives for Web ordering. For example, airlines may offer mileage bonuses, retailers an across-the-board 10-percent discount, and so on.
- ✔ Many customers prefer a dialogue with a real person, which translates into an agent-assisted telephone call.
- ✔ Some customers prefer an automated voice response system, so that they can push buttons on their own telephone to get the recorded information that they need.
- ✔ Everyone wants the option of switching channels when they require fast problem resolution. Companies that don't provide alternative contact information on their Web sites and e-mails score low marks with customers.

When you consider CRM, keep in mind that its successful implementation is as much a people process as it is a technology process. Having the right tools without a top-down commitment to training and motivating staff is a recipe for failure. As David Sims, a frequent writer on the topic of CRM, puts it, "The worst scenario is when a company purchases CRM software, opens the box, and then says 'Okay, now what are we going to do with it?'"

Part VI
The Part of Tens

The 5th Wave   By Rich Tennant

"Our customer survey indicates 30% of our customers think our service is inconsistent, 40% would like a change in procedures, and 50% think it would be real cute if we all wore matching colored vests."

In this part . . .

Just for good measure, we have added a few important topics that help round out your service education. The Part of Tens is a quick and easy way for you to brush up on the main points listed in this book — as well as a way to pick up some new tips and techniques.

Finally, you, like most people, want to receive the same good level of service that you provide. So, just to keep things in balance, we include a guideline in this part that helps you get the service you deserve when you're standing on the other side of the counter.

Chapter 22

Ten Major Don'ts of Customer Service

....

*E*very day you face situations when what you say to your customers makes or breaks the service interactions. That's why we decided to list ten phrases to avoid here in this chapter — because they drive customers nuts — along with our recommended alternatives for delivering the message in a more polite and helpful way.

1 Don't Know

Switch to: "I'll find out."

When you say "I don't know," your customers often hear it as, "I don't have the information you want, and I'm not going out of my way to get it." By offering to find the answer to your customers' questions, even if doing so means taking a little extra time researching or checking with another department, you score service points for going the extra mile.

No

Switch to: "What I can do is . . ."

Inevitably, you sometimes have to say no to a customer's request. Rather than using what we call a hard no — where no options or alternatives are provided — focus on what you can do for your customers. By starting your response with "What I can do is . . . ," you show customers that you're taking a problem-solving approach to their particular situations.

Check out Chapter 14 for more about how to successfully say no to customers when you have to.

That's Not My Job

Switch to: "This is who can help you . . ."

When customers ask you to do something that you don't have the authority or knowledge to carry out, become a catalyst by leading the customer to the person or department who can help him solve his problem.

You're Right; This Stinks

Switch to: "I understand your frustration."

Whenever a customer expresses annoyance at something another person or department has done, don't make matters worse by commiserating with him. Instead of agreeing by saying something like, "You're right, this place stinks," express empathy for the customer's feelings by saying "I understand how frustrating this must be." Empathy is showing care and concern without agreeing or disagreeing with what the customer is saying.

That's Not My Fault

Switch to: "Let's see what we can do about this."

If an angry customer seems to be accusing you of creating a problem for her, the natural reaction is to become defensive. However, if you allow that kind of reaction to take over, your mind becomes closed to hearing what the customer has to say. So when you find the words "That's not my fault" on the tip of your tongue, stop, take a breath, and then, with all the empathy you can muster, say, "Let's see what we can do about this." By resisting the urge to defend yourself, you can resolve the problem faster and with less stress.

Chapter 15 offers some great advice on dealing with angry and difficult customers.

You Need to Talk to My Manager

Switch to: "I can help you."

Customers sometimes ask you for things that are a little outside of company policy or procedure. At such times, quickly passing them off to your manager is tempting. Instead, focus on what you can do to help them. If your manager does need to be involved, take the initiative to go to him or her yourself and return to the customer with a solution in hand. Doing so makes you the service hero in the customers' eyes.

You Want It By When?

Switch to: "I'll try my best."

When customers make demands by asking you for something that is unreasonable and difficult to provide, your first reaction may be annoyance. However, because you have little control over your customers' requests, the best approach is to hold off on any negative judgments and try your best to accommodate the requests. Never promise something with only the hope that you can deliver. Giving customers unrealistic expectations may get them off your back in the short term, but it will blow up in your face later. Do make promises that you know you can accomplish and assure customers, with confidence and enthusiasm, that you know how important their deadlines are and that you'll try your best to meet them.

Calm Down

Switch to: "I'm sorry."

When customers are upset, angry, frustrated, or concerned, telling them to calm down is like saying that their feelings don't matter. If you want your customers to calm down, take the opposite approach and apologize. Apologizing doesn't mean you're agreeing with the customers' points of view or that you're admitting guilt, it means that you're sorry for what has happened and the negative impact it has had on the customer.

I'm Busy Right Now

Switch to: "I'll be with you in just a moment."

Stopping and assisting another customer who is asking for your help isn't always easy, especially when you're already in the middle of serving a customer. Some service providers handle this situation by tossing out a curt, "I'm too busy right now" at the customer, which is their way of saying, "Why are you bothering me, can't you see I'm busy?" Stellar service providers use a better approach by saying, "I'll be with you in just a moment." This little sentence, along with a pleasant tone of voice, tells your customer that you're aware of his presence and you'll help him as soon as you are able.

Call Me Back

Switch to: "I will call you back."

Some customer requests take time for you to research and investigate and require a further conversation at a later date. Follow-up phone conversations should always be initiated by you — not by the customer. When you're so busy that you're tempted to ask him or her to call you back, stop, be proactive, and take the initiative to call the customer back when you've taken care of the problem.

Chapter 23

Ten Tips for Constructive Conflict with Co-Workers

. . . .

In This Chapter

▶ Being assertive and dealing with conflicts directly

▶ Avoiding unnecessary negativity and judgments

. . . .

*O*ne significant difference between managing conflict with your co-workers and managing conflict with your customers is that customers come and go, but your co-workers are here to stay (more or less). Managing conflict with workmates can be more difficult because you have more contact with them, more often. All the skills you use to deal with difficult customers (check out Chapter 16) work just as well with difficult co-workers; however, you need a few additional skills when you're having a hard time communicating with co-workers. Establishing good rapport and finding out how to resolve conflicts with co-workers results in less stress for you and better service for your customers.

Assert Yourself

If you don't know how to strike that delicate balance between straightforwardness and tact, you can unintentionally create conflict. By flying off the handle and becoming aggressive, you force your co-workers into a defensive posture that makes hearing what you have to say difficult for them. The opposite stance is also ineffective; being too tentative when presenting your point may result in a co-worker not taking you seriously.

Knowing how to assert yourself can help you voice your thoughts, feelings, and opinions in a nonthreatening and balanced way. Here are some important tips on asserting yourself:

- ✔ **Be specific.** Make sure that you describe the situation in specific terms so that the other person knows exactly what you're talking about. For example, saying "You don't communicate" isn't as effective as saying "You didn't call me when you said you would."

- ✔ **Stick to the facts.** Don't become a mind reader and assign reasons, attitudes, or motives for why your co-worker behaved the way he or she did. Your co-worker will become defensive if you make incorrect assumptions about his or her feelings. Remember to describe only what is observable. For example, saying "You felt so guilty, you couldn't even look at me" isn't as effective as saying "After I spoke with you, you turned your back to me."

- ✔ **Never say never.** When you talk about the other person's behavior, stay away from absolute words such as "never" and "always," because those words usually are exaggerations of the facts. For example, saying "You always ignore me" isn't as effective as saying "You didn't do what I asked you to do."

Handle Most Conflicts Face to Face

As we discuss in Chapter 12, 55 percent of the message that people receive comes from body language. So although doing so may be more uncomfortable, dealing with conflict face to face whenever possible, rather than by e-mail or over the phone, is usually more effective. If face to face isn't viable, because of distance or schedules, the telephone is the next-best choice. Using e-mail to address conflicts is almost never a smart strategy, because the lack of body language and tone of voice almost always guarantee misunderstandings will take place. Some simple yet important tips to remember when managing conflict in meetings include

- ✔ **Making eye contact.** Let your co-worker know that you mean what you're saying by making direct eye contact with him. However, be careful not to stare him down, because doing so can be interpreted as overbearing and aggressive behavior.

- ✔ **Not fidgeting.** Avoid nervous habits, such as pacing, tugging at your hair, rattling change in your pocket, or tinkering with a pen. They are all distracting and weaken the impact of what you're saying.

- ✔ **Letting your face reflect your feelings.** Your face needs to reflect the message that you want to convey. For example, if you're angry, resist the urge to smile and make light of the situation. In this case, a look of concern is most appropriate.

Express Empathy for Other Viewpoints

A great deal of conflict can be nipped in the bud by providing your co-worker with a brief and sincere expression of empathy. By letting the other person know that you understand his or her point of view, even if you don't agree with it, you're already halfway to resolving the conflict. Empathetic phrases are a simple and easy way of conveying understanding. For example:

- ✔ I can see why you'd feel that way.
- ✔ I understanding what you're saying.
- ✔ That would upset me as well.
- ✔ I know this is really frustrating for you.
- ✔ I'm sorry.

By using a genuinely warm and caring tone, you enhance the meaning and effectiveness of empathetic phrases.

Avoid Fighting for the Last Word

Fighting for the last word is the vocal equivalent of dueling banjos. It usually begins when your co-worker makes a remark that you don't like, and you up the ante by coming back with a snappy, even more disrespectful reply. The other person takes offense and does the same back to you — only one better — and you're off! Before you know it, voices are raised, tempers are flaring, and the conversation is spiraling out of control. The following conversation is between Lauren and Jon, two systems programmers who share the same work area in a large insurance company.

Lauren: I can't believe you forgot to check the voice mail again.

Jon: Oh, yeah, like you never forget to check it!

Lauren: Actually, it's the first thing I do when I arrive in the morning.

Jon: Well, you're just so together, aren't you?

Lauren: Why are you always in such a bad mood?

Jon: If you don't like the way I am, then don't talk to me.

Lauren: No wonder nobody in the office likes you.

Jon: I haven't seen you winning any popularity contests lately.

If you find yourself in a conversation where things seem to be spiraling out of control, you can pull yourself out by backing off. End the contest by letting your co-worker have the last word. If you can drop your defensive posture, you'll be able to listen to his or her point of view, discuss it, and then present your ideas or opinions.

Rather than allowing the conversation to bounce back and forth with the speed of a ping-pong ball, stay quiet for five seconds before you respond to what your co-worker has said. A moment of silence usually gives you the time you need to stop zinging back with an automatic, negative response.

Don't Pretend Everything Is Okay

By burying your head in the sand and smoothing everything over, you fall into the trap of convincing yourself that nothing is wrong and that no conflict exists. On the surface, you seem to be avoiding confrontation with this strategy, but in reality, the situation is a conflict waiting to erupt. Eventually, the conflict will bubble to the surface when you least expect it. Here's a conversation between Cliff and Alex. Cliff is Alex's supervisor in the receiving department of a large consumer electronics company. Alex has fallen behind schedule but doesn't want Cliff to know.

Cliff: Did you inspect those amplifiers that came in yesterday?

Alex: Yes. They look fine.

Cliff: But some of the boxes haven't been opened.

Alex: Well, I've looked at most of them, and they were okay.

Cliff: How many did you look at?

Alex: Most of them.

Cliff: When will you inspect the rest?

Alex: Sometime today.

Cliff: We're expecting another shipment this afternoon, so all of them need to be checked before the next lot comes in. This job is really important, Alex, and I'm going to be very upset if it doesn't get done.

Alex: Don't worry; no problem.

Alex is avoiding telling his supervisor the truth because he wants the problem to go away without facing it head on. Alex believes that the situation will somehow miraculously fix itself when, in reality, it won't. Avoiding the conflict now only makes matters that much worse later when Cliff realizes that the next shipment has arrived and the amplifier inspection still isn't complete.

As soon as he knew that there was a possibility that his work would not get done, Alex should have notified Cliff. By doing so, the potential conflict could've been prevented and then a solution could've been reached for completing the inspection on time. Alex has another problem as a result of avoiding the conflict: His stress level will climb steadily as the new shipment arrival gets closer and makes focusing on his task more difficult and increases the possibility that unnecessary mistakes will be made.

If you find yourself in a situation where you're tempted to pretend everything is all right when it really isn't, take the following steps:

- ✓ **Don't assume it will get better.** Although hope springs eternal, the chances of an uncomfortable situation just blowing over are unlikely, so the sooner you come to terms with the situation, the sooner you resolve the problem.

- ✓ **Tell someone.** Find someone who can help you resolve the issue and tell that person exactly what is happening. He or she may get upset or react in a way that makes you feel uncomfortable at first, but a few minutes of direct heat is always better than several hours of slow simmering.

- ✓ **Pat yourself on the back.** After the situation is out in the open and resolved, notice how much lighter you feel. Recognizing and reinforcing that you had the courage to face the circumstances and deal with them is important. Give yourself a pat on the back for taking the burden off of your shoulders.

Look Below the Surface

In the previous example, Alex was avoiding conflict by pretending that everything was okay when it wasn't. His supervisor Cliff, on the other hand, has a role to play. Cliff was too easily diverted from getting to the facts by Alex's vague answers. Be sure to ask specific questions to get to the truth of the matter when dealing with a co-worker whom you suspect is saying things are okay when they're not. Both parties need to take action to keep from falling into this conflict trap. When you're in a situation where you suspect another person is smoothing over a problem to avoid a conflict with you, take these steps:

1. **Ask general questions.**

   Asking general questions can help you probe a little deeper into what the facts of the situation may be whenever you suspect that some important information is being left out.

2. **Ask specific questions.**

   Ask for details and don't settle for answers that seem too vague or general. Remember that when someone is holding something back, she probably is doing so because she wants to avoid conflict, not because she is dishonest. By keeping your tone soft and avoiding language that makes it sound as though you're accusing the other person, you make it easier for her to face the situation and tell you what you need to know.

3. **Act, but don't overreact.**

Assuming that the other person hasn't done something really bad, like blow up the mainframe computer, most conflicts can be resolved by simple communication. If you react by jumping up and down with steam coming out of your ears, you make fessing up unsafe for the other person the next time something difficult has to be dealt with. Instead, after the situation has been put on the table and discussed, look for mutual ways of resolving the problem.

Work with a Withdrawing Co-Worker

Withdrawal is a strategy some people use to keep conflict at arm's length so that it never has to be dealt with directly. The following conversation between Amber and Manuel, co-workers in the credit department of an auto parts company, shows what happens when one person withdraws from the conversation and just doesn't want to talk about the problem.

Amber:	Manuel, I really need your monthly statistics for my report.
Manuel:	*(busy working at his computer)* Later, okay?
Amber:	I need them today. This report is due soon.
Manuel:	I can't do it now, I'm busy.
Amber:	I want them by lunchtime.
Manuel:	*(getting up from his desk)* I'll see what I can do.
Amber:	*(frustrated)* This is the third time I've asked you for them.
Manuel:	*(leaving the office)* I have to go over to shipping, talk to me when I get back.
Amber:	*(loudly)* You're leaving? I can't believe it! You never want to deal with this problem or anything else!
Manuel:	*(looking back as he leaves)* There's no point in yelling. I'll be back in an hour.

If you have ever been in a situation like this one, you know how frustrating it can be. In this example, Manuel, for whatever reason, doesn't want to give Amber the time of day — or the statistics she desperately needs. Rather than directly confronting the situation, he withdraws from it by only half listening to what Amber is saying. Eventually, as she becomes more persistent, he physically leaves the room to avoid the conflict.

This conflict trap is difficult to manage, because if someone is really intent on withdrawing from the situation, you can't do a whole lot about it. However, here are some ways of talking to a withdrawing co-worker that can help you deal more directly with the situation at hand:

- ✔ **Resist the urge to push.** If a co-worker is starting to withdraw, resist the natural urge to chase after the response you want. The more you push your co-worker for an answer, the more he or she will pull back.

- ✔ **Use an empathetic tone of voice.** As you notice your co-worker beginning to withdraw, change your tone from one of frustration to one of understanding. Your co-worker always has a reason for not dealing with the issue at hand. Using an empathetic tone is often all you need to get a dialogue going.

- ✔ **Seek out your co-worker's advice.** After your co-worker lets down his guard a little, ask him what he would do — if he were you — to resolve the situation. By doing so, you gently nudge him out of withdrawal by helping him to be more sensitive to your predicament.

- ✔ **Set a specific time.** If the conflict can't be resolved right away, set a specific, mutually agreeable date and time when you can sit down and resolve the problem.

Avoid Serving Up Put-Downs

Verbal assaults used to invalidate the other person lead to conflict. Put-downs can be a co-worker's way of letting you know that she disagrees with something you've done or said. Because she wants to avoid direct conflict, she doesn't talk to you about the problem. Slowly, her unspoken feelings turn to resentment and eventually become outright attacks on your feelings, thoughts, and general character. The following conversation takes place between Mel and Betty, sales clerks at a retail furniture store.

Betty: Did you notice that I sold the walnut bedroom set?

Mel: All I noticed was the mess you made in the delivery book.

Betty: *(feeling put down)* I'm sorry. The customers were newlyweds, and they asked me so many questions I got confused.

Mel: It's a wonder you didn't scare them away. You always seem so put out when customers ask you a lot of questions.

Betty: *(hurt)* What do you mean? I'm never rude to my customers.

Mel:	You probably don't realize it when you are.
Betty:	Mel, you're the one who's being rude.
Mel:	No. I'm just calling it like I see it.
Betty:	You're so judgmental.
Mel:	See, there you go, you just can't take any criticism.

In this situation, Mel has an attitude about Betty before the conversation begins. No matter what Betty says, Mel uses it to find fault with her and invalidate her character and her achievements. The next time they speak, Betty will hide what she's really feeling, and the relationship between the two of them will rapidly deteriorate. By not dealing with the original conflict (whatever it was and whenever it happened), Mel internalized his disagreement and now it seeps out whenever an opportunity presents itself.

If you find yourself with a negative evaluation of a co-worker, remember that your attitude is your responsibility — not your co-worker's. Blaming the other person for a situation that you've been unwilling to confront never resolves anything. If, on the other hand, you're on the receiving end of a co-worker's negative evaluation, as Betty was, don't follow her example. Resist the urge to respond with more negativity, and try to get to the real issues that are causing the conflict. If you're in a situation where your co-worker is putting you down, do the following three things:

✔ **Don't get defensive.** Defending yourself against a co-worker's slurs never resolves the situation, because it fails to get to the real issues that are fueling the insinuations. You just end up feeling like a hamster on a wheel, spending lots of effort going round and round and getting nowhere.

✔ **Be interested.** Even though your co-worker is being indirect and may not be expressing himself well, he does have something to convey. Try to listen to the message underneath his negative evaluation and address that.

✔ **Get to the root cause.** Ask the other person whether something you did in the past has upset him.

By taking these actions, the conversation between Betty and Mel would be revised to sound something like this:

Betty:	Did you notice that I sold the walnut bedroom set?
Mel:	All I noticed was the mess you made in the delivery book.
Betty:	*(feeling put down)* I'm sorry. The customers were newlyweds, and they asked me so many questions I got confused.
Mel:	It's a wonder you didn't scare them away. You always seem so put out when customers ask you a lot of questions.

Betty now realizes that Mel has a negative evaluation about her and that getting defensive serves no purpose. Instead, she becomes interested in what Mel is saying.

Betty: What do you mean?

Mel: I've noticed that you can be snappy with customers sometimes.

Betty: Can you give me an example?

Mel: You were snappy with me last week.

Betty: I'm sorry. Have there been any other times when I've treated you rudely?

Mel: Yes, three months ago when I asked you whether you could work a Saturday for me, you jumped all over me.

Realize Mood Affects Receptivity

Your mood affects how receptive you are to input. For example, when you're angry, your attention is narrowly focused on the person or thing that is upsetting you. You probably have little room, if any, for input from another source. So when someone speaks to you when you're angry, you're more than likely unable to listen to or accept what he or she has to say.

The opposite is also true. When you're in a good mood, you're much more open to receiving input. The point is, don't approach your co-worker with a heavy-duty conflict-laden topic when she's in a bad mood, because you won't get the attention or receptivity you deserve.

Keep in Mind the Four Essential Truths of Human Interaction

Leading seminars for so many years has given us the opportunity to meet all kinds of different people, and we've discovered (sometimes the hard way) four basics truths that help you prevent unnecessary conflict:

✔ **Different people have different working styles.** Some people are precise and organized; others are vague and untidy. We all have different working styles (see Chapter 13), and remembering this fact gives you more patience and understanding with co-workers who think and act differently. Understanding and respecting these differences can help you to prevent conflicts caused by misunderstanding.

✔ **Be aware of your co-worker's sensitivity.** People get their feelings hurt more often and more deeply than they usually admit. Often, something said quite innocently can be taken as an offense by a co-worker. By being more sensitive to the feelings of others, you cut down the number of times you may inadvertently offend someone.

✔ **You prefer some people over others.** Don't expect to like all your co-workers equally. Some people you just click with, and others you don't. Chalk it up to chemistry. Conflict can usually be resolved by focusing on having respect for your co-worker's point of view instead of how much you like him or her.

✔ **You can't judge a book by its cover.** Sometimes you form a negative opinion about a co-worker because of your judgments about the way that person looks, talks, or where that person is from. If you get to know the person on a deeper level, you usually find out he or she is nothing like your mental picture. When dealing with other staff members whom you don't know well, be careful not to let the way they present themselves on the outside keep you from getting to know them on the inside.

Chapter 24

Ten Ways to Get Better Service as a Customer

In This Chapter

▶ Expressing yourself effectively

▶ Keeping the service provider on your side

*1*t's one thing to know what makes you a winner in the service game, but it's another to know how to get what you want as a customer. Get ready to switch gears and view life from the other side of the counter.

We've included this part on how to *get* good service in a book on how to *give* good service because we've found that the more you stand in your customers' shoes, the better you are at providing great service. The other reason is that if you're anything like us, you're equally interested in getting the best service you can when you're the customer. With this in mind, here are ten ways to making life on the other side of the counter less stressful and more successful.

Start Off on the Right Foot

When was the last time you walked into a department store and stood at the counter waiting to be waited on? Two sales associates were in clear view and were chatting away about their personal lives. Trying to be patient, you stood quietly waiting for them to notice you and offer a helping hand. After a while you started to think, "Do they see me, or are they still on break? What's going on here?"

How you initially approach service providers influences the entire interaction and its outcome. Don't let your time pressures or frustrations run away with you. You want to give the message to the service people that you view them as allies, not obstacles. Following are some easy and effective ways to convey this message:

✔ Make direct eye contact as soon as you have their attention.

✔ Greet the provider by saying, "Good morning" or "Good afternoon."

✔ Make a clear and direct request upfront, specifically stating what you want (see the next section for more details).

✔ Make it clear that you need their help.

✔ Use the word "please" within the first 30 seconds of the exchange.

Ask for What You Want

One of the best ways to get what you want is to ask for it! The more clear, concise, and direct you can make your request, the higher the chance that the service provider can deliver it. One of the biggest mistakes customers make is expecting the service provider to be a mind reader. Making clear requests saves you time and lessens the service person's frustration. Following are important elements to include in your request:

✔ Know the end result that you want and don't be afraid to ask for it. Never assume the service person already knows.

✔ If you have a time frame in mind, let the service person know what it is.

✔ Make sure the person who's helping you has the authority to do what you're asking.

✔ Be specific about any details that may vary from the norm.

Stand in Their Shoes

You may greet the sales clerks as warmly as you would your best friend, and you may make the world's clearest, most articulate and understandable request, however, sometimes the people helping you can't deliver 100 percent. The reason may be because they're simply having a bad day, or it might be that company rules and regulations have put them in a bind.

We've trained more than 30,000 staff members in our workshops and find that most people want to provide good service. The problem is that many people work for companies that are in-focused (refer to Chapter 2). Unfortunately these types of companies don't support, encourage, or empower their staff members to do what it takes to give you, the customer, great service. When faced with this situation, the best strategy isn't to shoot the messenger. Try to understand the parameters that the person is working within and enlist his help in getting through a system that you both probably feel doesn't work.

If you need help solving a problem, use the resources of the service person by asking:

- ✔ "What do you recommend?"
- ✔ "Do you have any suggestions?"
- ✔ "What would you do if you were in my situation?"
- ✔ "What's a good next step?"

On those occasions when you're dealing with someone who's obviously in a bad mood, try defusing the situation by recognizing their feelings and saying:

- ✔ "This situation must be tough for you."
- ✔ "You're doing a great job. I know this is a difficult situation."

You can make life much easier for yourself, and at the same time help the service person take better care of you, by doing one simple thing: Follow the instructions you're given. For example, if the form says fill out all the boxes, then fill out all the boxes! Why reinvent the wheel? If you follow the instructions and you still don't understand, ask for clarification. A minute you spend paying attention now will save you 30 minutes later.

Express Yourself in Style

In the movie *Network,* Peter Finch's character says, "I'm mad as hell, and I'm not going to take it anymore!" One thing we can promise you is that sooner or later, as a customer, you'll get angry at some individual serving you, sometime, somewhere. The range of your anger may be anything from mild annoyance to outrage. This anger is usually brought on by sheer rudeness, suffocating bureaucracy, complete incompetence, or a combination of all three, in which case you'll see shades of red not normally visible to the naked eye. At these times, the normal reaction is to pounce all over the service person (thinking she deserves it) and treat her as badly as you feel you're being treated.

Resist the temptation to pounce, and avoid the following:

- Threatening to sue as a tactic
- Yelling, screaming, or shouting
- Using foul language
- Threatening physical harm
- Claiming to know the owner of the company (when you don't) and saying that you'll speak to him about the incident

If any of the above worked, we'd recommend them. Unfortunately, as many of you know, they almost never do. More often than not, these strategies are counterproductive because they put the service person on the defensive. She becomes more interested in protecting herself than in helping you. The two of you will get further away from problem solving and move closer to taking opposite sides simply to avoid being in the wrong.

Sometimes you're justified in feeling angry and expressing that anger. Just be sure to express yourself in style, or as one of our friends says: "Stand up for yourself in an elegant way by expressing your needs and concerns in as reasonable a manner as you can muster."

Use "I" Messages

Parent effectiveness training teaches that by using "I" messages, instead of "you" messages, you can communicate your feelings honestly while minimizing the chance of putting the other person in a defensive posture.

"I" messages state feelings from your point of view and help to keep the other person from getting defensive because you are talking about how you feel, rather than blaming them. "I" messages begin, naturally enough, with the word "I." Examples include the following:

- "I feel frustrated that I can't get the answer I need from your company."
- "I don't feel comfortable with the way this situation is being handled."
- "I don't feel I'm getting the help I need."

By contrast, a "you" message states not what you're feeling, but instead states your opinion of the other person's behavior.

- "You're being very rude."
- "You're not being helpful."
- "You don't seem to know anything about this."

Take Control of the Telephone

The telephone is more pervasive in our lives, as customers, than ever before. On an average day, you may find yourself on the phone doing any of the following:

- ✔ Making a monetary transfer with the customer service representative at your local bank.
- ✔ Getting help from the technical support department of a software company on the new word-processing program you purchased.
- ✔ Ordering an item from a mail-order catalog.
- ✔ Tracking down the package you sent overnight to Botswana that hasn't yet arrived.
- ✔ Setting up an appointment with your local cable company for service.

Take note of what to do when you're faced with the following telephone situations:

- ✔ **When asked to hold:** When you call a company and the receptionist asks you to hold, but you don't want to, quickly respond by asking for the name of the person you want to speak with, followed, of course, by "please." Odds are you'll be transferred instead of being put on hold.

- ✔ **When you've been on hold for a while:** George Carlin, the comedian, used to do a great routine during which he joked that "hold is a lonely place." If you've been on hold forever, consider hanging up and calling back. Tell the receptionist how long you were waiting and ask if he can take a message for the person you're trying to reach.

- ✔ **When you've been transferred around:** Occasionally, you get a phone tour of a company by being transferred to all the departments — except the one you need. When this situation happens, ask to be connected back to the operator. Tell her you were transferred to the wrong person, and ask her to stay on the line until the transfer is complete. If she can't do that, ask for the direct number of the person you're calling. If all else fails, have the operator give the person you're trying to reach a message to call you back.

- ✔ **If you get stuck with voice mail:** If you can't reach a real person (which sadly happens all the time these days), try calling information and getting the company's main number. Ask for the fax number or e-mail address of the person you want to reach and send him a message.

- ✔ **If you're playing telephone tag:** If you find yourself playing telephone tag, take advantage of the alternative technologies available. Try sending the person you're trying to reach an e-mail or, if you're really desperate, a fax. You can often get a quicker response this way. Another idea is to leave a message on her voice mail system letting her know several, specific times when she can reach you.

Complain on the Spot

Okay, you smiled at the sales clerk when you approached her. You said please and thank you when you asked the gate agent which black hole your flight reservation disappeared into. You politely informed your waiter that you ordered sweet potatoes not sweetbreads. Unfortunately, these approaches have not worked. When all else fails, you may find yourself in a position where making a formal complaint is the next step.

The first ears that your complaint will reach are probably sticking off of the head of the service person you're talking to. If, after hearing your complaint, the service provider responds with a vacant stare or uncomfortable silence, you may have an overwhelming urge to speak. Don't. Learning to live with that silence will pay off. The server will feel more compelled to respond if you say nothing. This is the point when he is most likely to offer a suggestion or an alternative. Or, he may run, scream in horror, and then go look for his manager. If he does the latter, you can move your complaint up the corporate ladder (see the next section).

Move Your Complaint up the Ladder

If you've gone as far as you can go with the person helping you, ask for a supervisor or a manager. Don't put the person on the defensive by saying, "You're obviously not the right person to take care of this situation, let me speak to someone higher up!" A better approach would be to say: "I appreciate everything you've done, but I want to speak with your supervisor so that I can move this situation forward."

This approach gives the service person a way to turn you over to her manager without losing face.

Be prepared. If the person you're dealing with has a bad attitude, the supervisor or manager may be the same because the manager sets the departmental tone.

You have to walk a thin line when customers come to you and complain about the service they've received from one of your staff members. On the one hand, you need to support your staff person, and on the other, you need to empathize with the customers (see Chapter 15 for details on using empathetic phrases). In this situation, never criticize your employees in front of a customer and always apologize to the customer. Once the customer has gone, use the complaint as an opportunity to educate your employee. Help him see what he did right and how he could improve next time.

Write an Effective Complaint Letter

You want to believe that complaining to a manager is as high up as you have to go in order to solve a problem. Usually it is. However, when it doesn't pan out that way, you may decide to write a complaint letter to the president, the owner, or the executive of the company.

Complaint letters can be extremely effective in getting action if they're well-written and sent to the right person. The right person is usually the individual that has the power to do something about your situation. If you don't know who this person is, we recommend that you call the company's headquarters or corporate offices. Once you reach a live receptionist, briefly tell her your situation and ask for the person responsible for that area. If she doesn't know, ask to be transferred to someone who does.

Make sure you get the correct spelling of your contact person's name along with his or her title, address, and any necessary mail drop information.

Customers use the following two main styles in complaint letters:

- ✔ **The venting frustration style.** This getting-it-off-your-chest approach may make you feel better, but it won't produce the best results. In fact, you may be taken less seriously by the person reading it. Figure 24-1 is an example of this style.

  As you can see by reading the figure, passenger Bob doesn't need to take a class in assertive communications. However, even though Bob may have expressed his inner feelings and vented his frustration, not much else has been accomplished.

- ✔ **The action-oriented style.** The second style of complaint letter aims not only to express your feelings about the situation, but also to spark some kind of action on the part of the company.

You need to consider eight important items when writing an action-oriented complaint letter:

- ✔ Date of occurrence
- ✔ Time
- ✔ Names of those involved
- ✔ Your name and contact number
- ✔ Specific chronological events
- ✔ Your feelings
- ✔ Specific request for action
- ✔ Benefit to their company

Mr. Jim Smith, President
Friendly Airlines
777 Runway Ave
Houston, Texas 94943

Dear Mr. Smith:

Your company sucks.

I am appalled at the hideous service I received on my recent flight from San Francisco to New York. You obviously do not care about your customers.

I feel that it is only fair to tell you that after this experience, I will never fly your airline again.

Sincerely,

Bob Johnston
President
Conflict Resolutions Inc.

Figure 24-1:
Here's a get-it-off-your-chest complaint letter.

This type of letter reads something like the letter in Figure 24-2.

Jackpot tipping

Jackpot tipping is a technique that we learned from a friend on how to reward waiters and waitresses who give you extraordinary service. When you get the service that you expect, tip your server the standard 15 percent (or whatever you consider standard). If you receive substandard service, give him a reduced tip, say 10 percent. Now, here's the trick: Take the 5 percent difference and keep track of it (either mentally or by jotting it down). For example, if your meal came to $10 and the service wasn't up to par, you would tip 10 percent, or $1. The 5 percent difference (50 cents) goes into the jackpot. You keep adding money to the jackpot until the next time you get extraordinary service. Then the deserving waiter or waitress not only gets his or her 15 percent tip but also hits the jackpot and gets whatever has accumulated in your jackpot account.

You could end up giving someone a $10 tip for a $5 sandwich, but why not? Jackpot tipping is a great way to vote for excellence in a way that'll be noticed.

Mr. Jim Smith, President
Friendly Airlines
777 Runway Ave
Houston, Texas 94943

Dear Mr. Smith:

My name is Bob Johnston, and I am writing to inform you of my experiences on a recent flight with your airline. For your information, the flight was FA #101 from San Francisco to New York on July 3, 1995.

I think that you would be interested to know that this flight did not meet either my expectations for service or the level of service I am sure you wish to deliver. Specifically, the following occurred:

1. The plane was an hour late departing, but the gate agents made no announcement until 30 minutes after the flight was supposed to depart.

2. The ground staff underestimated the number of meals needed on the flight, so there were not enough meals to feed everyone on the plane. I, unfortunately, was one of the passengers who received no meal.

3. The sound on the movie was not working.

While these may seem like trivial occurrences, they made my flight very unpleasant.

As a long-time flier of your airlines, I found this level of service unacceptable and am requesting a ticket refund. For your convenience, I have enclosed a copy of my ticket receipt.

Please feel free to contact me at my office, ext. 7734, if you have any questions. I look forward to receiving a response from you before the end of this month.

Sincerely,

Bob Johnston
President
Conflict Resolutions Inc.

Figure 24-2:
Example of
an action-
oriented
complaint
letter.

Friendly Airlines sent passenger Bob two free first-class, round-the-world-tickets as an apology — *NOT!*

Acknowledge a Job Well-Done

Make a point of always acknowledging a service provider that does a good job. We are often quick to criticize when we don't get the service we want and not always as fast to praise when we do. By praising good service, you encourage those delivering it to keep up the good work.

Don't limit your praise to the spoken word only. Putting your praise in the form of a letter and sending a duplicate copy to the service person's supervisor is often beneficial. If you don't know who her supervisor is, you can call to find out. Or, send her two copies of the same letter with a request that she forward one copy to her boss on your behalf.

Twelve tips for surviving the 12 days of Christmas

While nothing may be further from your mind than the next holiday season, we felt it appropriate to provide some guidelines for dealing with what, for many, can be the most stressful time of the year. Dealing with travel, shopping, family and business obligations in a frantic two-week period, can stress even the most placid among us. You can enjoy the holidays and save yourself a lot of time and trouble by following some basic advice every busy business person and savvy consumer should know:

1. **Make a list of whom you need to buy presents for and from which stores.** Being organized will save you tons of time, money and stress just by knowing ahead of time who you want to buy gifts for and what you want to get them. Plan on spending a set amount of time on a given day at the stores on your list. If at all possible, go in the early morning or late afternoon and try to avoid shopping on the weekends from Thanksgiving through Christmas.

2. **Shop by mail or online.** Many catalog companies will wrap your gifts, include a personalized card, and ship them directly to friends and business associates. This is a great way to get all your holiday shopping done without ever leaving your house. Likewise, today you have more choices than ever about buying almost any gift you could imagine on the Internet. Want a best-selling book for your Uncle Neil? How about that hot new CD for Aunt Nancy? All of this and more can be purchased quickly with a credit card and a few clicks of the mouse.

3. **Stock up on basic items before the season rush begins.** This includes wrapping paper and ribbon, tape, cards, and tags — even candles and candy. The selection will be better, and you'll avoid having to fight the crowds and wait in long lines for just a few "small things."

4. **Call stores ahead of time if you're going to need special assistance.** During the holidays, most stores bring in temporary workers who don't know the ins and outs of the stores merchandise and policies and may not be able to give you the special attention you'll need. If you need the assistance of a knowledgeable sales person for a special purchase, make an appointment ahead of time by phone.

5. **Prepare your grocery list for the "big" holiday meal before you go shopping.** Divide the list by section and shop the store in that order. If there's a special item you'll need, call the store ahead of time to make sure it's in stock and ask them to hold it for you. If it's not in stock, ask them to special order it.

6. **Make restaurant reservations three weeks in advance of the holidays.** Don't leave booking that special restaurant till the last minute. Be sure to avoid problems by confirming all restaurant reservations at least one day before. If you have special food requirements, let the restaurant know this when you call to make the reservation.

7. **Plan on arriving 15 minutes early for restaurant reservations.** To avoid being late and losing your restaurant reservation, plan on arriving early. This allows for delays caused by holiday traffic, parking problems, and so on. Be aware that most restaurants, especially at the holidays, will hold a reservation only 10 to 15 minutes past the time set.

8. **If your flight is significantly delayed or canceled, don't stand in line.** Instead, use a nearby pay phone or cellular phone to call your travel agent or the airline. They'll make travel arrangements for you by phone much faster than a harried gate agent with 200 other people in line with the same problem to solve. In addition, we recommend that you use a hard ticket during the holidays and not an electronic one. If you need to switch airlines at the last minute, you won't have to get the ticket issued by the original airline first.

9. **Ship gifts ahead of time.** Why stress out yourself and anger other passengers by trying to stuff your gifts in an overhead compartment on a busy full flight? Instead, save yourself the trouble by mailing all packages to your final destination at least two weeks prior to the holidays. If you have to take last-minute gifts with you, wrap them carefully and check them at curbside.

10. **Always write down the name of whomever helps you.** This way, if there's a problem later on, after the holiday season, you'll be able to resolve it quicker when you can give the name of the specific person who provided you with the information or a promise.

11. **Use the knowledge of the service person to help you solve your problem.** If you need help in solving a problem, ask the service person "What would you recommend I do?" and then stay silent. If you give them a minute to think about it, they will often come up with a workable solution.

12. **Do business where you always do business.** Give your holiday business to the restaurants and stores that you know and that know you. An established relationship formed throughout the year will almost always lead to better customer service at holiday times.

Index

● *F* ●

• •

Notes

Notes

BUSINESS, CAREERS & PERSONAL FINANCE

0-7645-5307-0

0-7645-5331-3 *†

Also available:

- Accounting For Dummies †
  0-7645-5314-3
- Business Plans Kit For Dummies †
  0-7645-5365-8
- Cover Letters For Dummies
  0-7645-5224-4
- Frugal Living For Dummies
  0-7645-5403-4
- Leadership For Dummies
  0-7645-5176-0
- Managing For Dummies
  0-7645-1771-6

- Marketing For Dummies
  0-7645-5600-2
- Personal Finance For Dummies *
  0-7645-2590-5
- Project Management For Dummies
  0-7645-5283-X
- Resumes For Dummies †
  0-7645-5471-9
- Selling For Dummies
  0-7645-5363-1
- Small Business Kit For Dummies *†
  0-7645-5093-4

HOME & BUSINESS COMPUTER BASICS

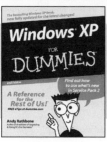

0-7645-4074-2

0-7645-3758-X

Also available:

- ACT! 6 For Dummies
  0-7645-2645-6
- iLife '04 All-in-One Desk Reference
  For Dummies
  0-7645-7347-0
- iPAQ For Dummies
  0-7645-6769-1
- Mac OS X Panther Timesaving
  Techniques For Dummies
  0-7645-5812-9
- Macs For Dummies
  0-7645-5656-8

- Microsoft Money 2004 For Dummies
  0-7645-4195-1
- Office 2003 All-in-One Desk Reference
  For Dummies
  0-7645-3883-7
- Outlook 2003 For Dummies
  0-7645-3759-8
- PCs For Dummies
  0-7645-4074-2
- TiVo For Dummies
  0-7645-6923-6
- Upgrading and Fixing PCs For Dummies
  0-7645-1665-5
- Windows XP Timesaving Techniques
  For Dummies
  0-7645-3748-2

FOOD, HOME, GARDEN, HOBBIES, MUSIC & PETS

0-7645-5295-3

0-7645-5232-5

Also available:

- Bass Guitar For Dummies
  0-7645-2487-9
- Diabetes Cookbook For Dummies
  0-7645-5230-9
- Gardening For Dummies *
  0-7645-5130-2
- Guitar For Dummies
  0-7645-5106-X
- Holiday Decorating For Dummies
  0-7645-2570-0
- Home Improvement All-in-One
  For Dummies
  0-7645-5680-0

- Knitting For Dummies
  0-7645-5395-X
- Piano For Dummies
  0-7645-5105-1
- Puppies For Dummies
  0-7645-5255-4
- Scrapbooking For Dummies
  0-7645-7208-3
- Senior Dogs For Dummies
  0-7645-5818-8
- Singing For Dummies
  0-7645-2475-5
- 30-Minute Meals For Dummies
  0-7645-2589-1

INTERNET & DIGITAL MEDIA

0-7645-1664-7

0-7645-6924-4

Also available:

- 2005 Online Shopping Directory
  For Dummies
  0-7645-7495-7
- CD & DVD Recording For Dummies
  0-7645-5956-7
- eBay For Dummies
  0-7645-5654-1
- Fighting Spam For Dummies
  0-7645-5965-6
- Genealogy Online For Dummies
  0-7645-5964-8
- Google For Dummies
  0-7645-4420-9

- Home Recording For Musicians
  For Dummies
  0-7645-1634-5
- The Internet For Dummies
  0-7645-4173-0
- iPod & iTunes For Dummies
  0-7645-7772-7
- Preventing Identity Theft For Dummies
  0-7645-7336-5
- Pro Tools All-in-One Desk Reference
  For Dummies
  0-7645-5714-9
- Roxio Easy Media Creator For Dummies
  0-7645-7131-1

SPORTS, FITNESS, PARENTING, RELIGION & SPIRITUALITY

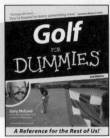

0-7645-5146-9

0-7645-5418-2

Also available:
- Adoption For Dummies
  0-7645-5488-3
- Basketball For Dummies
  0-7645-5248-1
- The Bible For Dummies
  0-7645-5296-1
- Buddhism For Dummies
  0-7645-5359-3
- Catholicism For Dummies
  0-7645-5391-7
- Hockey For Dummies
  0-7645-5228-7

- Judaism For Dummies
  0-7645-5299-6
- Martial Arts For Dummies
  0-7645-5358-5
- Pilates For Dummies
  0-7645-5397-6
- Religion For Dummies
  0-7645-5264-3
- Teaching Kids to Read For Dummies
  0-7645-4043-2
- Weight Training For Dummies
  0-7645-5168-X
- Yoga For Dummies
  0-7645-5117-5

TRAVEL

0-7645-5438-7

0-7645-5453-0

Also available:
- Alaska For Dummies
  0-7645-1761-9
- Arizona For Dummies
  0-7645-6938-4
- Cancún and the Yucatán For Dummies
  0-7645-2437-2
- Cruise Vacations For Dummies
  0-7645-6941-4
- Europe For Dummies
  0-7645-5456-5
- Ireland For Dummies
  0-7645-5455-7

- Las Vegas For Dummies
  0-7645-5448-4
- London For Dummies
  0-7645-4277-X
- New York City For Dummies
  0-7645-6945-7
- Paris For Dummies
  0-7645-5494-8
- RV Vacations For Dummies
  0-7645-5443-3
- Walt Disney World & Orlando For Dummies
  0-7645-6943-0

GRAPHICS, DESIGN & WEB DEVELOPMENT

0-7645-4345-8

0-7645-5589-8

Also available:
- Adobe Acrobat 6 PDF For Dummies
  0-7645-3760-1
- Building a Web Site For Dummies
  0-7645-7144-3
- Dreamweaver MX 2004 For Dummies
  0-7645-4342-3
- FrontPage 2003 For Dummies
  0-7645-3882-9
- HTML 4 For Dummies
  0-7645-1995-6
- Illustrator CS For Dummies
  0-7645-4084-X

- Macromedia Flash MX 2004 For Dummies
  0-7645-4358-X
- Photoshop 7 All-in-One Desk Reference For Dummies
  0-7645-1667-1
- Photoshop CS Timesaving Techniques For Dummies
  0-7645-6782-9
- PHP 5 For Dummies
  0-7645-4166-8
- PowerPoint 2003 For Dummies
  0-7645-3908-6
- QuarkXPress 6 For Dummies
  0-7645-2593-X

NETWORKING, SECURITY, PROGRAMMING & DATABASES

0-7645-6852-3

0-7645-5784-X

Also available:
- A+ Certification For Dummies
  0-7645-4187-0
- Access 2003 All-in-One Desk Reference For Dummies
  0-7645-3988-4
- Beginning Programming For Dummies
  0-7645-4997-9
- C For Dummies
  0-7645-7068-4
- Firewalls For Dummies
  0-7645-4048-3
- Home Networking For Dummies
  0-7645-42796

- Network Security For Dummies
  0-7645-1679-5
- Networking For Dummies
  0-7645-1677-9
- TCP/IP For Dummies
  0-7645-1760-0
- VBA For Dummies
  0-7645-3989-2
- Wireless All In-One Desk Reference For Dummies
  0-7645-7496-5
- Wireless Home Networking For Dummies
  0-7645-3910-8

HEALTH & SELF-HELP

0-7645-6820-5 *†

0-7645-2566-2

Also available:

- Alzheimer's For Dummies
  0-7645-3899-3
- Asthma For Dummies
  0-7645-4233-8
- Controlling Cholesterol For Dummies
  0-7645-5440-9
- Depression For Dummies
  0-7645-3900-0
- Dieting For Dummies
  0-7645-4149-8
- Fertility For Dummies
  0-7645-2549-2

- Fibromyalgia For Dummies
  0-7645-5441-7
- Improving Your Memory For Dummies
  0-7645-5435-2
- Pregnancy For Dummies †
  0-7645-4483-7
- Quitting Smoking For Dummies
  0-7645-2629-4
- Relationships For Dummies
  0-7645-5384-4
- Thyroid For Dummies
  0-7645-5385-2

EDUCATION, HISTORY, REFERENCE & TEST PREPARATION

0-7645-5194-9

0-7645-4186-2

Also available:

- Algebra For Dummies
  0-7645-5325-9
- British History For Dummies
  0-7645-7021-8
- Calculus For Dummies
  0-7645-2498-4
- English Grammar For Dummies
  0-7645-5322-4
- Forensics For Dummies
  0-7645-5580-4
- The GMAT For Dummies
  0-7645-5251-1
- Inglés Para Dummies
  0-7645-5427-1

- Italian For Dummies
  0-7645-5196-5
- Latin For Dummies
  0-7645-5431-X
- Lewis & Clark For Dummies
  0-7645-2545-X
- Research Papers For Dummies
  0-7645-5426-3
- The SAT I For Dummies
  0-7645-7193-1
- Science Fair Projects For Dummies
  0-7645-5460-3
- U.S. History For Dummies
  0-7645-5249-X

Get smart @ dummies.com®

- **Find a full list of Dummies titles**
- **Look into loads of FREE on-site articles**
- **Sign up for FREE eTips e-mailed to you weekly**
- **See what other products carry the Dummies name**
- **Shop directly from the Dummies bookstore**
- **Enter to win new prizes every month!**

* Separate Canadian edition also available
† Separate U.K. edition also available

Available wherever books are sold. For more information or to order direct: U.S. customers visit www.dummies.com or call 1-877-762-2974.
U.K. customers visit www.wileyeurope.com or call 0800 243407. Canadian customers visit www.wiley.ca or call 1-800-567-4797.